T0299813

CORRUPTION AND DEVELOPMENT

Of Related Interest

THE ROLE OF THE STATE IN DEVELOPMENT PROCESSES
edited by Claude Auroi (EADI Book Series 15)

POLITICAL CONDITIONALITY
edited by Georg Sørensen

AID AND POLITICAL CONDITIONALITY
edited by Olav Stokke (EADI Book Series 16)

FOREIGN AID TOWARDS THE YEAR 2000
Experiences and Challenges
edited by Olav Stokke (EADI Book Series 18)

FOOD SECURITY POLICY IN AFRICA BETWEEN DISASTER
RELIEF AND STRUCTURAL ADJUSTMENT
Relfections on the Conception and Effectiveness of Policies:
The Case of Tanzania
by Gabriele Geier (GDI Book Series No. 5)

BEYOND THE EMERGENCY
Development Within UN Peace Missions
edited by Jeremy Ginifer

Corruption and Development

edited by
MARK ROBINSON

Routledge
Taylor & Francis Group

LONDON AND NEW YORK

in association with
EADI The European Association of Development Research
and Training Institutes (EADI), Geneva

First published in 1998 in Great Britain by
FRANK CASS PUBLISHERS

Reprinted 2004 by Routledge
2 Park Square, Milton Park,
Abingdon, Oxon, OX14 4RN

Transferred to Digital Printing 2004

Routledge is an imprint of the Taylor & Francis Group

Copyright © 1998 Frank Cass & Co. Ltd.

Reprint 2002

British Library Cataloguing in Publication Data

Corruption and development
    1. Political corruption – Developing countries 2. Public
    institutions – Developing countries – Corrupt practices
    3. Political corruption – Developing countries – Public
    opinion
    I. Robinson, Mark
    364.1'323'091724

ISBN 0 7146 4902 3 (cloth)
ISBN 0 7146 4458 7 (paper)

Library of Congress Cataloging in Publication Data

Corruption and development / edited by Mark Robinson.
    p. cm.
    "First appeared in a special issue ... of the European journal of
development research ... vol. 10/1, June 1998"–T.p. verso.
    Includes bibliographical references and index.
    ISBN 0-7146-4902-3. – ISBN 0-7146-4458-7 (pbk.)
    1. Political corruption –Developing countries. 2. Business
ethnics–Developing countries. 3. Developing countries–Moral
conditions. 4. Economic development–Social aspects. I. Robinson,
Mark, 1961–   .
    JF1525.C66C67   1998
    364.1'322'091724–dc21   98–16986
                                                                                                    CIP

This group of studies first appeared in a Special Issue on 'Corruption and Development' of
The European Journal of Development Research (ISSN 0957-8811) Vol.10/1 (June 1998)
published by Frank Cass.

All rights reserved. No part of this publication may be reproduced, stored in or introduced into a retrieval system
or transmitted in any form, or by any means, electronic, mechanical, photocopying, recording or otherwise,
without the prior written permission of the publisher of this book.

Printed in Great Britain by
Antony Rowe Ltd., Eastbourne

Contents

Corruption and Development:
An Introduction

MARK ROBINSON

Corruption has become an issue of major political and economic significance in recent years. This has led to a resurgence of interest in analysing the phenomenon and the diverse forms that it assumes in developing countries with an expectation that democratisation and economic liberalisation offer potential routes to dealing with the problem. Anti-corruption strategies range from institutional reforms through to concerted efforts at the international level, but the efficacy of these approaches has not been subject to careful empirical research.

I. THE BROADER CONTEXT

In recent years corruption has become an issue of major economic and political significance in many countries across the globe, including a number of developed western states. Corruption scandals are a prominent source of media interest and newspapers frequently publish stories about illicit behaviour by politicians and public officials. Partly on account of heightened media attention there is a widespread perception that corruption is on the increase, both among the general public who demand effective action and politicians who are eager to derive political capital by adopting a forthright stance over the need to eliminate corrupt practices [*Heywood, 1997*]. This has resulted in the increased electoral popularity of political parties committed to fighting corruption and the launching of high profile anti-corruption campaigns by governments of various ideological hues. Specialised NGOs have been established in a number of countries to publicise the problem of corruption and mobilise public concern around cases of malfeasance as a means of provoking an official response. At the international level there is increased resolve on the part of inter-governmental bodies such as the OECD and the World Bank to

Mark Robinson, Fellow of the Institute of Development Studies at the University of Sussex. Most of the contributions were first presented at a workshop on 'Corruption and Development' organised by the IDS at the University of Sussex in May 1997. The workshop and resultant publication were made possible by generous financial support from the Government and Institutions Department of the UK Department for International Development (DFID).

tackle the problem of corruption in response to rising concern about aid effectiveness at a time of financial stringency and to public criticism.

While corruption is a feature of all societies to varying degrees, it is a particular concern for developing countries because it undermines economic growth, discourages foreign investment and reduces the resources available for infrastructure, public services and anti-poverty programmes. As noted by Johnston [*1997*], it may also undermine political institutions by weakening the legitimacy and accountability of governments. Corruption also reduces the effectiveness of aid-funded development projects and weakens public support for development assistance in donor countries. In short, it is inimical to sustainable development, poverty reduction and good governance, though it can also have the opposite effect by circumventing cumbersome regulations and facilitating business transactions [*Ades and Di Tella, 1996*]. Corruption not only affects poor people most directly, through the misallocation of public resources (including those derived from foreign aid) and routine exactions on the part of corrupt local officials, but it also keeps poor countries from becoming richer. For these reasons aid donors have focused increasingly on corruption and its impact on development and recognise the need to devise programmes to assist governments in tackling the problem [*World Bank, 1997a*].

The issue of corruption has assumed particular salience in developing countries in recent years because of the spread of democratisation and economic liberalisation. In theory the creation of democratic political institutions offers the potential for closer scrutiny of the actions of politicians and government officials by citizens, an independent media, NGOs and elected representatives. Yet opinion is divided. Some analysts argue that corruption is on the increase as a direct result of democratisation, since democratic political systems provide incentives and opportunities for corrupt practices. Others stress the potential of established democracies to devise institutions through which corruption can be tackled and contained. While it remains true that certain kinds of authoritarian regimes (for example in China and some Latin American countries) were able to check the incidence of corruption through political repression and by deploying harsh sanctions (usually for a limited period of time)[*Little, 1996; White 1996*], others, especially in sub-Saharan Africa and South Asia, utilised corruption as a means of distributing state patronage and ensuring regime continuity (see the contributions by Riley and Khan in this volume). The reality is that many new democratic states in Africa, Eastern Europe and Latin America are characterised by high and increasing levels of corruption, and that democratic structures have proved markedly ineffective in curbing the spread and tenacity of corrupt practices in developing countries [*Harriss-White and White, 1996; Little and Posada-Carbo, 1996*].

There is also an expectation that economic liberalisation has the potential to reduce corruption. The replacement of discretionary controls over prices and the production and distribution of goods and services with market mechanisms should limit the scope for rent-seeking behaviour by public officials. Prescriptions centre on economic policy reforms, institutional strengthening, and coordinated international action. But experience from developing countries which have undergone economic liberalisation does not provide firm support for the belief that the market can reduce the incidence of corruption. Instead it displaces it to other actors and spheres of activity [*Harriss-White and White, 1996;* Riley, this volume].

II. UNDERSTANDING CORRUPTION

It is difficult to generalise about the form that corruption assumes in different country contexts. There are differences between the form assumed by corruption in developing countries as compared to developed countries, and between forms of corruption that are growth-retarding or threaten political stability and those that are more benign and do not undermine the economic or political viability of nation states [*Johnston, 1996; Hutchcroft, 1997*]. A widely-accepted definition of corruption is the one offered by Johnston in his contribution to this volume, namely 'the abuse of public roles or resources for private benefit'.[1] However, while there is agreement, at least in broad terms, on what the term signifies, there are limitations on the extent to which an acceptable classification and analytical framework can be developed, though different approaches have been put forward.

Corruption may be categorised into three main forms: incidental (individual), institutional (for example, the police service) and systemic (societal). Some forms of corruption are confined to instances of malfeasance on the part of individual politicians or public officials, and are episodic rather than systemic. In other cases corruption pervades particular institutions or sectors of activity. For example, certain line ministries may be riddled with corrupt officials whereas in others the practice is much less pervasive, reflecting differential opportunities and controls. Corruption may also feature more routinely in sectors where it is easier for public officials to extract rents due to weaknesses in the prevailing system of controls and regulations.

In the third case corruption pervades the entire society and in the process becomes routinised and accepted as a means of conducting everyday transactions. This is what Johnston calls 'systemic' or 'entrenched' corruption, which affects institutions and influences individual behaviour at all levels of a political and socio-economic system. This form of corruption has a number of characteristic features: it is embedded in specific socio-cultural environments, and tends to be monopolistic, organised and difficult to avoid.

Entrenched corruption features in societies with the following characteristics: low political competition, low and uneven economic growth, a weak civil society, and the absence of institutional mechanisms to deal with corruption. In contrast, those societies which are relatively free of corruption are premised on respect for civil liberties, accountable government, a wide range of economic opportunities, and structured political competition, and are mainly, but not exclusively, characteristic of developed western states [*Johnston, 1997*].

The form which corruption assumes in different contexts also depends on whether politicians or bureaucrats take the lead, and whether key interest groups in civil society are actively involved through patronage and clientelism [*Hutchcroft, 1997*]. Corruption also varies in the direct impact it has on the lives of ordinary citizens: elite corruption may have corrosive economic effects, but does not directly affect many individuals, whereas everyday or 'petty' corruption involves public officials and ordinary citizens in regular but smaller scale transactions, which may have a more direct impoverishing effect.

While few analysts would dispute a definition of corruption as the abuse of public roles or resources for private benefit, there is little agreement on the nature and causes of corruption. Some of this disagreement emanates from the choice of analytical framework employed, since corruption can be analysed through a range of approaches drawing on different disciplines. Economic theories tend to be grounded in the rent-seeking approach advocated by public choice theorists. According to this corruption arises from interactions between clients, be they business people or ordinary citizens, and politicians and public officials who are assumed to be narrowly self-seeking in their behaviour [*Harriss-White, 1996; Philp, 1997*]. But public choice theory tends to be premised on a simplistic view of the state which assumes that state organisations and public officials are solely motivated by self-interest, and leaves little room for active and conscious intervention by state actors in combating corruption, or for uneven patterns of corruption both within and between institutions.

According to Galtung, this approach fails to take into account the role played by state officials in making appointments, and in setting penalties and incentives, and in shaping the institutional environment in which corruption takes place. Political scientists, in contrast, certainly those in the pluralist tradition, rely on a multi-tiered approach in which corruption is a function of the lack of durable political institutions and political competition, and a weak and undeveloped civil society. This approach often suffers from an excessive faith in the power of democratic politics and institutional reforms to effect durable changes in the behaviour of public officials and to limit the pervasiveness of corrupt practices. Others have a more functionalist interpretation in which corruption is viewed as a means of maintaining existing power structures and systems of political control, and for this reason would be sceptical of the potential efficacy of institutional and political reforms. Moreover, these approaches either seek to analyse corruption through the use of a simplistic model which is over-deterministic, as in the case of public choice theory, or rely on descriptive assessments informed by anecdotal evidence, which is characteristic of much political science writing in this field.[2]

An alternative approach grounded in political economy, along the lines developed by Khan [1996], emphasises differences in the political power of groups and resources allocated by the state as the key explanatory variable, and is based on the following premises: it acknowledges the complexity of corruption and accepts the existence of a wide diversity of forms; it focuses on the dynamics of power and agency rather than individual self-interest; and argues that a long-term perspective grounded in historical experience and political realities is of central importance in understanding corruption and the scope for designing effective measures to combat the phenomenon. Approaches to anti-corruption grounded in public choice theory emphasise economic reforms and downsizing the state as the principal route to reform, whereas the political economy approach advocates conscious political intervention as the primary vehicle for anti-corruption efforts. However, approaches rooted in public choice theory and the pluralist tradition tend to confine their analysis to particular countries and institutions and frequently overlook the role of international actors in shaping the form and content of corrupt practices at the national level.

Consequently the role of international factors as a central determinant of corruption have not been subject to careful scrutiny, at least until recently, despite the evident importance of foreign aid, investment and trade as sources of rent-seeking opportunities. While the role of aid donors and multi-national corporations was held to be an important contributory factor by more radical analysts, it is only in recent years that this dimension of the problem has received serious attention from among policy makers and given rise to concerted international efforts designed to combat the phenomenon (Galtung, this volume). International corruption takes the form of bribes and illegal payments in the context of trade, aid and investment flows between countries. It can entail preferential access to trading opportunities, favouritism in the processing of investment proposals, and kickbacks derived from the abuse of international procurement procedures, with significant economic repercussions.[3]

Quantitative research conducted by Johann Lambsdorff, the results of which are presented here, suggests that the degree of corruption of importing countries affects the trade structure of exporting countries. The explanation for this is held to lie in the inclination of exporters to offer bribes to public officials in importing countries. He argues that there may be a correlation between the level of corruption in exporting countries and the extent to which they are successful in markets where high levels of corruption prevail. The assumption is that firms willing to offer bribes are driving honest firms out of trade; hence if dishonest firms are properly regulated, a more level playing field will be created and honest firms will pick up a greater share of the trade. Such considerations underpin current efforts in the OECD to render international bribery illegal.

While international corruption has received due recognition in recent years there is a pressing need for studies to explain the diversity and incidence of corruption in the context of economic and political liberalisation, based on a comparative analysis of the changing social, political and economic characteristics of corruption within and between countries over time. But the study of corruption cannot be restricted to its contemporary manifestations without recourse to history; the evidence suggests that individual countries have exhibited variations in the form and incidence of corruption over time in response to changing political and economic factors. The same factors that promote corruption in the first place can also be instrumental in its demise. For instance, primitive accumulation is often based on discretionary access to public resources by private entrepreneurs, but as economic growth takes place, pressure for a functioning legal system to enforce contracts and regularise inheritance laws can emerge as business and political elites seek to ensure that the gains of illegal wealth are regularised. This highlights the importance of the historical context and the need to assume a longer-term perspective when assessing the scope for designing anti-corruption measures which are expected to generate positive results within a restricted time horizon.

According to some analysts the legacy of colonial rule is a significant factor in explaining variations in the intensity and prevalence of contemporary forms of corruption in Africa, Asia and Latin America. For example, it is sometimes argued that corruption in Latin America has been an endemic feature since the colonial period and reflects deep socio-cultural traditions that are resistant to change. Others contend that the root cause of corruption lies in the historic dominance of the state in economic and political affairs, a situation which has created opportunities for rent-seeking and weakened the ability of citizens to hold politicians and state officials accountable for their actions [*Little, 1996*]. In Africa entrenched corruption is a feature of countries which have experienced colonial rule, though corruption is also present in countries which did not undergo colonialism, such as Ethiopia and Liberia. Some features of former British colonies appear to render them less vulnerable to corruption than their Francophone counterparts: these include a tradition of press freedom, durable legal institutions, an emphasis on elite education and British civil service norms of probity and impartiality. This would appear to suggest that while contemporary manifestations of corruption in Africa cannot be explained by colonialism *per se*, colonial regimes left an institutional legacy which has shaped the subsequent form and extent of corrupt practices.[4] High levels of aid dependence are also an explanatory factor in the African context as these provide ample scope for rent-seeking opportunities when alternative sources of income are restricted.

According to Khan, the form and prevalence of corruption in Asia appears to be a function of the process of accumulation and evolution of property rights over time. The pattern of clientelistic relations established between emerging capitalist classes, politicians and the state bureaucracy, reflect underlying socio-economic factors which are the principal determinant of the forms assumed by corruption and its impact on economic growth. Rather than curbing corruption, economic and political liberalisation in South Korea has strengthened the bargaining power of the business sector in relation to the government, a situation which could lead to the persistence of the institutional foundations of corruption. However, this could be offset by demands for greater democratisation and public accountability in the context of growing economic crisis [*Kong, 1996*].

A final issue to consider when analysing the form and prevalence of corruption in developing countries is the relationship between economic growth and corruption. There are two contrasting perspectives on this relationship in the literature; one holds that corruption undermines economic growth through the extraction of rents, the other argues that corruption can improve social welfare and improve economic efficiency by overcoming bureaucratic hurdles [*Rose-Ackerman, 1978*]. Contrary to the expectations of conventional economic theory, East Asian experience indicates that the intensity of corruption does not necessarily assume an inverse relationship with economic growth. In some contexts it is argued that corruption can actually foster economic growth (or at least not undermine it) by facilitating inward investment, and by increasing the scope for collecting higher rents through taxation as a consequence. On the other hand, recent comparative evidence drawing on cross-country data points to a negative relationship between corruption and investment which has detrimental consequences for economic growth [*Ades and Di Tella, 1996*].

In an extension of this debate, there are also two contrasting views of the relationship between corruption and economic liberalisation. One approach, which is premised on the hypothesis that corruption hinders economic development, holds that economic liberalisation has the potential to reduce corruption through market mechanisms. Economic liberalisation is expected to reduce corruption through a combination of price reforms designed to deregulate prices, eliminate subsidies, and reduce tariffs, custom duties and other trade controls, and structural reforms aimed at reducing the size of the state through privatisation and by freeing up the banking sector. The expectation is that by reducing the size of the public sector and the direct involvement of the state in economic activity, opportunities for rent-seeking activities will diminish [*World Bank 1997b*].

But economic reforms can also have adverse consequences for corruption, at least in the short term. For example, in the absence of adequate enforcement mechanisms tax reforms designed to increase government revenues can increase incentives for corrupt practices (Toye and Moore, this volume). Privatisation in the absence of effective regulation has the potential for generating high levels of economic rent, especially in natural monopolies, and private appropriation of public assets through illegal means. Adherents of economic liberalisation argue that such problems arise as a result of poor implementation and weak capacity, rather than from structural causes. Critics point to the need for new sources of income and employment outside the public sector to reduce incentives for rent-seeking behaviour on the one hand, and for political reforms to provide an institutional environment through which corruption can be tackled directly on the other [*White, 1996; Kong, 1996*].

Taxation is one area where corruption can be especially damaging in economic terms since it reduces state revenues and limits government spending. Particular forms of taxation systems may be more conducive to corruption than others. Simplification of the tax system is considered to be effective in reducing corruption as it can replace overlapping taxes with a single broad-based tax regime. According to Toye and Moore value-added taxation is beneficial in this regard, though the implementation of such a system can be problematic in developing countries where there is widespread illiteracy and poor record-keeping on the part of retailers and owners of small businesses.

III. TACKLING CORRUPTION

In much of the existing literature the approach to analysing corruption determines the means advocated for tackling the problem. For example, advocates of public choice theory place their faith in economic liberalisation and curbs on the power of the state as a means of reducing the scope for rent-seeking activity [*Harriss-White, 1996*]. While economic liberalisation can help to reduce corruption by predatory state elites, there is a need for careful monitoring and regulation of the reforms to ensure that the benefits which accrue from this process (such as privatisation and removal of price controls) are not appropriated by these same elites. Moreover, the absence of alternative economic opportunities limits the scope for reducing corruption if the public sector remains a primary source of income and formal employment [*World Bank, 1997a*].

The pluralist approach, in contrast, assumes that political initiatives centred on the creation of new democratic institutions - such as elected legislatures, parliamentary committees and watchdog bodies - are central to the success of efforts to control corruption. Political reforms are thought to contribute towards an environment which is more conducive to reduced corruption because they can increase the responsiveness of political elites to the will of the people [*Little, 1996*]. But while political competition offers opportunities for new political elites to gain legitimacy by taking action against corruption, it can also enable such elites to secure greater access to existing rent-seeking opportunities as evidence from Africa appears to indicate. Moreover, comparative statistical evidence cited by Johnston suggests that democratic rights and processes do not make a significant contribution to corruption *per se*. Indeed there are many examples of countries where corruption has increased in spite of the existence of formal democratic institutions, India and Nigeria being prominent examples [*Singh, 1997*; Riley, this volume]. Johnston's argument is that the creation of democratic structures and special agencies to combat corruption will only succeed if citizens organise themselves effectively. In this respect he advances the notion of 'social empowerment', which he uses to refer to the range of political and economic resources and alternatives available to citizens, as an integral element of an assault on entrenched or systemic corruption. Actions by organised citizens can complement institutional reforms and provide them with a proper social foundation which is indispensable to their success.

Spontaneous public demonstrations against corrupt politicians have been effective in prompting authorities to remove them from office in some countries (the dismissals of the governments of Benazir Bhutto in Pakistan and Collor de Mello in Brazil are two recent prominent examples) but they do not tackle the root causes of the problem when it permeates all levels of government machinery. At best such actions can lead to a temporary abatement of the problem but it soon resurfaces in other guises or through other channels. Public action has to be established on a more permanent basis for citizen initiatives to succeed, and this in turn depends on the existence of organisations, enterprises and networks within civil society, which will vary significantly between countries. Groups and interests within civil society can play a role in monitoring the behaviour of individuals and officials and in fostering more regular interchange between private citizens and government as a means of reducing distrust and instilling greater public confidence in the duties and functions of state officials. But while some organisations within civil society can be a potent force for anti-corruption efforts, other groups benefit from corruption and are resistant to change. This suggests that autonomous action by independent civic groups has its limitations, and needs to be complemented by institutional interventions.

Anti-corruption efforts centred on institutional reforms are premised on a multi-pronged approach which combines reforms in the legal sphere (such as enforceable property and contract rights and measures to enhance the credibility of the judiciary), innovations in the governance sphere (strengthening mechanisms of accountability, controls over discretion and resource use, and improvements in terms and conditions of employment for civil servants) and specific institutional mechanisms (such as creating an anti-corruption agency, special courts to review corruption cases, and asset declaration for politicians and civil servants). For such efforts to succeed, a politically committed leadership, and public confidence in the sincerity of politicians to effect change (especially among politically and economically influential elites) is of central importance. However, the success of specialist anti-corruption agencies appears to be conditioned by a wider set of socio-economic factors, and the forms assumed by corruption in particular countries. Where corruption is entrenched, such agencies can only play a limited role, as their powers of investigation and enforcement may be constrained by influential politicians and civil servants who indulge in corrupt practices. As noted by Riley in this volume and Little [*1996*], the success of anti-corruption measures depends on political will, which in much of Africa and Latin America has not been readily forthcoming, largely because of the potential threat that it poses to the political and bureaucratic establishment.

Institutional corruption perhaps has most potential for support from external actors, such as international aid donors, but institutional reforms may not be as effective as political reforms for reducing corruption. Institutional reforms may be appropriate and effective in countries where corruption is not entrenched and where anti-corruption laws, agencies and organisations are in place and have broad public support. Such countries invariably tend to have the institutional trappings of democracy with governments that are subject to electoral contestation and popular accountability. But entrenched corruption limits the scope for effective intervention in the short term since it is deep-set and related to a complex set of societal features which may only change gradually over the longer term.

In some countries (such as China and Vietnam) attempts to fight corruption have taken the form of crack-downs and special tribunals with those found guilty of indulging in corrupt activity subject to the death penalty. But such campaigns are often politically orchestrated and are not easily sustained since they are designed to assuage public revulsion and reduce potentially negative political repercussions rather than to provide an enduring solution to the problem. Another problem highlighted by Galtung is that one-off initiatives often lack credibility, either because they cannot be legally enforced or are approved by parliaments that are perceived as weak or illegitimate. In other cases political initiatives may appear credible but are not feasible because they require a high degree of political commitment and administrative and legal capacity to implement. Moreover, as noted by Johnston, top-down actions may undermine political competition and the mobilisation of civil society which are vital to the success of anti-corruption efforts over the longer term.

Some observers are cautious about the potential effectiveness of political and institutional reforms since these will amount to little more than short-term palliatives in countries where corruption is embedded in deep-set social and economic structures that give rise to patronage and clientelism (Khan, this volume). For these reasons the objective of eliminating corruption may be unfeasible, though it may be possible to reduce corruption to acceptable levels where it does not threaten to undermine development or political stability. While this might not be readily acceptable to policy makers, it does accord with political realities and would ensure that efforts to combat the problem are founded on a realistic expectation of what can be achieved within a relatively short time span.

The limitations of institutional and political interventions, combined with a growing recognition of the importance of international factors as a contributory cause of corruption, have spawned a variety of international responses. Since corruption by firms in exporting countries can be an important contributory factor to the prevalence of corruption in importing countries (Lambsdorff, this volume), international efforts to make such transactions illegal can complement institutional and political reforms in the latter. The recent initiative of the OECD in this direction is a prominent example of such activity, though US corporations found guilty of indulging in bribery of foreign officials to obtain overseas contracts have been liable to criminal prosecution under the Foreign Corrupt Practices Act for over two decades. Similar initiatives are being pursued at the regional level within the European Union and Latin America, in the form of multilateral agreements which aim to control international and national corruption through extradition agreements and changes to legal assistance procedures.

International organisations, such as Transparency International (TI), can help to highlight the role of international factors in shaping corruption, and focus attention on the potential significance of concerted international action. One particular innovation examined by Galtung is the Integrity Pact promoted by TI where potential contractors or suppliers or suppliers of goods and services sign a statement that they will not offer any bribes in connection with official contracts in return for a commitment from the government that it will adhere to transparent procurement rules and commit itself to preventing extortion and acceptance of bribes by public officials. In some countries national integrity working groups have been formed bringing together stakeholders in government, civil society and the private sector to implement and sustain this approach.

IV. CONCLUSION

The contributions in this volume suggest that complementary strategies have to be devised to tackle forms of corruption at the international, national, local and institutional levels, involving government, civil society, the private sector and international actors. While experience suggests that sustainable anti-corruption efforts need to be country-specific, they can be informed by lessons from elsewhere and supported by concerted action at the international level. Clearly excessive reliance on one single strategy derived from the mode of analysis employed limits the scope and potential impact of anti-corruption efforts.

While there is now a voluminous literature on the subject, the scope for fresh research in this field has not been exhausted. A notable feature of much of the literature is the tendency to focus on definitions and models in the absence of much analytically informed empirical enquiry. In view of the political sensitivity and invisibility of the problem this is not altogether surprising, though more could be done by way of comparative analysis and systematic cross-country research to add weight to the rather slender corpus of evidence which exists at present in many developing countries.

One interesting avenue for comparative research is to examine the reasons for the low rates of corruption now prevalent in a number of western countries and to capture and account for variations between particular countries over time through comparative political economy. This would allow one to pinpoint more accurately the relative success of political and institutional reforms in tackling the problem as compared to longer-term socio-economic changes that shape the form and extent of corruption over time. Also of interest are contemporary success stories in developing countries, either in terms of particular countries which have managed to contain or overcome problems of systemic corruption, or specific institutions designed to tackle the problem directly. Both would offer insights that are potentially replicable in other situations, and highlight the extent to which the experience of one country or institutional innovation at a particular point in time and under a specific set of political and economic conditions is readily transferable. Research enquiry of this nature could also produce salutary evidence on the limitations of universal prescriptions grounded in a singular emphasis on economic liberalisation or political reform, and demonstrate the virtues of a multi-pronged and historically-sensitive approach.

There is also a need for more research and documentation of successful anti-corruption initiatives of a political or institutional nature, and on the efficacy of organised civic action as a means of tackling the problem within particular countries. At present, the evidence is largely confined to a few high-profile cases in East and Southeast Asia, with relatively sparse analysis of the impact and efficacy of institutional reforms elsewhere in the developing world.

A third potential avenue for research concerns the role played by international actors in combating corruption fostered through trade and investment flows in the context of globalisation, but also in the form of support for domestic anti-corruption initiatives. This could examine both the efficacy and limitations of multilateral agreements, and the extent to which external aid agencies can make a positive contribution to reducing corruption, though external intervention cannot be assumed a priori to be either benign or effective. At the very least, research of this nature could provide a useful corrective to the paucity of hard empirical evidence which characterises much of the literature on corruption and development, and offer some guidelines on the scope and potential limitations of external intervention.

NOTES

1. A more analytically grounded definition is that employed by Klitgaard, which derives from principal-agent theory, namely that corruption is 'monopoly plus discretion minus accountability' [Galtung, this volume; *Goudie and Stasavage, 1997*].
2. An important exception in this regard is the work of Robert Wade [*1985*] with his careful analysis of corruption in India.
3. For example, a recent cross-national econometric study conducted by Wei [*1997*] shows that corruption has a major taxation effect which discourages foreign investment.
4. I am grateful to Jean-François Médard for this observation.

REFERENCES

Ades, A. and R. Di Tella, 1996, 'The Causes and Consequences of Corruption: A Review of Recent Empirical Contributions', *IDS Bulletin*, Vol.27, No.2, pp.6–11.
Goudie, A. and D. Stasavage, 1997, 'Corruption: The Issues', Technical Paper No.122, OECD, Paris.
Harriss-White, B., 1996, 'Liberalization and Corruption: Resolving the Paradox (A Discussion Based on South Indian Material)', *IDS Bulletin*, Vol.27, No.2, pp.31–9.
Harriss-White, B. and G. White, 1996, 'Corruption, Liberalization and Democracy: Editorial Introduction', *IDS Bulletin*, Vol.27, No.2, pp.1–5.
Heywood, P., 1997, 'Political Corruption: Problems and Perspectives', *Political Studies*, Vol.45, No.3, pp.417–35
Hutchcroft, P. D., 1997, 'The Politics of Privilege: Assessing the Impact of Rents, Corruption, and Clientelism in Third World Development', *Political Studies*, Vol.45, No.3, pp.639–58.
Johnston, M., 1996, 'The Search for Definitions: The Vitality of Politics and the Issue of Corruption', *International Social Science Journal*, No.149, pp.321–35.
Johnston, M., 1997, 'What Can Be Done about Entrenched Corruption?', Paper presented to the Ninth Annual Bank Conference on Development Economics, The World Bank, Washington, DC, 30 April–1 May.
Khan, M.H., 1996, 'A Typology of Corrupt Transactions in Developing Countries', *IDS Bulletin*, Vol.27, No.2, pp.12–21.
Kong, T.Y., 1996, 'Corruption and its Institutional Foundations: The Experience of South Korea', *IDS Bulletin*, Vol.26, No.2, pp.48–55.
Little, W., 1996, 'Corruption and Democracy in Latin America', *IDS Bulletin*, Vol.27, No.2, pp.64–70.

Little, W. and E. Posada-Carbo (eds.), 1996, *Political Corruption in Europe and Latin America*, London: Macmillan.

Philp, M., 1997, 'Defining Political Corruption', *Political Studies*, Vol.45, No.2, pp.436–62.

Rose-Ackerman, S., 1978, *Corruption: A Study in Political Economy*, New York: Academic Press.

Singh, G., 1997, 'Understanding Political Corruption in Contemporary Indian Politics', *Political Studies*, Vol.45, No.3, pp.626–38.

Wade, R., 1985, 'The Market for Public Office, or Why India is not Better at Development', *World Development*, Vol.13, No.4, pp.467–97.

Wei, S-J, 1997, 'How Taxing is Corruption?', mimeo, Harvard University, Kennedy School of Government, Cambridge, MA.

White, G., 1996, 'Corruption and Market Reform in China', *IDS Bulletin*, Vol.27, No.2, pp.40–7.

World Bank, 1997a, *Helping Countries Combat Corruption: The Role of the World Bank*, Washington, DC: The World Bank.

World Bank, 1997b, *World Development Report 1997: The State in a Changing World*, New York: Oxford University Press.

Patron–Client Networks and the Economic Effects of Corruption in Asia

MUSHTAQ H. KHAN

Corruption is likely to be widespread during the early stages of capitalist development when capitalists enjoy low legitimacy and states face excess demand for the rights and resources they allocate. Yet the economic effects of corruption have differed greatly across Asian countries. The study argues that the differential economic performance of developers is related to the types of patron–client networks within which their corruption has been located. The type of patron–client network determines the types of rights exchanged through corruption and the terms of these exchanges. The study compares patron–client networks in the Indian subcontinent, Malaysia, Thailand and South Korea. Such an examination helps to explain why in some countries corruption has attended rapid growth while in others it has implied transfers which are very damaging for growth. This provides a more nuanced understanding of the causes and effects of corruption and one which must precede the construction of appropriate institutional and political responses.

Corruption has been associated with very different economic effects across Asian countries. In some North East Asian countries such as South Korea, widespread corruption has accompanied decades of very high growth. In others, such as the South Asian countries of the Indian subcontinent, corruption has been associated with relatively low growth. In a third group of countries in South East Asia, high levels of corruption have been associated with moderately high long-run growth rates. These differences could be the result of differences in underlying rates of growth. On the other hand they could also be the result of corruption having *differential* effects across countries (while their underlying growth rates can, of course, vary as well). Economic theory has identified a number of factors which could explain differences in the economic effects of corruption. However, economic explanations have given little attention to differences in the political power of the groups competing for resources allocated by the state.

Mushtaq H. Khan, Department of Economics, SOAS, University of London. The author is grateful to Mark Robinson for his comments as well as to the participants at the IDS Workshop on Corruption and Development.

This discussion argues that the distribution of political power is revealed in differences in the structure of patron–client networks across countries and these can be important for explaining the differential effects of corruption. The bargaining power of patrons and clients can explain differences in the rights and resources which they exchange (often in corrupt transactions). This in turn can contribute to our understanding of the differential effects of corruption. We will examine the patron–client networks linking states and competing groups of clients in the Indian subcontinent, Malaysia, Thailand and South Korea, and investigate the ways in which the structure of these networks can determine the economic effects associated with corruption in these countries.

Section I explains the structural pressures resulting in significant degrees of corruption in virtually every developing country. One reason why it has been difficult to allocate resources in developing countries in ways which are always strictly legal is that for a wide range of critical rights any state allocation would be perceived to be illegitimate. Economic development is characterised by the creation of new wealth-owning classes. The rights which underpin the emergence of these classes are by definition new and not widely perceived to be legitimate. The underlying problem of course is that in developing countries the result of these early developmental allocations are widely and correctly perceived to have consequences for generations to come when new classes stabilise. As a result many decisions made by states concerning the allocation of these critical rights cannot easily be made through strictly legal frameworks simply because a transparent allocative rule is often impossible to agree on. Thus, even in countries where rapid growth takes place, there has been a tendency for state allocations to be not fully exposed to public scrutiny and so susceptible to corruption. The interesting question is why some countries were more effective in generating growth despite these problems while in others wealth was transferred to relatively unproductive groups. Section II summarises a number of explanations offered by economists and develops one which has not received much attention: the relative political power of the different groups of clients demanding rights (and resources) from patrons in the state.

Section III compares several key differences in the patron–client networks in a number of Asian countries to show how differences in the distribution of power implicit in these networks may explain differences in the types of rights created and allocated by the state and thereby differences in their economic performance. In the South Asian countries of the Indian subcontinent, the patron–client networks reveal the substantial political power of clients from intermediate 'non-capitalist' classes. Attempts to accommodate the demands of these intermediate classes has resulted in interlocked patron–client transactions involving bureaucrats and politicians on the one hand and capitalists and non-capitalist clients on the other. These interlocked exchanges have meant that the rights created or allocated by the state became locked into enmeshed networks and were not easy to subsequently re-allocate. This in turn resulted in structural sclerosis. In contrast, in South Korea, patron–client exchanges were almost entirely insulated from the demands of intermediate classes because of the historical weakness of intermediate classes in that country. Politicians and through them the bureaucrats allocating new rights to capitalists could extract substantial payoffs from industrial groups. But here the networks through which these exchanges were organised allowed the re-allocation of these rights. This in turn created strong incentives for the state to re-allocate rights and resources in ways which maximised long-run growth.

South-East Asian countries present a number of interesting variants which in different ways resulted in more dynamic economies than in South Asia despite the presence of large intermediate classes and more complex patterns of patron–client exchanges than in South Korea. Malaysia inherited a large class of individuals whose demands could potentially have resulted in patron–client exchanges of the Indian variety. However, in Malaysia the clear ethnic division between intermediate classes who were largely Malay and a capitalist class which was initially largely Chinese paradoxically allowed the construction of a structure of patron–client exchanges which allowed fairly rapid growth. Instead of many decentralised patron–client exchanges between many different patrons and groups of clients, the ethnic redistribution adopted by the New Economic Policy in the 1970s allowed a centralised sharing of rents in Malaysia. This served to prevent structural sclerosis from developing along Indian lines.

Thailand provides yet another South-East Asian variant. Here Chinese capitalists were well integrated into local political elites and an ethnic-based patronage politics along Malaysian lines did not emerge. Instead, the relatively well-developed capitalist class took over patronage networks themselves. They became the patrons 'buying off' the demands of potential clients from amongst the aspiring intermediate classes and using this political power to bargain for resource allocation to their particular faction. The role of capitalists in Thai politics is apparent in the exceptionally large number of capitalists (by developing country standards) involved in Thai electoral politics. Here we have yet another structure of patron–client exchanges which allowed a relatively decentralised type of capitalism to thrive. These explorations suggest how the location of corrupt transactions within specific structures of patron–client exchanges can help to make sense of differential economic performance.

It may be utopian to believe that the transition to capitalism can be entirely just. Yet unless the transition process is widely perceived to be just, it is difficult for it to be organised in a legally regulated way in an open polity. External pressure to tackle corruption may help development only if such pressure contributes to the legitimisation of the processes through which capitalism is being created. On the other hand, it is very likely that anti-corruption strategies may sometimes make the problem of organising internal political stability more difficult during processes of capitalist transition which could in turn prolong instability and the perpetuation of underdevelopment. The issue of corruption thus brings to the fore the limits of attempts to establish high standards of justice in the transition to capitalism in the absence of any global political commitment to share equitably the costs of structural change.

I. CORRUPTION IN DEVELOPING COUNTRIES

It is not very useful to quibble over formal definitions of corruption. Most usually corruption is defined as the violation of the formal rules governing the allocation of public resources by officials in response to offers of financial gain or political support [*Nye, 1967; Khan, 1996b*]. However it is defined, corruption appears to be endemic in developing countries and indeed there are systematic reasons why this should be the case. Accumulation and the allocation of public resources in developing countries very frequently involves changes in established property rights and institutions or the creation of entirely new ones. To put it simply, the state is allocating rights and resources at a time when a new capitalist class is emerging. Given the long-run and even inter-generational consequences of these allocations, there are huge incentives to dispute, contest and attempt to change all such allocations.

For these processes *not* to involve corruption, the allocation and creation of these new rights would have to follow strict rules so that particular individuals could not change these allocations by bribing. The problem is that any such rules would themselves have to be set up publicly. Given the post-colonial political settlement in most developing countries, it is unlikely that explicit rules which aim to create new capitalist classes could be set up in such a way as to enjoy widespread legitimacy. If we recognise that what is happening in developing countries is the creation of new classes by the allocation and stabilisation of new rights, it is easy to appreciate the substantial difficulties in following a transparent and accountable route to the construction of capitalism even if developing country leaders had always been minded to follow such a route.

Suppose we were to try to construct a set of transparent and legitimate rules through which capitalist property rights were to be created. On the one hand, the *supply* of the resources through which the emergence of the new class is being encouraged is severely limited in developing countries. This is a manifestation of underdevelopment and poverty. On the other hand, there is likely to be a very great *demand* for access to these resources so that particular individuals can join this emerging class. Anti-colonial struggles mobilised large multi-class populist alliances in many developing countries and post-colonial states could not explicitly formulate rules of allocation which appeared to leave any of these groups out of the contest. Constitutions and laws enshrined principles of allocation which were egalitarian and fair at a time when underlying resource constraints made following such principles extremely difficult. The large gap between demand and supply has meant that the actual allocation of property rights often failed the principles of allocation which the law set out. Very great incentives were created for corruption. This was as true for the allocation of land, credit or licenses to emerging industrialists as for the allocation of irrigation water or credit to emerging capitalist farmers.

The contest over public resources is particularly severe because the early beneficiaries of these contests are winners in a game of class evolution which is likely to have consequences for generations to come. In many cases the individuals who succeed in establishing themselves at this critical stage only do so as a result of a great deal of good fortune, political connections, some initial wealth or corruption. None of these characteristics can legitimise the large differences in income and wealth which subsequently emerge. Given the inherent unfairness involved in these processes it has been relatively easy to organise opposition to these characteristics of the development processes in most developing countries. Opposition has typically been organised by members of emerging middle-class groups who have been left behind in the development process and is therefore more intense in societies where these groups are better organised and entrenched.

Paradoxically, the opposition of these groups has often resulted in a second set of structural pressures generating high levels of corruption in developing countries. The opposition of organised groups has often had to be bought off by payoffs from existing elites or directly from the state to the most troublesome or vociferous opponents in an attempt to 'purchase' support or legitimacy. This type of corruption is more overtly political in motivation as opposed to the corruption which results from the excess demand for publicly allocated resources and rights. Here the state allocates resources to those with the greatest ability to create political problems rather than to those who have the greatest ability to pay (see Khan [1996a] for a discussion of the significance of the distinction). Political corruption too results in surreptitious transfers because (in most cases) payoffs to opponents in proportion to their ability to make trouble could not by its nature be publicly recorded in the budget.

This is the general background against which we need to examine the evolution of patterns of corruption in Asian countries. The approach in this paper will be to locate the processes of corruption in the context of the very different routes through which classes and property rights have been evolving in developing countries. We argue that by so doing we are better able to account for the differences in the apparent effects of corruption across countries. The processes of accumulation have been quite different across Asia. The rights which were being created for emerging capitalist classes and the terms under which these rights were being created differed greatly. Since the social utility of property rights depends quite a lot on which rights are created and the terms of their creation it is not surprising that the processes of corruption in these countries were associated with a very wide range of economic performance. To say this is not to justify corruption even under those conditions where it was associated with rapid growth. Rather it is to point out that corruption can have much more damaging effects in contexts where it is associated with growth-retarding patterns of accumulation. It is also to point out that corruption is often integrally linked with the political processes through which capitalism is being constructed rather than simply being an excrescence which can be easily excised.

The literature on corruption has been concerned from the outset with whether corruption was beneficial or harmful and under what circumstances. However, the circumstances were typically so broadly defined that in effect competing models appeared to show that corruption was likely to be either generally harmful or generally beneficial. For instance, in an early contribution Leff [1964] argued that corruption was likely to have beneficial effects in developing countries suffering from restrictive private monopolies and state intervention. By allowing entrepreneurs to side-step restrictive rules, Leff argued that corruption could result in more efficient resource allocation. Since virtually every developing country could be described as having restrictive rules in key sectors as well as private monopolies, Leff's argument suggests that corruption could be generally beneficial in a large number of countries. In fact, in the African countries Leff was particularly interested in, the beneficial effects of corruption were least in evidence.

In contrast Myrdal [1968] argued that the possibility of corruption may induce bureaucrats to introduce legislation which created new obstacles. Myrdal's argument anticipates some of the rent-seeking literature which appeared in the 1970s and 1980s. Since bureaucrats can always create new possibilities of extracting bribes by creating new restrictions, Myrdal, and the rent-seeking literature generally are suspicious of *any* corruption. This type of argument suggests that in general corruption signals harmful rent-seeking by state officials who have deliberately created value-reducing restrictions whose effects leave society worse off. Neither can this approach do justice to the widespread evidence of substantial corruption in many developing countries which enjoyed high rates of growth. Indeed historical evidence suggests the presence of widespread corruption in the currently advanced countries at an earlier stage of *their* development. The gradual reduction of corruption in the successful developers may have been the *result* rather than the precondition of successful development.

Clearly we need to have an analytical framework which allows corruption to have different effects in different countries. If indeed corruption has a uniform effect (whether good or bad) everywhere, this should be the conclusion reached at the end of a process of evaluation and analysis rather than a presumption made at the outset. If on the other hand, corruption can have variable effects, identifying these differences could be of great policy importance. Even if all corruption is equally undesirable on moral grounds, the differences between them in terms of their *economic* effects may inform the direction of policy and institutional attention. Two sets of observations constitute the starting point of our enquiry: (1) the association of corruption with poor performance in the South Asian countries; and (2) the comparatively much better performance of East and South-East Asian countries despite the prevalence of substantial corruption there.

Informal journalistic evidence suggests that corruption has been widespread in virtually all developing countries. This view is corroborated by the subjective responses of foreigners who have done business in these countries. These responses are summarised in the *Business International* corruption index which is reported in Table 1 for our sample of countries for the period 1980–83. Table 1 shows that for this group of countries, the extent of corruption correlates very poorly with economic performance. The differences between subjective corruption indices ranging from 6 to 4 are not necessarily significant but the table does suggest that over the relevant period, very corrupt Thailand did not perform significantly worse than apparently less corrupt South Korea and probably better than less corrupt and more resource-rich Malaysia. As a group, these countries combined good performance with high levels of corruption. The South Asian countries fit more closely with the

TABLE 1
CORRUPTION AND ECONOMIC PERFORMANCE

Country	Corruption Index 1980–83	GDP Growth Rates	
		1970–80	1980–92
Malaysia	6.0	7.9	5.9
South Korea	5.7	9.6	9.4
India	5.25	3.4	5.2
Pakistan	4.0	4.9	6.1
Bangladesh	4.0	2.3	4.2
Thailand	1.5	7.1	8.2

Note: A Corruption Index of 10 indicates 'No Corruption', an Index of 0 indicates 'Maximum Corruption'.

Sources: Mauro [*1995*]; World Development report [*1994*].

perception that corruption is associated with poor performance. But even here, more corrupt Pakistan appears to have performed somewhat better than less corrupt India.

Some of the differences in performance between these countries may be accounted for by variations in economic variables such as investment rates. However, we will concentrate on factors which may explain why corruption is itself associated with differential effects across countries.

II. SOME DETERMINANTS OF THE EFFECTS OF CORRUPTION

The overall economic effect of corruption can be broken down into two components. The first is the economic effect of the bribe. The resources transferred in the bribe itself often results in a reduction in social value and is therefore an economic cost for society. In theory, however, bribes could be pure transfers which simply redistribute wealth but keep total wealth unchanged. In this rare case the bribe itself may be costless for society. In the more usual case, bribes from industrialists or other social actors to state officials represent a social cost of variable magnitude as social wealth is reduced to a greater or lesser extent. This is typically the case if the bribe-giver would otherwise have invested the bribe in production whereas the transfer to the official typically results in consumption with possible value-reduction for the economy over time. This is the first effect of corruption which is the effect of the flow of resources from social actors to state officials shown by the higher arrow in Figure 1.

The second effect of corruption is the economic consequence of the new rights or reallocations of rights brought about by state officials as the quid pro quo of the bribes they have received. This is the effect of the rights created or transferred by state officials in response to the bribe which is shown by the lower arrow in Figure 1. This part of the analysis is much more complicated as it is not always the case that the changes brought about as a result of, or in association with, corruption are always value-reducing for society. (Leff's argument was a simple version of the value-enhancing possibility.) There is also a problem of choosing the benchmark quite carefully (the structure and allocation of rights which would have existed *in the absence* of corruption) to judge this effect correctly [*Khan, 1996b*]. Clearly Figure 1 is a simplification of the possibly complex flows of bribes and payoffs from social actors to state officials on the one hand and flows of rights, subsidies and allocations of public resources from officials to social actors on the other. We examine some of these complexities in greater detail later.

The overall effect of corruption is the joint effect of the direct implications of the bribe and the effect of the rights created or transferred as a result. Differential effects across countries can be due to differences in either or both

FIGURE 1
THE TWO ECONOMIC EFFECTS OF CORRUPTION

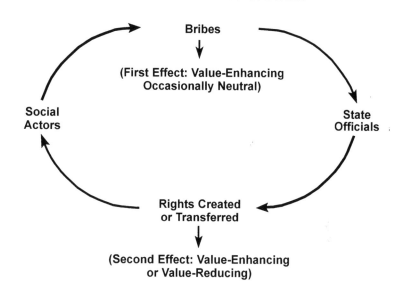

of these effects [*Khan, 1997*]. In some cases corruption may be damaging mainly because the bribes are large or may have particularly damaging effects on the economy because of lost opportunities for investors or the use made of the bribes by recipients. In other cases the significant negative effect of corruption may be due to the types of rights created, whom they are created for and the terms under which they are created. The patron–client networks which we will concentrate on in this article have implications for the effects of corruption particularly because of their role in determining the second effect, that is in determining the types of rights which are created or transferred through corrupt transactions.

Patron–client networks describe a set of transactions which may overlap with and yet are analytically distinct from corruption. Patron–client relationships are repeated relationships of exchange between specific patrons and their clients. A number of features distinguish patron–client exchanges from other types of exchange. First, such exchanges are usually personalised. They involve an identifiable patron and an identifiable set of clients. Entry and exit is considerably less free compared to normal market transactions. Second, the exchange is between two distinct *types* of agents, distinguished by status, power or other characteristics [*Schmidt et al., 1977: xiii–xxxvii*]. Typically the superior member is the patron and the inferior member the client. Clearly a wide range of exchanges in developing countries between state officials and privileged groups of clients can be described in these terms. Nevertheless, the power or status of the patron can vary across a broad range and these differences may be important for understanding the types of exchanges taking place within different patron–client networks [*Khan, 1996a; 1996b*]. It is this insight which makes patron–client networks interesting for the study of corruption. The type of network can give us critical additional information about the types of rights being transacted and the terms on which these transactions take place. Some characteristics of patrons and clients which are likely to influence the economic implications of the transactions are easily dealt with by economists; others are less simple to model.

Objectives and Ideologies

Economists normally assume that actors in state and society will want to maximise value for themselves. At the very least, they will want to maximise value for someone. In fact both state officials and social actors may be motivated by ends which are primarily non-economic such as race or ethnicity. To the extent that transactions between patrons and clients reflect such non-economic goals, economic value may obviously not be maximised [*North, 1981; 1995*].

The objectives of state officials and social actors determine their goals while their ideologies (shared assumptions about how the world works) influence the ways in which they attempt to achieve them. Exchanges within patron–client networks can only be value-maximising if the partners to the exchange want to achieve value maximisation for themselves or at least for others. It is not necessary that they be totally motivated by value maximisation as long as a substantial part of decision-making is motivated by it. If transactions are value-maximising for individuals they may also, under certain conditions, be value-maximising for society. On the other hand, transactions which are not even value-maximising for the transactors are very unlikely to be value-maximising for society. Apart from being motivated (to a large extent at least) by economic value-maximisation, it is also necessary that the participants have ideologies which enable them to learn rapidly so that they do not hold on to beliefs about causes and effects which do not stand up to repeated experience. North [*1995*] has recently stressed the importance of ideologies and learning processes in explaining differences in performance across countries. Ideologies could therefore have some role to play in explaining why both corrupt and non-corrupt transactions within patron–client networks may differ across countries. While ideologies and learning processes may be important it is likely that their importance has been exaggerated in some recent work [*Khan, 1995: 79–85*].

Numbers of Clients

The numbers of potential clients of each type can affect their success in organising collective action in bargaining with patrons. If small groups with specific interests are more successful in organising collective action, they may bribe or lobby more effectively than bigger groups and indeed the rest of society [*Olson, 1965; 1982*]. This could result in rights being created to favour small groups even when they are value-reducing for society as a whole. However, small numbers are only part of the story. In most developing countries, resources have to be directed to and rights created for small numbers of emerging 'capitalists'. But in fact their expected advantage in lobbying or bribing due to their small numbers is often over-ridden by the bargaining power of other groups such as the urban middle classes or rich peasants whose power is often based on their *large* numbers. Thus while numbers are important, their effect on bargaining power is more complicated than is suggested by the simplest interpretations of Olson's model.

The Homogeneity of Clients

This too may determine the chances of successful collective action by different groups of clients. More importantly, the homogeneity or otherwise of particular groups may determine the relative transaction costs facing state officials or political patrons in collecting bribes from that group. If some clients are relatively easy to transact with (say because they are of the same ethnic group as the patrons), the latter may prefer to deal with them even if others may notionally have been willing to pay more. Thus, for instance, the relative homogeneity of small groups demanding value-reducing rights may be successful while less homogenous larger groups demanding value-enhancing rights may fail. The relative transaction costs of dealing with different groups of clients may be relevant for explaining some outcomes of patron–client exchanges in developing countries [*Khan, 1997*].

The Institutions through which Patrons and Clients Interact

These include in particular the institutions of the state through which patrons and clients negotiate and carry out exchanges. Institutions can influence both the 'demand' for new rights (the flow of bribes to state officials) as well as influencing the 'supply' of rights (the flows of rights from patrons to those offering bribes). On the demand side, institutions may allow or prevent particular groups of clients to compete for new rights or resources. They also describe the rules of the game which define how clients who bribe can expect their chances of winning to change as a result. These institutional features determine the magnitude of the bribes offered by particular groups of clients demanding particular rights or re-allocations of rights [*Mueller, 1989: 229–35*]. On the supply side, the degree of fragmentation of institutions may determine how easy it is for different patrons to coordinate their transactions. A failure to coordinate may sometimes result in lower valued rights being created even though patrons might collectively have extracted bigger bribes by collectively creating higher valued rights [*Rose-Ackerman, 1978; Shleifer and Vishny, 1993*]. Institutional structures can thus play an important role in determining the outcomes of patron–client exchanges.

The Relative Political Power of Patrons and Clients

The potential role of relative political power in determining the types of rights transacted between patrons and clients has not been adequately recognised in the literature. The relative political power of clients determines the *type* of payoff they can offer to the patron. If clients are politically weak, the patron is likely to extract the maximum *economic* payoff from the client in the form of a bribe commensurate with the right being created or transferred. At the other extreme, if the patron is politically weak, the client may instead be offering political support rather than an economic payoff. The payoff to the patron in this case is not just the value of the bribe paid to state officials and politicians but also the political support (or absence of political opposition) which is often also offered [*Khan, 1996a; 1996b*]. We argue that a critical factor determining differences in the rights which are transacted between patrons and clients in different settings is the relative power of competing groups of clients and their patrons in the state.

One reason why political power has received little attention from economists is that it is relatively difficult to define. Steven Lukes distinguished between power defined as a *collective capacity* which he called *power₁* and power defined as an *asymmetric relationship* between individuals or groups which he called *power₂* [*Lukes, 1978: 636*]. The first type of power is relevant when we want to discuss power as a transformative capacity. However, for our purposes, the relevant notion of power is *power₂* in Lukes' terminology. *Power₂* determines whether clients are able to bargain a more or less attractive deal with their patrons. Udehn [*1996: 150*] suggests an even narrower version of *power₂* which he calls *power₃* and defines as the capacity of some actors to reward and/or punish other actors. *Power₃* and its determinants may be most relevant for looking at differential bargaining outcomes within patron–client networks. The determinants of *power₃* determine the extent to which clients are able to inflict political costs on patrons if they are ignored. The greater the power of clients in terms of the second and third definitions, the more likely is it that patrons will be offering powerful groups of clients rights in exchange for political support rather than economic payoffs.

Differences in the power of specific groups of clients across countries may then be important for understanding differences in the bargains they are able to strike with their patrons. It may determine whether patrons are primarily motivated by economic or political considerations when negotiating with clients. When clients lack political power in the form of *power₃*, patrons can focus on economic considerations alone. Other things being equal (the factors discussed earlier), a patron allocating a right will prefer to allocate or create rights for clients who add the most value. This is because these clients will in principle be able to offer the biggest bribes. In contrast when clients have the power to disrupt or otherwise impose political costs on patrons, purely economic considerations are not enough. We have elsewhere described the costs which clients can threaten to impose as *transition costs* [*Khan, 1995: 81–3*]. To avoid these costs, rights may be created for or allocated to clients on the basis of their relative power to disrupt. Thus this type of power may have implications for the rights which are created through patron–client transactions including those involving corruption.

III. CORRUPTION AND POWER IN PATRON–CLIENT NETWORKS

Exchanges within patron–client networks are in reality much more complex than the neat bilateral exchanges shown in Figure 1. While some of these complexities may be usefully abstracted from, others are critically important for picking up economically relevant differences in a comparative analysis. In particular, the position of different types of clients and actors within the state and their bargaining relationships need to be identified even if in a highly simplified way in different contexts. Nevertheless, the basic format of the implicit exchanges outlined in Figure 1 can still be used to keep track of what is going on in transactions involving several groups of patrons and clients.

In what follows, we identify what we think are key features of exchanges within patron–client networks in several Asian countries. The characteristics identified are based on the work of political scientists and political economists and refer to exchanges which may be described as typical of those countries without suggesting that these are the only types of patron–client exchanges occurring. We then identify why these patterns may be relevant for understanding the economic performance of these countries, and therefore the economic consequences of the associated corruptions.

South Asia

Despite important differences between India, Pakistan and Bangladesh there are substantial similarities in the predominant types of corruption observed in these three populous South Asian countries. The basic patterns of subcontinental corruption were described by Wade in his classic studies of corruption in the irrigation bureaucracy of a South Indian state [*Wade, 1984; 1985; 1989*]. The distinguishing characteristic of corruption in the Indian subcontinent is the close intermeshing of economic and political calculations in exchanges between patrons and clients at different levels.

A number of factors have contributed to the evolution of complex networks of interlinked exchanges in the Indian subcontinent. The factor which is

28   CORRUPTION AND DEVELOPMENT

probably the single most important one for the exchanges which concern us is
the political importance of intermediate classes in the Indian social structure.
Important groups of clients in the Indian subcontinent have been drawn from
these intermediate or 'middle' classes. Often the professional members of
these groups have been recognised as equal members of the dominant class
coalition in India, along with capitalists and landlords [*Bardhan, 1984*].
However, for our purposes it is useful to distinguish between the capitalist
members of the dominant coalition and the much larger non-capitalist section
which consists of emerging middle class groups, the educated sections of the
population, both employed and unemployed and others who use political
power to get access to resources. The importance of these non-capitalist
intermediate classes in the subcontinental political space far outweighs their
numbers which in any case would run into many millions.

The relevant power of this latter group is very largely the third type of
power discussed earlier. It is a power which is based fundamentally on their
organisational and political ability to disrupt and challenge the legitimacy of
patrons who fail to deliver [*Khan, 1989*]. This is reflected in a state tradition
of rapid and ongoing accommodation and incorporation of emerging
intermediate groups even while fairly ruthless suppression appears to be taking
place. One of the most important mechanisms of incorporation is the transfer
of surpluses to these classes through patron–client exchanges, some of which
are perfectly legal (such as subsidies) while others are corrupt and involve
illegal transfers of resources or the transfer of resources which were illegally
generated.

Both Pakistan and India and subsequently Bangladesh inherited the effects
of a deep-rooted anti-colonial political mobilisation which empowered their
emerging 'middle classes'. They inherited a tradition of political activity on
the basis of a wide variety of emotive symbols including language, caste and
religion and these patterns of mobilisation were widely accepted as legitimate
in the post-colonial society. Politics based on these symbols has not enriched
the vast majority of the populations of these countries but *has* enabled
successive layers of emerging middle class groups to get access to public
resources on the basis of their ability to organise much more numerous groups
below them. Those amongst the intermediate classes who happened to be in
power found it necessary to organise transfers to the most vociferous of the
excluded groups in ongoing processes of accommodation and incorporation.

What is important is that a large part of the transfer (whether legal or
illegal) from patrons to intermediate classes of clients has been based on the
political bargaining power of these pyramidally organised groups of clients.
These transfers in turn have had to be financed and patrons had to find the
resources for such transfers either in general taxation or through exchanges
with other groups of clients. The inadequacy of general fiscal resources is an

important part of the reason why we observe a complex intermeshing of political and economic exchanges in patron–client networks in the Indian subcontinent. Political elites have often found the resources with which they 'finance' their political survival in their economic exchanges with other groups of clients, in particular the slowly emerging class of industrial capitalists. This is an important factor explaining the dense structure of interlinked economic and political exchanges which Wade identified but did not adequately explain. Political 'corruption' led to economic corruption as each group of politicians organised their own networks of resource collection and distribution.

The interlocked networks based around each political faction in turn have had important implications for the rights which are created or allocated to capitalists and which in turn have implications for long-run performance. Capitalists too are rational political actors and in a context where no political actor or bureaucrat is able to operate without satisfying their constituencies, it has been relatively easy for capitalists to ensure that they too were funding powerful constituencies so that their interest in leading the easy life could not be challenged. As a result the politicians and bureaucrats who have organised their political survival through such localised arrangements are often unable to change the structure or allocation of rights to capitalists even when this would raise value. The difficulty of *changing* the structure of rights because of such interlinked patron–client exchanges thus serves to block structural change and productivity growth when growth requires the creation of new rights or the re-allocation or alteration of existing rights.

Figure 2 shows the potential complexity of the flows of resources between patrons and clients in the political context typical of most South Asian countries. Bureaucrats and politicians constitute two parallel hierarchies and at each level bureaucrats or politicians may be patrons for lower level colleagues or for groups elsewhere in society. For simplicity Figure 2 only distinguishes between two social groups, the capitalist and non-capitalist clients of the state, the latter being the intermediate classes discussed earlier. The most successful non-capitalist clients often become political leaders or even capitalists over time. The most distinctive feature of these patron–client exchanges are the transfers going from politicians at different levels to different groups of non-capitalist clients. The quid pro quo from these clients to the state is not shown in Figure 2 because it is typically not an economic payoff but rather a 'payoff' in the form of political quiescence or support.

The resources for the economic payoffs to the intermediate classes come from the rest of society in the form of taxes or transfers from other groups of clients. If we look at the nodes representing the 'capitalist' clients of the state, we see a number of transfers going the other way, this time from these clients to patrons in the bureaucracy and in the political structure. Emerging capitalists are willing to make these transfers to politicians and bureaucrats

FIGURE 2
PATRON–CLIENT NETWORKS IN THE INDIAN SUBCONTINENT

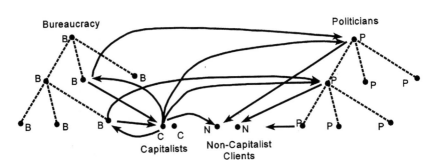

because they too are often receiving subsidies, allocations of valuable property rights or at the very least the protection of their property rights. Emerging capitalists in both India and Pakistan have received large subsidies and were allocated scarce resources such as land, credit and foreign exchange on a preferential basis. This was justified by the claim that these were transfers which would induce industrialisation or agricultural growth which in turn was perceived by the respective states as essential for the survival of the economy and of their country's sovereignty. The kickbacks from industrialists have in turn been an important source of finance for the political survival strategies of subcontinental politicians.

While the networks of corruption and political payoffs in India have often been commented on, the economic implications of these complex networks have not been analysed. An important consequence was that allocations of rights and subsidies which were to create a new capitalist class rapidly got embroiled in the networks of transfers which maintained political stability. As a result any particular allocation proved very difficult to change once it had become established as change provoked opposition from many different quarters. Economic allocations to particular capitalists were soon difficult to separate from the political payoffs to the non-capitalist clients who had been accommodated through interlocking transfers. The eventual result was the emergence of persistent subsidies for poorly performing industries and sectors which were difficult to change in response to performance failures or changes in technology and markets.

This result was common to both India and Pakistan in the 1960s and beyond despite the institutional and policy differences between Nehru's Five Year Plans and Ayub's authoritarian industrial policy. Declining economic performance combined with a sustained growth in political demands from emerging middle classes led to dramatic political crises in the Indian subcontinent. These twin features characterised the dismemberment of Pakistan in 1971, ethnic violence in post-1971 Pakistan, deep-seated political instability in Bangladesh and the growth of centrifugal political forces in India as linguistic and regional forces gathered strength in the 1970s and 1980s.

South Korea

The revelations of corruption in South Korea which have begun to emerge in the 1990s suggest that corruption in North East Asia has probably been as extensive in terms of the relative magnitudes of the transfers as it has been in South Asia. On the other hand, the pattern of resource flows appears to be both different and simpler. This seems to have been particularly the case in the early days of industrial policy in the 1960s [*Kim, 1994: 59–70; Kong, 1996*]. There is evidence, however, that political power has become more dispersed over the 1980s resulting in more complex patterns of transfers [*Ravenhill, 1997*]. The broad features of the South Korean case suggest a much higher degree of concentration of political power which allowed the political executive to extract rents from beneficiaries of new rights without having to make political side-payments to non-capitalist clients to anything like the extent which we observe in South Asia.

FIGURE 3
PATRON–CLIENT NETWORKS IN SOUTH KOREA

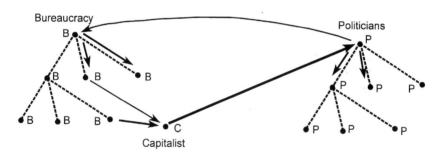

Figure 3 is a simplified picture of resource flows within patron–client networks in South Korea. Given the lesser importance of non-capitalist clients of the state in this case, we simplify by excluding non-capitalist clients from the figure. This outline is consistent with Amsden's [*1989*] account of the flows associated with industrial policy in South Korea and is in its main features corroborated by a number of subsequent observers [*Kim and Ma, 1997*]. The main features of the state-society transfers taking place were first the transfer of large subsidies from the state to emerging capitalists. These are shown by the arrows from different sets of patrons in the bureaucratic apparatus to specific clients in the industrial sector. We now also know that there were in exchange substantial kickbacks from these favoured industrial groups to the political leadership as rents from the growing industrial sector were re-distributed to the political leadership and through this route to bureaucrats as well [*Kong, 1996*]. The revelations of the last two years suggest that part of these rents were later distributed in a relatively orderly fashion down the higher levels of the political and bureaucratic hierarchies.

The centralised rent collection and distribution of industrial rents by the peak political leaders created powerful incentives to allocate and create rights in ways which maximised these rents over time. Rents are maximised *over time* if growth is maximised. This is simply saying that the economic ability of investors to pay bribes is proportional to the productivity of the investor. Recalling the factors considered in section II, in the absence of a short time horizon or other constraints on allocation, even politicians or officials who are merely concerned with maximising bribes over time will allocate rights or subsidies in such a way as to maximise growth. This involves making sure that the most productive entrepreneurs are favoured and the less productive ones are weeded out. The top politician in the South Korean state was able to operate in this way because the political bargaining power of unrelated individuals to bargain for payoffs was virtually absent during a critical phase of the country's development when key property rights were being established and developmental resources were being allocated for rapid industrialisation [*Woo-Cumings, 1997*]. The absence of a powerful intermediate class which could demand payoffs from the state at this critical stage of industrialisation can in turn be traced to Korea's social history and the nature of the Japanese colonial impact which prevented these classes from developing or consolidating [*Kohli, 1994*].

Malaysia

The South-East Asian countries provide interesting intermediate cases. Unlike South Korea and Taiwan with their fairly exceptional social structures formed under the Japanese colonial impact [*Kohli, 1994*], the South East Asian countries were closer to the South Asian pattern. Although less powerful and entrenched than in the Indian sub-continent, emergent middle classes in these countries possessed a greater ability to organise political opposition and thereby demand political payoffs compared to their North Asian counterparts. The political and institutional responses in these South East Asian countries show a wide range of variation in terms of the patterns of political side-payments organised to maintain political viability. Malaysia and Thailand provide two interesting contrasts to the South Asian case. In both these countries political payoffs and corruption were very important but did not prevent rapid accumulation and growth.

Malaysia inherited an ethnic problem which could have spelt disaster. In the 1960s it possessed an enterprising capitalist sector based on small scale trade and production but this sector was dominated by ethnic Chinese capitalists. An emerging Malay middle class was increasingly willing to use its political muscle to organise the Malay majority to get a larger share of the pie for itself. Fortunately for Malaysia, the coincidence of ethnic identities with class ones to some extent helped the organisation of political payoffs in a centralised way. The orderly solution to the legitimation problem emerged as an unintended consequence of the 1969 riots and the adoption of the New Economic Policy. The political bargain between patrons in the state and politically powerful claimants for resources was resolved through centralising the demands of the emerging Malay middle classes in an ethnically aligned political system. This allowed the state to organise political transfers centrally without constructing decentralised and interlocked exchanges between competing groups of political factions, their intermediate group clients and particular subsets of capitalists. The de-linking of political payoffs from economic corruption allowed in turn a greater degree of rationality in the allocation of subsidies and the protection of capitalist property rights than was possible in the Indian subcontinent [*Khan, 1997; Jomo and Gomez, 1997*].

FIGURE 4
PATRON–CLIENT NETWORKS IN MALAYSIA

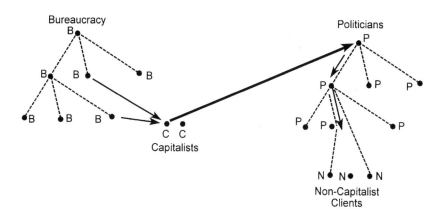

The characteristic features of the economic flows between patrons and clients in post-1969 Malaysia are shown in Figure 4. The most important transfers are shown in the arrow from the (largely) Chinese capitalists to the political leadership of the Malay party UMNO which dominated the political system. These transfers included both taxes and illegal extractions. The rents extracted were then centrally distributed through the political apparatus to the non-capitalist clients of UMNO shown by the arrows cascading down the political apparatus to non-capitalist clients. In return domestic capitalists received protection and increasingly, assistance for moving into high technology industries through the provision of good infrastructure and the negotiation of backward linkages between the state and the multinationals operating in Malaysia. These quid pro quo payoffs to Malaysia's capitalists were typically not large explicit subsidies (as in South Korea) but they were nevertheless of economic significance; these are indicated in Figure 4 by arrows from the bureaucracy to capitalists. The distinctiveness of this system, compared to the South Asian system was that rent extraction from the Chinese capitalists was centralised and, initially at least, direct links between particular capitalists and political factions in the Indian manner did not exist. This has changed to some extent over time as the Malaysian economy has grown and with it the political power of competing Malay factions within UMNO. But the picture sketched above is reasonably accurate for the late 1960s and early 1970s when Malaysia began its economic takeoff.

One feature which distinguishes Malaysia from the South Asian countries and partly explains why Malaysia's clientelist politics was able to coexist with a more dynamic and competitive capitalist sector is that country's vast resource wealth. This has allowed the distribution of political payoffs to the emerging Malay middle class on a large enough scale to keep them satisfied. It is doubtful whether the small productive sector in any of the post-colonial South Asian countries could have transferred rents to the state for centralised distribution on a scale that would have satisfied all the demands being made. On the other hand, the bipolar ethnic dimension of the conflict in Malaysia helped rather than hindered the construction of an efficient solution to the clientelist problem. It allowed the construction of a fairly explicit and centralised 'tax' system which taxed capitalists for the benefit of emerging intermediate groups. The language of ethnic deprivation allowed a high proportion of these exactions to be legitimised and therefore organised through centralised and legal party and state structures without secret deals and personalised bargains. This is consistent with the observation that Malaysia is the least corrupt of the group of countries shown in Table 1 according to subjective corruption indices. A non-ethnic and purely welfarist argument for transfers would not have been equivalent because it would have required that the bulk of the transfers went to the poorest groups in Malaysia and not necessarily to the leading factions of the intermediate classes who had the greatest political power. Given this problem facing a purely welfarist argument, it is difficult to imagine an equivalent ideology in India which could have served to justify a similar centralised transfer from capitalists to the leaders of India's contesting and diverse intermediate groups.

The accommodation of the Malay intermediate classes through the centralised collection and distribution of rents prevented the build-up of dense localised networks of exchanges between patrons and clients along the Indian pattern. This in turn allowed the structure of rights and subsidies allocated by the state to remain relatively fluid and allowed structural change without insuperable resistance being offered by large collections of localised intermediate groups. This fluidity has undoubtedly decreased somewhat over time as factions of intermediate groups within UMNO have become more powerful over time and have established decentralised alliances with large Chinese capitalist groups [*Jomo and Gomez, 1997*]. Second, by satisfying the Malay intermediate classes through rent transfers from Malaysian Chinese capitalists and by deploying natural resource rents, the Malaysian state could offer multinationals locating in the country a credible level of security for property rights and profits which was untypical by developing country standards. This, too, proved to be of great importance in encouraging relatively high-technology firms to locate in Malaysia in the 1970s and late 1980s and engage in backward linkages with Malaysian firms.

Thailand

In contrast to Malaysia, the Chinese capitalists of Thailand were much more ethnically integrated with the Thai middle class. The Malaysian pattern of patron–client exchanges which separated political from economic exchanges along ethnic lines could not therefore emerge in Thailand. Thailand was also different from all the countries discussed so far in not having experienced direct colonial occupation and rule. The absence of anti-colonial mobilisations explains why the political leadership of its emerging intermediate classes appears to have been weaker compared to the Indian subcontinent or even Malaysia. On the other hand, its intermediate classes were not as atomised as they were in South Korea which was subjected to Japanese colonial strategies. Unlike South Korea where Japanese land reform displaced rural power blocs, Thailand had powerful networks of rural politicians who had to be accommodated at a much earlier stage of development. Thus, despite its differences with India, it is quite possible that decentralised networks of patronage may have developed in Thailand to meet the political demands of powerful and largely rural clients. Instead, over the last 20 years Thailand seems to have witnessed a gradual taking over of localised political networks by local capitalists.

The key arrows in Figure 5 are the ones showing transfers from capitalists to political factions which allowed many Thai capitalists (almost uniquely in the Asian development context) to take over and run their own political factions. Thailand has the highest number of businessmen in parliament in the region [*Sidel, 1996*]. The most important feature distinguishing the Thai

FIGURE 5
PATRON–CLIENT NETWORKS IN THAILAND

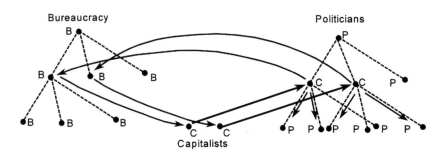

political system has been the ability and willingness of its capitalists to buy
their own political factions. Control over their own factions has not only given
Thai capitalists places in parliament. It has also given them the political power
to gain direct access to favoured subsidies and the allocation of rights, for
instance in the form of franchises and licenses [*Doner and Ramsay, 1997*].
Uniquely perhaps in Asia, the political power of Thai capitalists frequently
places them in the position of patrons within their own patron–client networks.
While Thai capitalists, like their counterparts in the other Asian countries, have
had to make transfers to the political system as part of the maintenance cost of
their property rights, their payoffs were managed by the 'private' political
networks which they controlled.

The Thai pattern of patron–client exchanges (both legal and illegal) has
also had identifiable and important effects in Thailand. The fact that Thai
capitalists have been directly involved in the protection of their property rights
meant that resources were not centrally controlled or allocated by the state to
quite the same extent as in the other countries. As a result Thai capitalism has
been based on the acquisition of relatively small scale technology with
property rights over these assets being protected in a decentralised way by this
type of political corruption and patron–client exchanges.

The number of capitalists entering the political fray in Thailand has also
been large, the result of a history of accumulation by small-scale immigrant
Chinese traders many of whom became extremely wealthy over a long period
of time. This has ensured vigorous political competition between capitalists for
the spoils of power which has prevented the political system from being
monopolised by any particular capitalist faction. Instead there has been
vigorous competition for entry into markets through political competition
between competing factions in the parliament and the bureaucracy. Although
the political costs of this competition have been high in the form of rampant
corruption and political instability, the long-run economic performance of

Thailand has been relatively better than that of its South Asian neighbours. If political stability does not collapse entirely, long-run economic growth may eventually make it possible to attenuate the worst effects of Thai political corruption through constitutional and political reforms.

CONCLUSION

The proposition discussed in this study has been that the existence and effects of corruption cannot be properly studied outside the context of capitalist accumulation and the political contests which it faces from other emerging classes in the surrounding social milieu. Economists have typically examined the economic incentives promoting corruption while leaving to political scientists the task of analysing its political roots. This paper argues that the forms of economic corruption and their effects are closely tied to the forms of political corruption. This approach raises fundamental dilemmas for policy approaches to corruption. The public face of corruption is clearly unacceptable and in the long run it may destroy the limited legitimacy of some developing country states. On the other hand, the visible face of corruption is often an integral part of processes of accumulation and social compromise which are no less ugly in themselves.

Capitalist accumulation in its early phases creates new classes of privileged property holders whose justifiable claim to be in this position instead of many other potential contenders may be very limited. The contests they face from emerging middle classes may be difficult to deal with other than through political side-payments. These side-payments are in turn difficult to organise publicly and from funds which are open to public scrutiny except to a limited extent in rare cases such as Malaysia where a convenient legitimising ideology for such transfers can emerge. This is because while the demands of the intermediate classes may be perfectly understandable and may occasionally be considered legitimate, they may nevertheless be difficult to justify on welfare grounds in the face of widespread and much more serious poverty. Yet payoffs to some members of these classes may be a necessary part of the social compromise through which the process of transition is negotiated. Thus corruption of different types may emerge in these contexts as part of a range of exchanges which makes these systems work despite the obvious economic costs which we can identify by looking at parts of the system in isolation.

Drawing the line between 'acceptable' types of accumulation in early capitalism and 'unacceptable' types is never going to be easy. The more interesting question is to distinguish between situations where corruption has impoverishing effects from those where corruption allows rapid growth. We have argued that there are good reasons why corruption in South Korea may not have been that damaging for growth. While there may be other reasons for

South Korea's performance as well, our argument suggest that we do not need to rely entirely on these compensating factors to explain why this economy performed well despite the presence of substantial corruption. In fact a fair amount of corruption was involved during the transitional phases of all countries. The real issue is why the transition process is blocked in some developing countries as in South Asia. Here we have argued that the *patterns* of corruption may be integrally implicated which are in turn determined by the distribution of power between the state, capitalists and intermediate classes. The economic (as opposed to moral) problem is not corruption *per se* but the political structures which generate growth-retarding corruption. This analysis suggests that anti-corruption strategies which are concerned with the possible effects of corruption on development have explicitly to identify the underlying political problems. If corruption is politically generated and if the political structure of societies determines the economic effects of the ensuing corruption, in countries where development is blocked the only long run solution may be to provoke a sustained public discussion of such arguments so that new political arrangements can eventually be constructed.

REFERENCES

Amsden, A., 1989, *Asia's Next Giant: South Korea and Late Industrialization*, Oxford: Oxford University Press.

Aoki, M., Kim, M.-K. and M. Okuno-Fujiwara, 1997, *The Role of Government in East Asian Economic Development: Comparative Institutional Analysis*, Oxford: Clarendon Press.

Bardhan, P., 1984, *The Political Economy of Development in India*, Oxford: Basil Blackwell.

Doner, R.F. and A. Ramsay, 1997, 'Rents, Collective Action and Economic Development in Thailand', in Khan and Jomo [*1997, forthcoming*].

Jomo, K.S. and E.T. Gomez, 1997, 'Rent-seeking and the Creation of Efficient Rights: The Malaysian Dilemma', in M.H. Khan and K.S. Jomo (eds.), *Rents and Rent-Seeking*, forthcoming.

Khan, M.H., 1989, 'Clientelism, Corruption and Capitalist Development', unpublished Ph.D. dissertation, University of Cambridge.

Khan, M.H., 1995, 'State Failure in Weak States: A Critique of New Institutionalist Explanations', in J. Hunter, J. Harriss and C. Lewis (eds.), *The New Institutional Economics and Third World Development*, London: Routledge.

Khan, M.H., 1996a, 'A Typology of Corrupt Transactions in Developing Countries', *IDS Bulletin*, Vol.27, No.2.

Khan, M.H., 1996b, 'The Efficiency Implications of Corruption', *Journal of International Development*, Vol.8, No.5.

Khan, M.H., 1997, 'Rent-Seeking as Process: Its Inputs, Outputs and Differential Effects', in Khan and Jomo [*1997, forthcoming*].

Khan, M.H. and K.S. Jomo (eds.), forthcoming, *Rents and Rent-Seeking*.

Kim, H.-K. and J. Ma, 1997, 'The Role of Government in Acquiring Technological Capability: The Case of the Petrochemical Industry in East Asia', in Aoki, Kim and Okuno-Fujiwara [*1997*].

Kim, Y.J., 1994, *Bureaucratic Corruption: The Case of Korea*, Seoul: Cho Myung Press.

Kohli, A., 1994, 'Where Do High Growth Political Economies Come From? The Japanese Lineage of Korea's "Developmental State"', *World Development*, Vol.22, No.9.

Kong, T.Y., 1996, 'Corruption and its Institutional Foundation', *IDS Bulletin*, Vol.27, No.2.

Leff, N., 1964, 'Economic Development through Bureaucratic Corruption', *American Behavioral*

Scientist, reprinted in M. U. Ekpo (ed.), 1979, *Bureaucratic Corruption in Sub-Saharan Africa: Towards a Search for Causes and Consequences*, Washington, DC: University of America Press.

Lukes, S., 1978, 'Power and Authority', in T. Bottomore and R. Nisbet (eds.), *A History of Sociological Analysis*, London: Heinemann.

Mauro, P., 1995, 'Corruption and Growth', *Quarterly Journal of Economics*, Vol.110, No.3.

Mueller, D.C., 1989, *Public Choice II: A Revised Edition of Public Choice*, Cambridge: Cambridge University Press.

Myrdal, G., 1968, *Asian Drama: An Inquiry into the Poverty of Nations*, New York: Pantheon.

North, D.C., 1981, *Structure and Change in Economic History*, New York: Norton.

North, D., 1995, 'The New Institutional Economics and Development', in J. Hunter, J. Harriss and C. Lewis (eds.), *The New Institutional Economics and Third World Development*, London: Routledge.

Nye, J.S., 1967, 'Corruption and Political Development: A Cost-Benefit Analysis', *American Political Science Review*, Vol.61, No.2.

Olson, M., 1965, *The Logic of Collective Action*, Cambridge, MA: Harvard University Press.

Olson, M., 1982, *The Rise and Decline of Nations*, London: Yale University Press.

Ravenhill, J., 1997, 'Rents, Corruption and Development: Yes, No and Maybe', in Khan and Jomo [*forthcoming*].

Rose-Ackerman, S., 1978, *Corruption: A Study in Political Economy*, New York: Academic Press.

Schmidt, S.W., Guasti, L., Landé, C.H. and J.C. Scott (eds.), 1977, *Friends, Followers, and Factions*, Berkeley, CA: University of California Press.

Shleifer, A. and R.W. Vishny, 1993, 'Corruption', *Quarterly Journal of Economics*, Vol.108, No.3.

Sidel, J.T., 1996, 'Siam and its Twin? Democratization and Bossism in Contemporary Thailand and the Philippines', *IDS Bulletin*, Vol.27, No.2.

Udehn, L., 1996, *The Limits of Public Choice: A Sociological Critique of the Economic Theory of Politics*, London: Routledge.

Wade, R., 1984, 'The System of Administrative and Political Corruption: Canal Irrigation in South India', *Journal of Development Studies*, Vol.18, No.3.

Wade, R., 1985, 'The Market for Public Office: Why the Indian State is not Better at Development', *World Development*, Vol.13, No.4.

Wade, R., 1989, 'Politics and Graft: Recruitment, Appointment, and Promotions to Public Office in India', in P.M. Ward (ed.), *Corruption, Development and Inequality: Soft Touch or Hard Graft?*, London: Routledge.

Woo-Cumings, M., 1997, 'The Political Economy of Growth in East Asia: A Perspective on the State, Market and Ideology', in Aoki, Kim and Okuno-Fujiwara [*1997*].

World Development Report, 1994, *Infrastructure for Development*, Oxford: Oxford University Press for the World Bank.

An Empirical Investigation of Bribery in International Trade

JOHANN GRAF LAMBSDORFF

It is shown that the degree of corruption of importing countries affects the trade structure of exporting countries. Whereas Sweden and Malaysia experience disadvantages with corrupt counterparts, the exports of Belgium/Luxembourg, France, Italy, the Netherlands and South Korea are positively related to the level of corruption of importing countries. While we controlled for geographic, sectoral, idiomatic and other influences, it is concluded that these findings are due to the differentiated inclination of exporters to offer bribes.

I. INTRODUCTION

> Whose is the greater blame in a shared evil?
> She who sins for pay, or he who pays for sin?

(Sor Juana Inés de la Cruz, seventeenth century, Mexico)

At a Summer School in Management[1] participants were asked how they would react to a foreign business partner who demands a bribe. This question stimulated a controversial debate. Some Southern European participants argued in favour of giving bribes, arguing that this may be the only way to seal a contract. This contrasted with the ambiguity of some Scandinavian participants who felt uneasy about bribes. Whatever the cause of these different attitudes, they represent a characteristic of international trade relations which has recently aroused controversy among trading partners. This study investigates these differences empirically.

Empirical research into corruption is quite a new undertaking. The starting point for cross–country analysis is usually some professional assessment of the degree of corruption in various countries. Such assessments are sometimes

The author is assistant professor at Göttingen University, Germany. He would like to thank Carsten Ackermann, Laurence Cockroft, Cheryl Gray, Fritz Heimann, Michael Johnston, Daniel Kaufmann, Guy Pfeffermann, Susan Rose-Ackerman, Mike Stevens and Robert Williams for critical comments. None of them necessarily endorses the results. Earlier versions of this work were presented as a paper at the Institut für Statistik und Ökonometrie, Göttingen University, Germany, the 'Workshop on Corruption and Development', IDS, Sussex and the 'Second EA-Convention for the Advancement of Social Sciences', Nicosia, Cyprus.

conducted by Risk Service Agencies and sold to investors. These data have recently been employed in academic research. Some academics have attempted to determine the negative effects of corruption on investment and growth [*Mauro, 1995*].[2] Its effects on the composition of government expenditure and foreign direct investments have also been scrutinised [*Mauro, 1996; Wei, 1997*]. Other contributions focus on the causes of corruption by investigating the impact of political competition and the extent of a country's openness on the level of corruption [*Ades and di Tella, 1995*]. Another line of research takes a corruption index as its starting point to describe qualitative differences between political systems [*Heidenheimer, 1996; Johnston, 1996; Bardhan, 1997; Wedeman, 1996*]. Closer to the approach adopted in this study is that of Hines [*1995*] who showed how improved legal standards with respect to bribery in international trade resulted in a fall in US aircraft exports and foreign direct investments after 1977. Whether these legal standards disadvantage US exports compared to those of other exporting countries however needs to be analysed within a cross-country analysis, a task which this analysis will undertake.

Section II provides a broad assessment of the current political discussion, focusing on legal aspects, real business behaviour and the question of responsibility. In section III the extent to which corruption in importing countries affects the trade structure of leading exporting countries is demonstrated. Section IV presents our conclusions.

II. THE CURRENT DEBATE

The Legal Viewpoint

With the imposition of the Foreign Corrupt Practices Act in 1977, the USA started to campaign for stronger international regulation of bribery of foreign officials. However, most trading partners did not endorse the US proposal to end tax deductibility and to impose legal sanctions. The usual line of reasoning is that imposing stricter national regulation hurts the export industry[3] while favouring competing countries' exports, especially of those countries with a lower standard of business ethics. Apparently we face a prisoner's dilemma: while all export nations may profit from transparent procurement and good codes of conduct it appears profitable to be the only one deviating from such behaviour. Complaints abound in the US concerning the corrupt trade practices of partners who are considered to give them an 'unfair' advantage. When a US power-generating company withdrew after being asked for a $3 million bribe in the Middle East, a Japanese company quickly stepped in. Whereas Lockheed was convicted of making payments of $1.5 million to an Egyptian government official in 1995 and fined $24 million,[4] the corrupt activities of

European and Asian competitors usually comply with domestic legal standards. In October 1995 Commerce Secretary Ron Brown presented a CIA report to the US Congress, claiming that between 1994 and 1995 the US lost $36 billion of business deals due to bribery and corruption by its competitors.[5] The report urged the US government to pressurise trading partners into a joint initiative to 'level the playing field for all competitors'. The then US Trade Representative Mickey Kantor picked up this initiative and threatened sanctions against countries which condone bribery.[6]

At the same time the OECD countries launched a joint initiative to improve the conduct of their export business. In May 1994 the Council of the OECD on Bribery in International Business Transactions recommended that each member country examine its criminal, civil and tax laws in order to prevent the bribing of foreign officials [*Transparency International, 1995: 87–8*]. In May 1996 the OECD members went one step further and agreed to 'criminalise the bribery of foreign officials in an effective and co-ordinated manner' and to re–examine the tax deductibility of bribes where this was still permitted (*Transparency International Newsletter*, June 1996). In May 1997 an agreement was signed by ministers of the 29 members of the organisation to enact laws by April 1998 making bribery a punishable offence and to open talks on an anti-graft pact.[7]

Arguably, the current debate focuses on legal standards.[8] What is missing in this context is an assessment of the actual behaviour of the business sector. Legal sanctions may play a major role in determining such behaviour, but many possibilities still exist to substitute bribery[9] of foreign officials with other dubious payments which are accepted under the existing legal standard, or which cannot be prosecuted and appropriately penalised.[10] Instead of bribing directly, exporters may hide their favours by granting expensive foreign trips or by donating scholarships to family members of the foreign official. Alternatively, they may just delegate the bribery to local agents and claim ignorance when this is uncovered.[11] In this way, bribery may be disguised as a legal commission. Similarly, a local agent may act as an 'intervening purchaser', bribing for the acquisition of a contract and then selling the contract to the foreign exporter (*The Wall Street Journal*, 29 Sept. 1995). Another means of disguising corruption is by designing a joint venture and giving 'free' shares to local commissioners, public officials and politicians.

Arguably, legal standards can be bypassed if private firms put their efforts into designing alternative payment schemes. Levelling the playing field only with respect to legal standards might be insufficient if exporters differ in their inclination and capability to develop such techniques and if regulating authorities differ in their rigour to counter such behaviour. In order to provide a benchmark for levelling the playing field, it is therefore essential to determine real business behaviour, which this study will undertake.

The Question of Responsibility

In order to justify corrupt export promotion, industry representatives often point to an alleged cultural acceptance of corruption in the importing countries. In this way responsibility is shifted to the takers of bribes, who many prefer to locate in the less developed countries. From a systematic viewpoint, this simply repeats the 'they–us dimension', which assumes a higher degree of corruption in foreign countries than at home.[12] By contrast, people from less developed countries point to the difficulty of establishing an honest administration and a transparent political environment when low-paid public servants are constantly offered side payments by business people from industrial countries.

This study takes up this second viewpoint and shows to what extent exports are affected by corruption. The aim is to assess the active involvement of exporting nations in the payment of bribes. The actual behaviour of the business sector is therefore not simply assumed to follow the cultural standards of the importing countries. Nevertheless, from a theoretical point of view, it is legitimate to ask whether differences in export behaviour can actually occur. If a firm acquires extra profits by means of bribery, will not other firms be inclined or even forced to follow suit and adjust their moral standards downward? From the viewpoint of methodological individualism there are no impediments to do so and profit maximisation may require this adjustment. Organisational difficulties, however, may restrict a firm's inclination to engage in illicit activities. Particular organisational capacities have to be built up in order to organise any kind of criminal activity.

With respect to bribery, firms have to open hidden accounts, which are known to only a few insiders within the firm. At the same time employees may use their insider knowledge to obtain extra income for themselves and to skim off the quasi rents of a project. Quite often kickbacks paid to high-ranking foreign public officials and politicians are partly diverted back into the private accounts of the firms' employees. Special safeguards have to be devised against this kind of fraud. Furthermore, a firm engaging in bribery might be exposed to denunciation and extortion.[13] Again, special safeguards have to be devised in order to keep employees loyal.[14]

In addition, corrupt agreements cannot usually be legally enforced. A potential risk is that public servants fail to deliver after receiving a bribe. Some firms may be more reluctant than others to run such a risk. In this way morality is incorporated within specific organisational structures, which distinguishes firms significantly by their inclination to give bribes for the acquisition of exports. Forbidding employees to bribe foreign officials in this respect may be in line with maximising behaviour.[15]

III. THE TRADE PERSPECTIVE

Corruption can significantly affect trade. The most obvious kind of influence relates to goods which are imported by the public sector. The extent of corruption among public officials and politicians influences which competitor is most likely to win a contract. Tendering procedures can be falsified and contracts awarded in favour of those competitors who offer the highest bribes. However, private sector imports – and even imports by subsidiaries of multinational companies – can also be influenced by the extent of corruption prevalent in a country. On the one hand, the extent of corruption at all state levels which regulate and control external trade – such as customs, trade ministry and trade regulation authorities – impact on this kind of business, and those exporting countries which are inclined to engage in corrupt practices obtain a competitive advantage. On the other hand, employees of private firms may also request bribes in return for awarding contracts. In so far as the corruption index is a good proxy for the extent of private forms of corruption, this influence is captured here. The following empirical investigation shows that the degree of corruption of importing countries has significant explanatory value for the trade structure of some exporting countries.

The dollar value of bilateral trade flows is commonly explained as depending on the size (as measured by GDP) and income (as measured by GDP per head) of both the exporting and the importing countries, as well as geographic distance and some further explanatory variables.[16] Two problems arise when incorporating an index of corruption of the importing countries into this approach. First, multicollinearity between the corruption index and GDP per head of the importing countries may pose problems to the regression. However, this influence proved less important with a correlation coefficient of 0.78. A more severe problem was presented by multicollinearity between the corruption index and the error term. An underestimation of the total exports of a country by the explanatory variables can in this case influence the coefficient of the corruption index: for countries whose exports exceed the value predicted by the model a positive influence of the corruption index is obtained, since this (strictly positive) series can capture the estimation error. Such an approach inevitably confuses the good performance of an exporting country with a tendency to avoid corrupt countries.

I have therefore decided to adopt a simpler approach. Instead of determining the nominal value of trade flows, I determine the share of the import market which an export country is able to obtain, and in order to achieve a relatively good fit for each exporting country, the determinants of market shares for each exporting country are investigated separately.[17]

The Data

The investigation was carried out for the 19 biggest exporting countries, using trade data for the four-year period 1992–95. Extending the investigation to these four years has been favourable with respect to avoiding outliers and small-term influences. Appendix 1 (Table 2) lists overall exports from these countries as reported by the importing countries. The biggest 87 importing countries are included in the investigation (see Appendix 2 for a list of the countries). Each of the 19 exporting countries obtains a certain share of each of the 87 import markets. For example, for India data were obtained according to Figure 1.[18]

FIGURE 1
SHARES OF THE INDIAN IMPORT MARKET

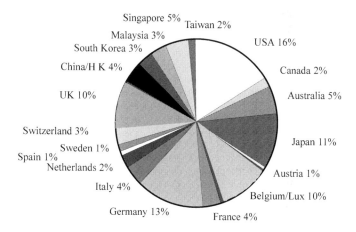

Hence 86 numbers for each exporting country were obtained, each number representing the corresponding share of the import market, leaving out the respective home market.[19] From this a distribution of market shares for each of the 19 exporting countries can be extracted. A typical distribution of market shares (MS) is presented in Figure 2 for the case of Germany. Undoubtedly, the data are not normally distributed but appear to be close to a log–normal distribution. The following function determines a transformed series of the market shares: MST = log(MS+C). This series is closer to a normal distribution and will be used in all regressions.[20]

FIGURE 2
MARKET SHARES OF GERMAN EXPORTS

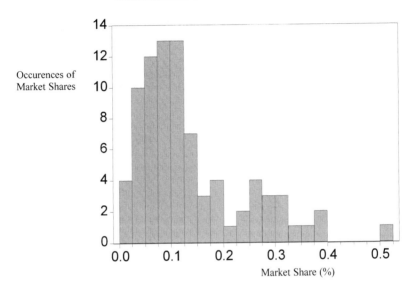

For each of the importing countries the level of corruption by public officials and politicians was determined, see Appendix 2. We define corruption in this context as the 'misuse of public power for private benefits' and the data represent the subjective evaluation of business people.[21] The values refer to perceptions obtained between 1993 and 1996. Since there may be a time lag between actual corruption and its perception, it appears reasonable to regress these data with trade data referring to 1992–95.

The share of the import market will evidently be lower the longer the distance is to the respective market. Figure 3 demonstrates this relationship, with distances determined as the geographic distance between the demographic centres of the respective countries.[22] With respect to the appropriate functional form the logarithm of the distance was included as an explanatory variable in the test equations. This was supported by the better performance of the logarithmic term in White heteroskedasticity tests.[23]

Market shares may also be influenced by the particular kind of product an exporter is offering. Such an influence might be relevant to our analysis if the structure of imports correlates with the degree of corruption.[24] For example, it is argued that the export of capital goods in particular is exposed to corruption, especially when purchased by governments and when a certain degree of secrecy is required [Moody-Stuart, 1996: 135; Shleifer and Vishny, 1993: 613]. In order to control for such an influence we will include an index of 'sectoral-fit' into our regression.

FIGURE 3
MARKET SHARE AND GEOGRAPHIC DISTANCE FOR GERMANY

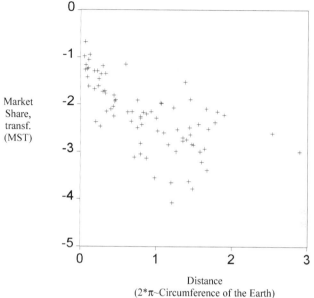

According to the Standard International Trade Classification (SITC) Figure 4 presents the average structure of imports for all 87 countries. Many exporters have a structure which is quite comparable to this sectoral distribution. However, Australia and to a lesser degree Canada and Malaysia are particularly strong in exporting crude materials and fuels. Japan exports mainly machines and transport equipment, China and Hong Kong have an emphasis on miscellaneous manufactures, Switzerland is strong in exporting chemicals and the Netherlands in exporting food and live animals. It is straightforward to assume an advantage for these countries in import markets which more closely fit their export structure. From the structure of imports and exports we determine the index of 'sectoral-fit', which represents the expected market shares as a function of the sectoral distribution of products. For exporting country i and all importing countries j this is determined by the following equation:

$$sectoral - fit_{ij} = \sum_{k=0}^{9} \frac{M_{jk} X_{ik}}{M_j X_k}$$

with M_j representing the $ value of imports into country j, M_{jk} those of category k, X_{ik} country i's exports of category k and X_k all 19 countries' exports of category k.[25] The equation determines the share of **all** sectoral exports country i is able to obtain (X_{ik}/X_k) and multiplies the result with the respective import share of country j (M_{jk}/M_j). The sum of these values gives the expected total market share. To give an extreme example, Australia is expected to obtain 4.7 per cent of the Indian import market but only 1.1 per cent of the Argentinean, since the latter's import structure differs considerably more from the Australian export structure. In a number of cases the variance of this index is very low.[26] This resulted in some insignificant coefficients of this index, and if not at least weakly significant, this variable was omitted. The index will be included into the regression in logarithmic form, which is preferable with respect to heteroskedasticity.

FIGURE 4
STRUCTURE OF IMPORTS (SITC), AVERAGE FOR 87 COUNTRIES

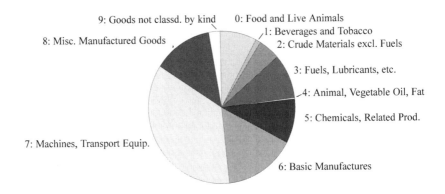

Additionally, the regressions filter out advantages arising from a common language.[27] Included is a dummy variable which has the value 1 for countries who share a common language with the exporting country, be it officially or as a result of a high representation in the media, business or education sector. If (weakly) significant, the dummy is included and reported in Table 1.[28] For some importing countries a common language also hints at some sort of political influence which it is aimed to filter out: (post-) colonial dependence. Whether colonialism as such should be regarded as an unacceptable way to promote exports is not the concern here. It is the outcome of questionable political considerations, but surely it must be distinguished from the bribery of public officials and politicians that it is aimed to identify here. For countries outside the European Union there seem to be trade disadvantages with EU members. We therefore include a dummy variable which has the value 1 for EU member countries.[29] Other political organisations, such as the Commonwealth of Nations, were insignificant to the regressions.

Empirical Results

Surely, any geographic, sectoral or idiomatic conditions may confront some exporters with the need to give bribes more than others. In trying to determine the active role of exporters this has to be filtered out by the inclusion of these explanatory variables. The relationship we aim to obtain is whether there is a tendency for some countries to export into corrupt markets. For each exporting country (i) we apply an ordinary least squares regression for the import shares according to the following function:

$$MST_j = c_1 + c_2 \bullet \log(distance_j) + c_3 \bullet EU - dummy_j + c_4 \bullet corruption - index_j + c_5 \bullet language - dummy_j + c_6 \bullet \log(sectoral - fit_j) + \mu_j.$$

The results are reported in Table 1.[30] Figures below the coefficients indicate the corresponding t–statistics. The geographic influence is negative, as expected, and highly significant in all cases. The European Union exerts a significantly negative influence on the exports from Austria, Canada, Japan, South Korea and the USA. This may be due to import barriers which impose a trade disadvantage as compared to EU members. The language–dummy is significantly positive for the old colonial powers: France, Spain and the UK. Also (weakly) significant values have been obtained for the USA, China/Hong Kong, Singapore, Australia and Belgium/Luxembourg.

The index of sectoral fit is (weakly) significant for Australia, Japan, Netherlands and Canada – countries with export structures which differ considerably from the average export structure. Weakly significant results were also obtained for the USA, France and Malaysia whose structure is closer to the average.[31] As can be seen, the coefficient for the corruption index is close to zero in a number of cases. Significant negative coefficients on a 95 per cent significance level have been obtained for Belgium/Luxembourg, France, Italy, the Netherlands and on a 90 per cent significance level for South Korea. A positive coefficient on a 90 per cent significance level is obtained for Sweden only.

The last columns of Table 1 report the R^2 and the Jarque–Bera coefficient. Some regressions have a rather low R^2, indicating that the independent variables may only partially explain the variations of the dependent variable. The low values in the case of Taiwan, Switzerland and Canada indicate particularly that important explanatory variables are still missing. In the case of Taiwan one may suspect the political confrontation with China to contribute to this outcome. With respect to the regressions for Canada and Switzerland there are no *ad hoc* explanations for their poor performance. The low R^2 should

TABLE 1
DETERMINANTS OF BILATERAL TRADE FLOWS

Country	Constant	Distance	EU-Dummy	Corruption Index	Language Dummy	Sectoral Fit	R²	JB
Australia	-0.78	-2.69	0.27	0.048	0.49	0.78	0.51	2.9
	-0.54	-6.97	0.65	0.86	1.74	2.18		
Austria	-5.53	-1.00	-0.76	0.012			0.73	4.0
	-40.52	-13.76	-3.33	0.41				
Belgium/Lux	-0.07	-0.35	0.34	-0.080	0.26	1.05	0.48	0.6
	-0.03	-4.24	1.42	-2.69	1.60	1.36		
Canada	-1.33	-0.88	-0.69	-0.019		0.97	0.30	1.0
	-0.96	-5.06	-2.73	-0.54		1.94		
China/HK	-3.02	-0.43	-0.21	-0.045	0.32		0.26	2.0
	-18.65	-3.59	-0.89	-1.36	1.95			
France	1.39	-0.46	0.09	-0.072	1.22	1.62	0.62	0.6
	0.57	-5.23	0.34	-2.44	5.80	1.71		
Germany	-2.42	-0.59	-0.15	-0.026			0.64	1.8
	-23.90	-10.33	-0.82	-1.21				
Italy	-2.65	-0.54	-0.28	-0.068			0.49	1.5
	-23.87	-8.42	-1.41	-2.87				
Japan	0.48	-0.64	-0.57	-0.017		1.17	0.34	3.2
	0.46	-4.73	-2.54	-0.55		2.54		
Malaysia	-3.35	-1.30	0.12	0.067		0.46	0.56	0.8
	-2.23	-9.88	0.38	1.48		1.12		
Netherlands	-2.02	-0.39	0.24	-0.060		0.36	0.62	1.1
	-3.17	-7.73	1.57	-3.35		1.63		
Singapore	-4.54	-1.08	0.10	-0.025	1.04		0.71	3.3
	-26.85	-9.73	0.40	-0.72	5.90			
South Korea	-3.33	-0.60	-0.66	-0.057			0.34	1.6
	-21.24	-4.69	-2.87	-1.80				
Spain	-4.43	-0.97	-0.27	-0.048	1.53		0.65	2.4
	-28.00	-9.00	-0.93	-1.54	8.28			
Sweden	-4.81	-0.59	-0.16	0.065			0.43	2.4
	-31.41	-5.88	-0.63	1.95				
Switzerland	-4.19	-0.36	-0.25	0.006			0.25	2.9
	-32.66	-4.42	-0.99	0.21				
Taiwan	-4.29	-0.69	-0.46	0.061			0.31	4.1
	-23.15	-5.50	-1.64	1.61				
UK	-3.17	-0.52	0.12	-0.053	1.04		0.42	1.6
	-21.16	-4.71	0.39	-1.63	6.33			
USA	5.11	-0.80	-0.79	0.007	0.29	3.67	0.46	3.2
	2.20	-6.70	-4.29	0.27	2.26	2.86		

Note: No data have been reported for the exports from Malaysia to Israel, South Korea to Cuba, Singapore to Bolivia and Austria to Gabon, which might be due to very low values. These countries have been omitted in the regressions. Cuba and Libya represented outliers to the regression of the USA (in the sense that their inclusion yields a high Jarque–Bera coefficient) and have been omitted. The regression for Belgium produced many outliers. The Bahamas, Vietnam, India, Israel and Zaire have been omitted without affecting the coefficient of the corruption index.

be borne in mind when interpreting the results. The Jarque-Bera coefficient is smaller than 5.99 in all cases and normal distribution of the residuals (μ_j) cannot be rejected on a 95 per cent significance level.[32]

Although significant results on a 95 (90) per cent significance level were only obtained for four (six) countries, by comparing directly between countries further significant differences between countries can be determined. This can be done by jointly testing two regressions and applying a Wald–test for the restriction that the coefficients of the corruption index are equal.[33] In this way the null-hypothesis of equal export behaviour of, for example, Malaysia and the United Kingdom can be rejected on a 95 per cent level. It is possible to conclude that the results prove a significant inclination of the United Kingdom to export more into corrupt countries than Malaysia. The same applies to Germany compared with Sweden and on a 90 per cent significance level to South Korea compared with Australia.

IV. CONCLUSIONS

The low involvement of, for example, Swedish exports in corrupt import countries came as no surprise and appears to reflect business perceptions. This does not mean however, that Swedish firms would never offer bribes to promote their exports.[34] However, these instances will occur to a much lesser extent than in the first group of countries which show a significantly negative coefficient of the corruption index: Belgium/Luxembourg, France, Italy, the Netherlands and South Korea. For all these countries the regressions allow for the null-hypotheses, that is, that exports are not promoted by the degree of corruption in the importing country, to be rejected on a 95 (90) per cent level. Figure 5 presents an overview of the results.[35] The corruption coefficient has been adjusted, that is, multiplied by 20, to allow the presentation in a single graphic. A coefficient of –0.08 for Belgium/Luxembourg indicates that, with a rise of the corruption index by one degree (out of ten) the logarithm of the export countries' import share decreases by eight per cent. For example, an increase in the performance of India from the current 2.63 to 3.63 would reduce the Belgian share of the import market from 10.3 per cent to 9.5 per cent. What can be the explanation for this decline?

Without doubt, even in highly corrupt countries some firms acquire contracts without paying bribes. Arguably this applies to large and prominent firms and to those with a technological advantage. In cases where the quality of a product is outstanding, such firms may resist demands to share their quasi-rents with corrupt politicians and public servants. In cases of prominent firms with good access to the media, politicians may risk their reputation by asking for a bribe. Although convincing, this argument does not contribute to this analysis and does not explain the differences found. Large, prominent and

FIGURE 5
THE INFLUENCE OF CORRUPTION ON THE EXPORT STRUCTURE

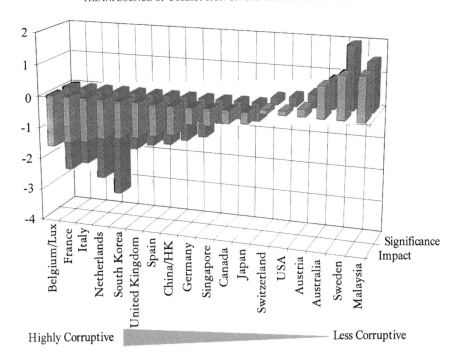

technologically advanced firms have a competitive advantage in all import markets and no tendency to export into more or less corrupt markets can be derived from this argument.

Alternatively, the political power of exporters may play a major role in determining market shares.[36] In this scenario, an exporter may trade in diplomatic support, military assistance, donor help or other 'political goods' for exports. Surely this might be an important mechanism for the acquisition of contracts. However, this is relevant to the analysis here only if countries which are perceived to be corrupt are more open to this kind of influence than others. This may sound convincing but our results do not necessarily support this viewpoint: small exporting countries with rather limited political influence can be found to have a significantly better performance in the import markets of corrupt countries than political heavyweights such as the USA.

Finally, trade relations cannot be established within a few years. The reputation of providing good quality and service may underpin the dominance of big exporters for a long time. It has been argued that the spread of corruption in international trade relations originated in 'non–traditional companies, trying to break into fields which had been dominated for many years by a small number of companies from an even smaller number of countries' [*Moody-Stuart, 1996: 152*]. If this argument still holds, we would expect the East Asian countries to have larger market shares in corrupt countries than in less corrupt countries. However, this is not supported by empirical findings either. Traditional exporters can be found on both sides of the scale, just as newly-exporting countries.

Since the arguments presented are not convincing and particularly since the most obvious variables were controlled in the regressions, it appears more convincing to relate the observed differences to a parameter which is actively set by the exporting business. Corruptive measures in the promotion of exports will be more effective in countries with a high level of local corruption in public administration and politics. Likewise, promoting exports by giving bribes will not be an effective means in countries with transparent procurement regulations and a high level of integrity. Therefore, the observed differences in market shares are most likely to originate in the differentiated behaviour of the business sector of exporting countries: the varying inclination to offer bribes.

An improvement in the corruption index of India will therefore reduce the market share of Belgium/Luxembourg by reducing the chances of obtaining contracts by offering bribes. Other countries whose companies are less inclined to offer bribes, such as Sweden, will likewise profit from less corruption in India.

The results for the USA deserve more detailed explanation, since the high legal standards of the USA may have implied an even better result. Running the same regression for the USA with 1972/73 trade data – a time when US companies did not anticipate the enactment of the Foreign Corrupt Practices Act (FCPA) – the coefficient of the corruption index is lower, that is, -0.038. While the difference is noteworthy it is not significant on a 90 per cent level. Therefore, it is not possible to provide statistical proof for the effects of the FCPA and Hines' [*1995*] results cannot be reproduced here. Surely this should not lead to the conclusion that the effects of the FCPA have been limited. The high support by internal activities of US firms proposes a considerable effect of the legal standards in the USA. It cannot be ruled out that in the case of the USA political power represents an advantage for exporting to corrupt countries and represents some sort of substitute for the bribery of their firms. Whatever the explanation, the results for the USA should be kept in mind when discussing ways of levelling the playing field.

What remains to be answered is who actually bears the 'responsibility' for business conduct in international trade. This study cannot answer a question that is moral by nature, however, as exporting countries apparently exhibit different patterns of behaviour, it can be concluded that exporting countries do not simply take the cultural climate as given and adjust their ethical standards accordingly. In so far as export behaviour differs across nations, the inclination to offer bribes emerges as the sovereign choice of the exporters. To that extent, exporters will have to share the 'moral' burden.

NOTES

1. 'International Business Strategy', Summer School in Management, London School of Economics, 1996.
2. Mauro's [1995] findings have been queried by Wedeman [1996]. An approach incorporating corruption among other explanatory variables is employed by Knack and Keefer [1995].
3. 'The moral problem to me is simply jobs' was the argument used by Lord Young, former British Cabinet Minister, BBC World Report broadcast, May 1994.
4. See The Wall Street Journal, 29 Sept. 1995.
5. See The Wall Street Journal, 12 Oct. 1995. Later publications even raised the losses to $45 billion, The Straits Times, Singapore, 8 March 1996.
6. See The Straits Times, Singapore, 8 March 1996 and The Financial Times, 26 July 1996. However, threatening to impose sanctions may not be the general position of the US government.
7. See The Times, London, 28 May 1997, The Financial Times, 24 May 1997; The Straits Times, Singapore, 25 and 28 May 1997.
8. For a comparative overview of legal standards in OECD countries, see Wiehen [1996] and Geiger [1995].
9. The terms 'corruption' and 'bribery' are used synonymously throughout this study.
10. See LeVine [1989: 689] for a description of the behaviour of multinational companies with respect to bribery. On the relationship between legal standards, real business behaviour and bribery, see Rosenthal [1989].
11. In February 1996, following corruption charges, Singapore imposed a five-year ban on public contracts with the German Siemens, the Italian Pirelli, the British BICC Supertension Cable and the Japanese Marubeni and Tomen. When asked about this measure, Siemens declared that it was not informed about what local agents did with the $20 million paid for 'project co–ordination'. See The Straits Times, Singapore, 14 Feb. 1996 and Frankfurter Allgemeine Zeitung, Frankfurt, 14 Feb. 1996.
12. For a detailed description of this 'xenophobic' phenomenon, see van Duyne [1996].
13. It was reported to me that an employee of a German firm was convicted of having diverted kickbacks to Chinese officials into his Hong Kong bank account. He reacted by threatening to reveal his Chinese counterparts to Chinese authorities, exposing them to harsh penalties and making future business in China impossible. The case was dropped as a consequence.
14. For a theoretical enquiry into these institutional aspects see Husted [1994] and Rose–Ackerman [1989: 663–9].
15. This argument is particularly valid with respect to stockholder interests as opposed to top manager interests [Rose-Ackerman, 1989: 667].
16. A possible specification of this is given by the gravity model:

$$X_{ij} = k_1 Y_i^{k_2} (Y_i / P_i)^{k_3} Y_j^{k_4} (Y_j / P_j)^{k_5} D_{ij}^{k_6} A_{ij}^{k_7} \mu_{ij},$$

with X_{ij} being the US dollar value of the trade flow from country i to country j, Y_i and Y_j the nominal GDP in countries i and j, P_i and P_j the population in countries i and j, D_{ij} the distance between countries i and j. A_{ij} is any other factor influencing bilateral trade flows and μ_{ij} a normally distributed error term. See Bergstrand [1989; 1985] for an overview of the literature. Bergstrand [1989] proposes three dummies for the EU, the EFTA and the neighbouring countries to be considered as important other factors (A_{ij}).

17. With respect to the gravity model this approach allows us to delete Y_j and Y_j/P_j from the test equation and to substitute Y_i and Y_i/P_i by an individual constant for each test equation. As a result, the explanatory power (R^2) of our regressions will be lower than the usual values in gravity models (which are approximately 0.8), without losing explanatory power with respect to differences in the structure of exports.

18. Imports from other than the 19 biggest exporters are not considered here.

19. For China and Hong Kong only 85 numbers can be obtained since both home markets are left out.

20. As some values of MS are zero, especially in the case of smaller importing countries, a constant C is included in the transformation. The constant C has been chosen so as to minimise the Jarque–Bera coefficient. Therefore the monotonous transformation aims at a normal distribution of the dependent variable. The Jarque-Bera coefficient tests whether a series follows a normal distribution by evaluating its skewness and kurtosis. It is distributed χ^2 with 2 degrees of freedom. The constant and the Jarque-Bera coefficients are reported in Appendix 1.

21. For a full description of the data and the methodology, see Lambsdorff [1997] and Lancaster and Montinola [1997].

22. The demographic centres were estimated with the help of PC Atlas 1.0 and the distances determined according to spherical trigonometry.

23. Heteroskedasticity has mostly been eliminated by making use of the logarithmic term. Only in the case of France, Singapore and Sweden did a simple linear form perform better, whereas the logarithmic form yielded significant heteroskedasticity. In order to preserve methodological consistency, the regressions have been conducted throughout with logarithmic terms. It should be noted that for Singapore this did not change the value of the corruption coefficient. However, using simple linear terms for France and Sweden the coefficients were higher, that is, -0.038 and 0.117, and the t-statistics amounted to -1.4 and 3.2 respectively.

24. Such a correlation however lacks empirical support. For example, Mauro [1996] did not find a significant correlation between corruption and the share of government expenditure on military products.

25. The data are taken from the *International Trade Statistics Yearbook* 1994, Volume I, United Nations, New York. Where 1992 data are not available the closest alternative year has been chosen. No data were available for Angola, Lebanon, Russia, Taiwan and Vietnam so data have been substituted by the average given in Figure 4.

26. This is particularly the case where the export structure is close to the average of all exporting countries or where deviations coincide with relative constant import shares for this product.

27. This is also done by Wei [1997].

28. For Belgium all three official languages, French, Dutch and German, were considered. Chinese turned out to be insignificant for all countries. However, the English language has been significant for Singapore and China/Hong Kong and the results are reported in Table 1. Canada has been attributed a value of 0.5 for the English and the French language-dummy. Portuguese turned out to have a similar influence as Spanish on the exports from Spain. The language-dummy for Spain therefore has a value of 1 for Spanish and Portuguese speaking countries. All these considerations have been important in yielding a high R^2 and a low Jarque–Bera coefficient. However, the influence of the corruption index has not been changed considerably by these adjustments.

29. Since Austria, Sweden and Finland joined the EU in 1995 a quarter of the trade data might be affected by this membership. Hence these countries have been attributed the value 0.25.

30. All regressions have been conducted with Econometric Views, Version 2.0, Quantitative Micro Software, Irvine/California, 1995.

31. The variable 'sectoral-fit' represents an expected value for the market share. Therefore the constant is mostly insignificant if this variable is included. Note in passing that the inclusion of this variable had only minor effects on the coefficients of the corruption index.

32. Each of the regressions has been conducted independently and we only required methodological consistency with respect to the functional form of the regressions. This contrasts with the gravity model, where the coefficients, e.g. for the distance, language and EU variables, are forced to have the same values for all countries. One may question, whether our specification is relevant to the results we obtained. Alternatively we can jointly test the trade structure of all exporting

countries with the following system of equations:

$$MST_{ij} = K_i + V_1 \cdot \log(distance_{ij}) + V_2 \cdot language - dummy_{ij} + V_3 \cdot EU - dummy_{ij}$$
$$+ V_4 \cdot adja - dummy_{ij} + V_5 \cdot \log(sectoral - fit_{ij}) + C_i \cdot corruption - index_j + \mu_{ij}, \forall i,$$

with K_i being a constant and C_i a coefficient of the corruption index for each exporting country (i). Treating the countries uniformly, we can include the language-dummy and the sectoral-fit variable for all countries. Following Bergstrand [1989] this approach also allows us to include an 'adjacency'–dummy, indicating a common border between trading partners. In contrast to our previous approach and following the specification of the gravity model, most coefficients are now forced to have the same value for all exporting countries. However, our results remain largely unaffected. In particular, the values of the corruption index are largely reproduced and the significance is mainly even higher in this approach. For the sake of brevity we will not report these results.

33. Under the null-hypothesis, the resulting coefficient is asymptotically distributed as χ^2 with 1 degree of freedom.

34. A recent case involved allegations that the Swedish L.M. Ericsson colluded with senior ministers and officials in Zimbabwe [Transparency International, 1995: 11]. Other charges concern the activities of the armaments manufacturer Bofors in India [Heidenheimer, 1996: 344].

35. Taiwan is not included in the figure. We had subjective doubts whether the business reputation of Taiwan is in line with the high value of the coefficient of the corruption index. As an explanation for the results it might be assumed that corrupt importing countries can more easily be influenced by Chinese political pressures which attempt to inhibit exports from Taiwan.

36. '... many Europeans also argue that U.S. military and political power gives American businesses an unfair advantage. Americans say their country's leading role just as often sets them at a disadvantage – for example, when Washington puts pressure on China to improve its record on human rights and weapons proliferation and European governments seek commercial favor by keeping quiet.' (The International Herald Tribune, 4 April 1997).

REFERENCES

Ades, A. and R. di Tella, 1995, 'Competition and Corruption', draft, Keble College, Oxford University, Jan.

Bardhan, P., 1997, 'Corruption and Development: A Review of Issues', Journal of Economic Literature, Vol.35, pp.1320–46.

Bergstrand, J.H., 1985, 'The Gravity Equation in International Trade: Some Microeconomic Foundations and Empirical Evidence', Review of Economics and Statistics, Vol.67, pp.474–81.

Bergstrand, J.H., 1989, 'The Generalized Gravity Equation, Monopolistic Competition and the Factor–Proportions Theory in International Trade', Review of Economics and Statistics, Vol.71, pp. 474–81.

Geiger, R., 1995, 'Statement', in J. Holtz and M. Kulessa (eds.), Korruption als Entwicklungshindernis, Bonn: Gemeinsame Konferenz Kirche und Entwicklung, pp.16–18.

Heidenheimer, A.J., 1996, 'The Topography of Corruption: Explorations in a Comparative Perspective', International Social Science Journal, Vol.158. No.3, pp.337–47.

Heidenheimer, A.J. Johnston, M. and V. LeVine (eds.), 1989, Political Corruption – A Handbook, New Brunswick, NJ: Transaction Publishers.

Hines, J.R., 1995, 'Forbidden Payment: Foreign Bribery and American Business after 1977', National Bureau of Economic Research Working Paper, No.5266.

Husted, B.W., 1994, 'Honor among Thieves: A Transaction–Cost Interpretation of Corruption in Third World Countries', Business Ethics Quarterly, Vol.4, No.1, pp.17–27.

Johnston, M., 1996, 'Public Officials, Private Interests, and Sustainable Democracy: Connections between Politics and Corruption', draft, Colgate University, New York, April.

Knack, St. and P. Keefer, 1995, 'Institutions and Economic Performance: Cross–Country Tests Using Alternative Institutional Measures', Economics and Politics, Vol.7, No.3, pp.207–27.

Lambsdorff, J. Graf, 1997, 'The TI Corruption Perception Index 1996', in J. Pope and C. Mohn (eds.)

Transparency International Report 1997, pp.61–6, Berlin, April. The data can be obtained via internet: http://www.uni-goettingen.de/~uwvw.

Lancaster, T. and G. Montinola, 1997, 'Toward a Methodology for the Comparative Study of Political Corruption', *Crime, Law and Social Change* (Special Issue on 'Corruption and Reform'), forthcoming 1998.

LeVine, V., 1989, 'Transnational Aspects of Political Corruption', in Heidenheimer, Johnston and LeVine (eds.) [*1989: 685–99*].

Mauro, P., 1995, 'Corruption and Growth', *Quarterly Journal of Economics*, Vol.110, No.3, pp.681–712.

Mauro, P., 1996, 'The Effects of Corruption on Growth, Investment and Government Expenditure', *International Monetary Fund Working Paper*, No.96/98.

Moody-Stuart, G., 1996, 'Grand Corruption in Third World Development', in *Uganda International Conference on Good Governance in Africa*, edited by the Inspectorate of Government, Government of Uganda in co-operation with Transparency International, Berlin, pp.122–59.

Rose-Ackerman, S., 1989, 'Corruption and the Private Sector', in Heidenheimer, Johnston and LeVine (eds.) [*1989: 661–83*].

Rosenthal, M., 1989, 'An American Attempt to Control International Corruption', in Heidenheimer, Johnston and LeVine (eds.) [*1989: 701–15*].

Shleifer, A. and R. W. Vishny, 1993, 'Corruption', *Quarterly Journal of Economics*, Vol.108, pp.599–617.

Transparency International, 1995, *Report 1995*, Berlin, March.

van Duyne, P. C., 1996, 'Organized Crime, Corruption and Power', draft, Katholieke Universiteit Brabant, Tilburg University, The Netherlands.

Wedeman, A., 1996, 'Looters, Rent–Scrapers, and Dividend–Collectors: The Political Economy of Corruption in Zaire, South Korea and the Philippines', paper presented at the 1996 annual meeting of the American Political Science Association, San Francisco, Aug.

Wei, Shang-Jin, 1997, 'How Taxing is Corruption on International Investors', draft, Harvard University and NBER, Feb.

Wiehen, M., 1996, 'OECD Recommendations and Enquiry', in *Uganda International Conference on Good Governance in Africa*, edited by the Inspectorate of Government, Government of Uganda in co-operation with Transparency International, Berlin, pp.115–22.

APPENDIX 1
THE NINETEEN LARGEST EXPORTING COUNTRIES

Table 2 reports data from the *International Monetary Fund*, Direction of Trade. The figures represent exports between 1992 and 1995 to the 87 largest importing countries, according to their import statistics (with an export volume of US$186.293 million Saudi Arabia could have been included in the list of major exporting countries; however, the analysis of raw materials exporters would have raised further questions with respect to comparability). These 19 countries make up 78 per cent of all imports into the 87 largest countries. Imports originating from other exporting countries are not considered in the analysis. We jointly investigated China and Hong Kong, since exports from China are often traded via Hong Kong and available statistics vary as to whether to treat these as exports from Hong Kong or China. This does not imply that these countries necessarily share the same pattern of export-behaviour. The number reported does not include trade between Hong Kong and China. Except for Canada and Sweden, the hypotheses of a normal distribution of the dependent variable (MST) cannot be rejected on a 95 per cent level, since the critical value for the Jarque-Bera statistic is 5.99.

TABLE 2
THE 19 LARGEST EXPORTING COUNTRIES

Country	Exports (in million US$)	Constant	JB
USA	2,080,857	0.02263	0.2
Japan	1,623,068	0	1.8
Germany	1,617,657	0	0.9
France	909,425	0	3.7
United Kingdom	763,406	0	0.9
Italy	704,786	0.00860	1.7
China/HK	650,686	0.00219	0.0
Canada	64,526	0.00013	21.2
Netherlands	548,242	0.01144	1.5
Belgium/Lux.	483,390	0.00371	0.0
Taiwan	371,879	0.00038	0.1
South Korea	353,118	0.00182	0.0
Switzerland	315,517	0.00003	0.2
Spain	274,921	0.00087	1.3
Singapore	274,045	0.00019	1.4
Malaysia	250,828	0.00015	0.1
Sweden	238,321	0	9.3
Australia	183,848	0.00016	1.1
Austria	177,113	0	5.0

Source: International Monetary Fund, Direction of Trade.

APPENDIX 2
TRANSPARENCY INTERNATIONAL CORRUPTION PERCEPTION INDEX 1996

Representing the subjective evaluation of business people, Table 3 reports countries' assessment with a maximum score of 10 (totally clean) and a minimum of 0 (totally corrupt). The Transparency International Corruption Perception Index provides an average score for 54 countries. The index is a 'poll of polls', using 10 surveys and professional assessments. The data refer to the subjective evaluation of almost 10,000 business people. A full description of the data, methodology and sources is provided in Lambsdorff [1997]. For a comment on the methodology see Lancaster and Montinola [1997]. Although the author was in charge of designing the index, the figures for any individual country do not necessarily reflect the author's personal opinion. The TI-index was determined by including three sources from the World Competitiveness Report, Institute for Management Development, Lausanne, three sources from the Political & Economic Risk Consultancy Ltd., Hong Kong, one small survey by Peter Neumann, published in the monthly German magazine, 'Impulse', No. 4/1994, two assessments by DRI/McGraw-Hill Global Risk Service and by the Political Risk Services, East Syracuse, NY and finally contributions to a survey of Göttingen University. Each of the sources has been normalised to the same mean and standard deviation as the according sub–sample of countries in other sources. In order to produce reliable results, at least four sources were required for a country to be included into the TI corruption index. As a result, many large importing countries could not be included. Hence, for another 31 countries the respective corruption value has been determined with the same technique. However, since fewer sources were used the data may be less reliable. This seemed preferable to omitting big importing countries.
     The second column indicates the country's position in the TI-index; the third column gives the actual index value as an average of the existing sources; the fourth column reports the number of sources available. Generally, all countries whose annual imports exceed $2 billion have been included in the analysis. Liberia has not been considered, since its import structure has been so unusual that it constantly produced outliers. Some additional African countries – Cameroon, Ethiopia, Gabon,

Ghana, Senegal, Tanzania, Uganda and Zaire – have been included in order to provide a better coverage of that continent. Yugoslavia and Bulgaria have been omitted owing to lack of data.

TABLE 3
CORRUPTION INDEX

Country	TI-Pos.	Score	Surv.	Country	TI-Pos.	Score	Surv.
Algeria		3.17	3	Kenya	52	2.21	4
Angola		2.46	3	Kuwait		3.94	3
Argentina	35	3.41	6	Lebanon		3.17	2
Australia	10	8.60	6	Libya		3.16	3
Austria	16	7.59	6	Malaysia	26	5.32	9
Bahamas		4.49	1	Mexico	38	3.30	7
Bahrain		3.58	2	Morocco		3.03	3
Bangladesh	51	2.29	4	Netherlands	9	8.71	6
Belgium	20	6.84	6	New Zealand	1	9.43	6
Bolivia	36	3.40	4	Nigeria	54	0.69	4
Brazil	40	2.96	7	Norway	6	8.87	6
Brunei		4.86	1	Oman		3.34	2
Cameroon	49	2.46	4	Pakistan	53	1.00	5
Canada	5	8.96	6	Peru		4.07	3
Chile	21	6.80	7	Philippines	44	2.69	8
China	50	2.43	9	Poland	24	5.57	4
Colombia	42	2.73	6	Portugal	22	6.53	6
Costa Rica		6.18	3	Romania		4.28	3
Cuba		3.34	2	Russia	47	2.58	5
Cyprus		6.21	2	Saudi Arabia		1.82	3
Czech. Rep.	25	5.37	4	Senegal		2.89	3
Denmark	2	9.33	6	Singapore	7	8.80	10
Dominican Rep.		3.91	3	South Africa	23	5.68	6
Ecuador	39	3.19	4	South Korea	27	5.02	9
Egypt	41	2.84	4	Spain	32	4.31	6
Ethiopia		4.04	3	Sri Lanka		2.60	2
Finland	4	9.05	6	Sweden	3	9.08	6
France	19	6.96	6	Switzerland	8	8.76	6
Gabon		0.93	2	Syria		4.05	3
Germany	13	8.27	6	Taiwan	29	4.98	9
Ghana		3.41	3	Tanzania		2.76	3
Greece	28	5.01	6	Thailand	37	3.33	10
Guatemala		1.17	1	Tunisia		4.08	3
Hong Kong	18	7.01	9	Turkey	33	3.54	6
Hungary	31	4.86	6	Uganda	43	2.71	4
India	46	2.63	9	United Arab Em.		2.73	3
Indonesia	45	2.65	10	United Kingdom	12	8.44	7
Iran		1.89	3	USA	15	7.66	7
Ireland	11	8.45	6	Venezuela	48	2.50	7
Israel	14	7.71	5	Vietnam		2.51	3
Italy	34	3.42	6	Yemen		2.65	1
Ivory Coast		2.93	3	Zaire		–0.39*	3
Japan	17	7.05	9	Zimbabwe		2.99	3
Jordan	30	4.89	4				

* Although generally restricted to values between 0 and 10 due to the adjustment process a negative value has been obtained.

Taxation, Corruption and Reform

JOHN TOYE and MICK MOORE

Corrupt tax officials often collude with taxpayers to understate tax liabilities. What can governments of poor countries do to reduce this collusion? This study argues that their incentive for anti-corruption reform of their tax systems increases with their dependence on revenues that are 'earned', in the sense that their collection requires substantial political and organisational inputs from the government. It further argues that the redesign of tax systems, and specifically their simplification, can reduce corrupt leakages. The Indonesian tax reform of the 1980s, including its adoption of a simple value added tax, is referred to for illustration of these arguments.

INTRODUCTION

What is the scope for governments of poor countries to reform taxation systems to reduce corruption? That is our central question. It can be divided into two somewhat more precise questions, that are treated in the first and second halves of this study respectively. In what circumstances will governments be likely to take effective action against corruption in tax collection? And how might the re-design of existing tax systems help the governments of poor countries to achieve that goal?

Our objective is to suggest useful ways of thinking about these questions from a political economy perspective. For the subject of tax reform has so far been treated mainly in technical terms. Yet it is primarily a political topic. We suggest that an understanding of the politics of government revenue and taxation systems can help us move towards a more practical appreciation of the circumstances in which reform might be achieved. Our main point here concerns the political and economic character of governments' revenue bases. These vary widely in respect of the amount of effort expended by the state to raise revenue. These variations – expressed in terms of relative dependence on 'earned' and 'unearned' income – affect both the scope for reform and the

John Toye and Mick Moore, Institute of Development Studies at the University of Sussex. The excellent research assistance of Francis Hutchinson and Garett Pratt is gratefully acknowledged. The authors have benefited from the extensive comments on an earlier draft by participants in a DFID-sponsored Workshop on Corruption and Development that was held at IDS in May 1997. Special thanks are owed, for their most helpful comments, to Ajay Chibber, Satya Mohanty, Mark Robinson and an anonymous referee. The usual disclaimer applies.

incentive for governments to embark on reform. Governments dependent on 'earned' income are likely to be best placed and best motivated to reduce corruption in tax collection.

How should they go about doing so? Can existing tax systems be re-designed in ways that squeeze out corruption, and particularly that most intractable form of it, collusion between officials and taxpayers wrongly to lower assessments? Our main point here, illustrated by the Indonesian case, is that progress can be made in this direction by reforms that give a greater revenue-raising role to a value-added tax. However, no purely technical re-design can wholly eliminate collusive corruption.

We recognise that the background against which we reach these conclusions is one where the published literature on corruption and taxation in poor countries is rather sparse. Academic writing on wrongdoing in the revenue collection business refers mainly to OECD countries, and official methods of combating tax evasion on the part of taxpayers. But tax evading behaviour on the part of citizens and companies may interact with corrupt behaviour on the part of tax bureaucrats: the two can cut deals at the cost of the public treasury. There is no necessary or tight connection: in some circumstances taxpayers can evade taxation despite the best efforts of honest tax collectors; in others they might dutifully hand over money that goes into the officials' private pockets. However, we have chosen to focus here on the interaction between corruption on the part of officials in poor countries' taxation systems, and tax evasion on the part of taxpayers. The 'deals' of collusive corruption are the most intractable of the problems that tax reformers in developing countries have to face.

Why do we know so little about corruption and taxation in poor countries? Part of the reason is that, if we are to define 'knowledge' as having detailed information about methods, channels, dynamics and quantities, we have little knowledge about corruption of any kind. Wade's [1985] explanation of the way in which official posts were allocated and re-allocated on a purchase basis within the Irrigation Department in a South Indian state is highly unusual in that it provides these kinds of detail. Another reason for our ignorance lies in the dominant role of the International Monetary Fund in framing debate about public revenue issues in poor countries. To a greater extent than the World Bank, the Fund avoids public engagement with 'political' issues. The literature and discussion on taxation that it generates and stimulates is predominantly technical in orientation. We refer to some of that literature here, but prefer to begin from a political economy perspective.

THE POLITICAL ECONOMY OF 'EARNED' AND 'UNEARNED' STATE
INCOME

Do Fiscal Deficits Motivate Tax Reform?

In what circumstances are governments of poor countries likely to make the
effort substantially to reduce corruption in tax collection? Would that an
important component of the answer were: 'When taxpayers become incensed
about the issue and become influential through electoral and pressure group
activity.' Unfortunately, this happens all too rarely in poor countries. There are
several reasons. First, direct taxpayers typically comprise only a very small
proportion of the population. Second, they often benefit from collusion with
tax officials in assessment and collection, at the expense of the public treasury.
Third, tax bureaucracies can strike back at those who lead public campaigns
against corruption: a special investigation of an individual's tax affairs is easy
to justify and can be made very costly to the victim, even where there has been
no wrongdoing.

The most likely factor motivating governments to tackle corruption and
other leakages in revenue collection would seem to be a perceived fiscal deficit
arising from some combination of a fall in revenues or an increase in
expenditure commitments. The proposition that governments will reform
when they need money most desperately is intuitively appealing, and no doubt
contains some truth. Unfortunately, it is not a proposition with a very high
predictive value. Some governments preside over long-term declines in
revenue in much the same way that they continue to resist economic reform
more generally, that is, long after the point at which it appeared to outsiders
that they had no choice but to reform. For example, the Peruvian government
took radical, effective action to increase tax collection in 1991 only when tax
revenue had fallen steadily from 20-22 per cent of GDP in the 1960s to less
than four per cent of GDP [*Thorp, 1996*]. Clearly, factors other than fiscal need
affect the willingness of governments to tackle tax reform in general, and
corruption in tax administration in particular, and many of the factors are
specific to particular circumstances.

Defining Earned and Unearned State Income

We suggest that it is possible to develop some initial propositions on the
propensity to fiscal anti-corruption reform by categorising states according to
the different sources of state income. In this we take our cue from Rudolf
Goldscheid, who sketched the outlines of a grand theory of societal
development in which the sources of public finance played the same critical
role in driving social change as social class and class struggle did in Marxist
analysis. His theme was that:

the pattern of public finance has at all times had a decisive influence on national and social evolution. Tax struggles were the oldest form of class struggle, and fiscal matters were an important contributory cause even in the mightiest spiritual movements of mankind [*Goldscheid, 1958: 202*].

Goldscheid's work is now unread, and largely deservedly so. Yet it does foreshadow recent developments in the political analysis of states and state development. Through a variety of channels, political scientists and historians are beginning to recognise that the politics and institutions of public finance play a significant but under-appreciated role in the formation and evolution of states.[1] The field as yet has no specific conceptual tools of its own. There is however a conceptual framework latent in some of the relevant literature. In particular the concept of 'rentier states' appears very useful for present purposes: the notion that state income can be categorised on a continuum between 'earned' and 'unearned'.

The term 'earned income' is not used normatively but as a positive description. It refers here to the notion of 'having to work for' something, that is, having to put purposive effort into attaining a goal.[2] The contrast is with income that is unearned, because it is received passively, without any work or effort. This idea of 'effort' must be clearly distinguished from the term 'tax effort' which has been much used in studies sponsored by the IMF. These studies measure the amounts of revenue raised in relation to the size of available tax bases (for example, customs duties in relation to the size of the foreign trade sector, excise duty in relation to luxury consumption) to give an overall indicator of aggregate 'tax effort'. In the conventional terminology, 'tax effort' refers to an output or result more than to an input. We use it here in a more political and organisational sense, to refer to the input made by government to raise revenue. The effort required to exploit some types of tax bases is much greater than the effort that is required to exploit others. It takes more effort to collect ten per cent of the value of imports as customs duties than it does to collect ten per cent of the value of oil production as a petroleum revenue tax. Tax bases can be graded according to the effort required to capture x per cent of each as revenue. Any measure that adds up the actual percentages of revenue collected into an aggregate measure of 'tax effort' will, therefore, be misleading, precisely because it fails to make any distinction between the different efforts involved.

The 'tax effort' that concerns us specifically is the effort made by the state in relation to the mass of its citizens or subjects (henceforth, citizens). There are two fiscal criteria that we can use to judge how far any state is engaging with the mass of its citizens. One is the extent to which state income is earned, and this in turn depends on:

(i) *Organisational effort*: How large, efficient and differentiated is the bureaucratic apparatus that the state deploys to collect its income? A state that has a number of distinct and effective services to assess and collect, for example, income, property, and turnover taxes, is working much harder for its income than is a state that receives a large annual cash subvention from an oil-rich neighbour and collects the remainder through a flat rate import duty.

(ii) *Reciprocity*: How far are citizens obtaining some reciprocal services in return for their tax contributions? This fiscal criterion of the degree of state engagement with the mass of its citizens concerns its expenditure priorities, and harks back to the voluntary exchange theory of taxation. 'Reciprocal services' range from (a) what we may term 'rudimentary' (a state apparatus that does not coercively and arbitrarily exploit citizens when collecting taxes or otherwise interacting with them); through (b) a 'minimal contractual relationship' (the provision of law, order, justice and security); to (c) 'extended reciprocity' (for example, the services associated with 'welfare' and 'developmental' states).

In this study, we do not further consider the expenditure side of the budget, or the reciprocity criterion. On the income side, however, criterion (i) – organisational effort – needs further elucidation. It is not a matter of the state deploying a large organisation as such. Size is not a criterion on its own, for the obvious reason that a large bureaucracy is quite capable of sitting in its offices, making little impact on the potential tax payers and raising a small amount of revenue at a very high administrative cost. But neither is efficiency of collection a criterion on its own, because it is clear that the most efficient forms of taxation, at least in terms of the smallness of the average cost of collection, are precisely those which require hardly any interaction with citizens. Differentiation is not a criterion on its own, because it may result in both extra inefficiency of collection and additional leakage of revenue through corruption. On the other hand, it is unlikely that any state would wish to earn all its revenue from only one or two types of taxes. Earning state income, therefore, requires the deployment of instruments which, taken together, are large, efficient and differentiated.

This multiplex criterion allows us, in principle, to rank different types of taxes on a scale of the degree of 'earnedness'. The deployment of a relatively elaborate bureaucratic apparatus to nurture, monitor and tax a concentrated, major income source (for example, a large phosphate deposit) would lead to a lower ranking on the 'earnedness' scale than would an equivalent revenue raising effort that was more widely dispersed (for example, collecting an urban property tax). Efforts to establish a good relationship with a major foreign aid donor would rank low on the scale for the same kinds of reasons. One indicator of the extent to which state income is earned is the proportion of potential income providers throughout the whole country who are brought into the revenue net.

Our earlier argument about the different effort required to raise a given percentage of any tax base as revenue can be extended to apply to different variants of the same type of tax. The extent to which one generic source of state income – say, property tax – is earned may vary from one situation to another depending on local factors: the concept of 'earnedness' refers to relations between state and citizens, and what appears to be the 'same' tax may have very different implications for state-society relations in different contexts. Differences between societies in the distribution of real property and in the nature of the classes and groups who own real property will mean that the 'earnedness' of a three per cent property tax is likely to vary from one country to another. For this and other reasons, the statistical information currently generated on state income sources, organised as it is by general descriptive categories, can provide us with only the crudest indications of the 'earnedness' of particular state income sources. Thus all that we can attempt here is to make some generalisations about where particular sources of government income are likely to be located on the 'earnedness' scale.

(1) *Sources of government income that are generally earned to a relatively high degree*: business turnover taxes; income taxes; property taxes; head taxes; contributory social security funds; profits from state ownership of productive enterprise, especially activities that are organisationally and technically demanding and non-monopolistic; and commercial borrowing.

(2) *Sources of government income that are generally earned to an intermediate degree*: commodity export taxes; control of location-specific physical infrastructure (canals, oil transmission lines, military facilities for other states, airports, harbours); and monopoly state activities which are relatively low technology but require active 'husbandry' (commercial forestry with protection and replanting; liquor sales monopolies).

(3) *Sources of government income that are generally unearned*: direct grants and the concessional element in soft loans; profits from maintaining fixed, overvalued exchange rates; royalties, fees and taxes from authorising the extraction of natural resources – oil, timber, minerals, etc.

Even these broad categories are not clearly distinguishable in standard public finance statistics. For example, income from oil or other natural resources appears in very different forms in the accounts of different governments. Any attempt to map the dependence of different categories of state on income classified on the 'earnedness' scale is necessarily done on a broad-brush basis. The results are however striking: the 'earnedness' of state income is positively and strongly related to levels of national income. Governments of poorer countries are highly dependent on unearned income, especially mineral revenues and foreign aid. Moore [1998] took 53 countries for which relevant data were available for 1988. The countries were classified in a four-by-four table: by income level and by degree of 'earnedness' of state income. The government of the average low income country obtained 43 per cent of its income from the least 'earned' income source (foreign aid), and only 14 per cent from the most 'earned' income source (taxes on income, profit and capital gains, and social security contributions). By contrast, the government of the high low income country obtained 58 per cent of its income from the most 'earned' income source.

This result is not wholly surprising, since one of the criteria for the allocation of foreign aid by country is a fiscal 'gap' that may be larger because of the difficulty of raising 'earned' income. The room for manoeuvre to do this may be very limited, because (in the case of sub-Saharan Africa, for example) shifting cultivation and pastoralism make rural direct taxes much harder to levy than in countries with permanently settled agricultural populations. But there may also be a moral hazard effect of foreign aid, that it relieves recipient governments of the need to seek out all possible sources of 'earned' income.

It is argued more fully elsewhere [Moore, 1998] that the 'earnedness' of state income is a significant political economy variable: that earned income is positively and causally associated with states that are (a) effective, in the sense of exercising sovereignty, and (b) responsive to citizens, partly to the extent of being more democratic. We argue here that the same conceptual framework can help us understand how states treat their taxation systems and bureaucracies, and, therefore, the ways in which they may respond to pressures or opportunities to reform those systems to reduce corruption.

How is Taxation-Corruption Organised?

The literature yields only sparse information about corruption and taxation in developing countries. We can however combine fragments of information on taxation with (a) the earned-unearned income framework set out above and (b) some knowledge about how corruption mechanisms operate (from, for example, Wade [1985]) to produce some hypotheses about how and how far taxation systems may be corrupt in particular circumstances. These ideas may at least serve to guide further research, and provide some ideas about which anti-corruption mechanisms might work.

For these purposes, it matters little whether we conceive of states as coherent organisations or simply as sets of powerful self-interested individuals. Where states depend heavily on 'earned' income, the taxation system receives considerable attention from the political leadership. First, it is considered important that the taxation apparatus is manned and led by competent bureaucrats. Honesty, in the citizens' sense of the term, may not be important. In so far as the taxation system is also used as a source of illicit revenue for political parties and elites, what matters is not that the tax bureaucracy should be honest, but that it should be dishonest in a predictable, controllable fashion, that is, that the understood percentages should be paid over to the right people at the right time.

Second, because political parties and elites are relatively dependent on the taxation apparatus for their illegal incomes, they tend to develop an interest in how it is managed. In these circumstances, the primary political function of the tax assessment and collection system is revenue collection. Most of that revenue goes to the public treasury. The revenue that is used illicitly is channelled in a relatively centralised fashion: it is first transferred up to high levels in the taxation apparatus, and then handed over to high level politicians (or bureaucrats in other agencies). Local and low-level politicians are not much involved directly, although they may share in redistribution effected by high level politicians. The corruption networks involved tend to be relatively wide-ranging, stable, homogenous and widely understood.

There is a considerable amount of knowledge about the 'value' of particular posts and activities: the post of Chief Tax Inspector at P is 'worth' about T thousand dollars a year, and one can expect to pay about U thousand dollars for a two-year transfer there; a front line Tax Inspector in a particular post may expect to pay about V thousand dollars to his boss each year simply to remain in post and free of trouble. The local Chief of Police may expect about W per cent of estimated 'revenues' each year to guarantee that there is no trouble. At the top, the Minister of Finance has a good idea of how much he should receive each month from each taxation agency. In this kind of system, there is no contradiction involved in one corrupt person accusing another of being a cheat. Given broad political stability, overall patterns of relationships in relation to taxation-corruption will remain relatively stable. There will however be instability in the laws, rules and procedures relating to assessment and collection: the state has both revenue motives to change the system (that is, there always seems scope for collecting a little more money) and corruption motives (that is, introducing changes in liabilities and collection procedures gives more scope to extract a surplus from tax payers).

Let us now look at the opposite situation, where governments depend heavily on unearned income. A few of these governments are also notoriously wealthy. The Saudi or Kuwaiti regimes may spend vast amounts of money on large, non-meritocratic, inefficient bureaucracies that reallocate state mineral wealth to large sections of the population [*Chaudhry, 1989*]. While it is often true that unearned state incomes are also large incomes, especially where oil is the source, it is helpful to separate source from size when assessing the consequences for corruption and tax reform.

Unearned sources of state income tend to be concentrated: a few mines or wells and the foreign companies which operate them; a canal; or a few foreign aid donors. Governments tend to concentrate their most effective public servants on tapping these sources. These are the main wellsprings of public revenue, political funds and private surplus for members of the political elite. Most areas of the taxation system are of little interest to state elites from a revenue perspective. They come instead to be treated largely as a source of political patronage: appointment to posts in the tax bureaucracy is a way of rewarding supporters (and potential opponents), and providing them with resources on a continuing basis. Several things follow.

The corruption networks – the number of people who share in any corrupt appropriation – tend to be relatively narrow, fragmented, heterogeneous and secret. Chief Tax Inspector X makes one set of arrangements with colleagues, friends, relatives and members of political or other bureaucratic networks in his locality; Chief Tax Inspector Y may make a very different set in his domain. As individual bureaucrats are moved around, the 'system' might change. There are continual processes of individual renegotiation, fuelled by the dearth of information about how the cake is being shared, and dearth of norms, based on 'common practice', about how it should be shared. No one has general oversight or insight into the system. The political elite has little direct interest in the revenue that is generated through routine taxation because it is feeding from elsewhere. As the elite and the state have neither a powerful corruption or revenue interest in tax assessment and collection, there is little incentive to amend legislation, ordinances or formal procedures.

Implications for Reform Initiatives

What does the previous discussion imply about the prospects for reducing corruption in tax collection in different public finance regimes? The scope for steady, incremental improvement is greater in situations where governments are dependent on earned incomes. There are two reasons for this. One is that the tax bureaucracies tend to be relatively meritocratic, competent and disciplined. The underlying structure of the tax collection system is relatively sound, and therefore amenable to gradual improvement. The other reason is that dependence of governments on earned income actively fosters interaction between state and society, and these interactions tend to promote demands for improved accountability of the state apparatus. Taxpayers are likely to exercise some voice, and that is likely to contribute to dampening down corruption in tax collection.

The dependence of states on earned income leads to the existence of effective accountability of the state to societal forces. One would expect to observe this effect over time in individual countries: regimes that become more dependent on earned income should become more accountable, possibly even democratic. We do not have the data needed to demonstrate this point conclusively.[3] There is however some striking supporting evidence from Indonesia, a country which has had much the same political system – and to a large extent the same political leaders – for the 30-year period since the mid-1960s, but has experienced major changes in the sources of public revenue. The 1970s was a period of booming oil revenues, when the regime became largely autonomous of other social and economic forces, including private capital [*Winters, 1996*].

Unlike many other regimes dependent on mineral wealth, the Indonesian government foresaw a future when it would have greater need of what we have here called earned income, and prepared for this through tax reforms in the 1980s. When oil revenues began to decline in the 1980s, taxpayers were obliged to substitute. Indonesia is far from a democracy, but has a growing democratisation movement, that has received considerable stimulus from the effectiveness of the new, broad-based tax system: democrats have explicitly linked their demands for political rights to the fact that the regime is now levying taxes on the population to a much greater extent than before [*Winters, 1996: 161*]. The old logic of 'no taxation without representation' seems to be at work here.

Indonesia is unusual in the extent to which the government prepared for the decline in unearned income and made a smooth transition to earning income from large numbers of its citizens. Regimes which are very dependent on unearned income are very vulnerable. On the one hand, the major unearned income sources – mineral revenues and aid – are unstable and prone to sudden declines. On the other hand, states which have lived from unearned income rarely have a tax bureaucracy of sufficient competence to switch quickly to earned income sources. For them the choice may lie between not replacing lost revenue or adopting the 'autonomous revenue agency' model that has become more popular in recent years. In collecting customs revenues, the autonomy stems from the employment of a foreign company to assess and/or collect duties on an incentive basis – the more the revenue collected, the greater the company's reward (Indonesia, Mozambique).

For 'internal' revenue, the preferred model is a new public agency, with highly paid staff, and considerable political and legal authority to collect taxes. This approach has resulted in considerable improvements in revenue collection in Ghana, Peru and Uganda. To some extent this may result from reducing levels of corruption in tax collection. But, after some period of time, the autonomy enjoyed by these agencies begins to lead their staff into corrupt practices. Autonomous, authoritative revenue agencies may be an essential first step in a crisis situation, but the long term problems of corruption and non-accountability in tax collection remain. There are various options open to policy-makers to address these problems by improving the structure of incentives that tax officials face, such as making bonus payments to them that are related to the amount of tax that they collect or legislating a more effective combination of penalties for corrupt collusion between them and the evading taxpayers. We do not examine these policy options which are well discussed by Bardhan [*1997: 1320–46*]. Instead we ask the question whether one particular more radical approach, that of re-designing the whole system of taxation to make it less corruption-friendly, would be likely to succeed.

CORRUPTION AND THE DESIGN OF TAX SYSTEMS

Political and Administrative Biases in Tax Design

We have argued that a collapse of unearned income that forces the state to substitute 'earned' tax revenues for the lost unearned income reduces the degree of insulation of the government from the governed. It creates a possibility for taxpayers to call the government to better account for its spending. To the extent that the government decides to respond to these demands, the basis exists for the growth of government accountability, and therewith the growth of government legitimacy. Indeed, such demands and responses have historically led on towards the emergence of more democratic types of government.

However attractive such an evolution may seem, and however much one would wish to encourage it, it is also true that democracies have drawbacks of their own in the matter of revenue raising. Politicians in a democracy tend to think that they have to be concerned more with what the taxation system looks like to the median voter than with how it actually performs in terms of criteria of net revenue raised, horizontal and vertical equity and its distorting effects on the economy.[4] They will, therefore, be inclined to prefer taxation that is as invisible to the general public's eye as possible, and when visible as equitable-looking as possible. Thus politicians will favour indirect taxation over direct, since the former tends to become consolidated into the purchase price of the taxed goods and services. They will also favour cascading indirect taxes to VAT, because the headline rate per unit of revenue is lower [*Due, 1976: 86*]. In direct taxes, steep progression of rates with numerous detailed exemptions will be preferred to mild progression or proportionality with no exemptions, because the former appears to be less harsh on the median voter.

Thus we caution against exaggerated expectations of rational taxation in new democracies. But whether the over-arching political constraints are set by an autocrat or by democratic politicians, it is important to be aware that, within those constraints, the detailed design of particular taxes can be shaped to fit the preferences of the tax officials themselves. Is this such a bad thing? The answer depends on what assumptions one makes about what the preferences of the tax officials themselves are likely to be. We assume the existence of corrupt tax officials, as well as dishonest taxpayers [*Besley and McLaren, 1993: 120 n.2*].

If tax officials are corrupt, or would seriously like to become so, a discreetly manipulative approach to tax design is an important lever to advance their purposes. Corrupt officials will have their own favoured methods for collecting any tax. Essentially, their collection methods should be complicated enough for them to be able, without undue difficulty, to make the life of the honest taxpayer miserable. If they can do that, then they will be able to turn some honest taxpayers into dishonest taxpayers who will collude in a secret agreement that, if their tax assessments are wrongly reduced, part of the revenue that the state loses thereby will be paid to the tax officials themselves. Both dishonest parties can secure private benefits at the expense of the state.

In order to structure incentives in a way that will promote such dishonest bargains, corrupt tax officials will prefer particular methods of tax collection. Four of these preferred methods are:

(a) multiple, overlapping tax jurisdictions (not unified jurisdictions);
(b) complex eligibility criteria (not simple ones);
(c) discretionary procedures (not automatic ones);
(d) full investigation of cases (not summary disposals).

These features can readily be legislated into any tax system, whatever the balance between direct and indirect taxes and whatever the nature of the separate tax bases [*Toye, 1989: 811*]. Moreover, either singly or in combination, they effectively set up a situation in which the typical encounter between tax officer and citizen has the following characteristics: (1) relevant information will be grossly asymmetric, in favour of the tax officer; (2) more than one type of tax officer can be involved in settling an individual case; (3) one or more face-to-face meetings may take place before the assessment is confirmed; (4) the severity of the assessment can vary widely without any breach of the tax rules. Such an encounter will contain ample scope for oppressive behaviour intended to induce collusion, the actual offer of bribes in return for a reduced assessment, and punitive sanctions on those honest taxpayers who still refuse to bribe.

To lend some verisimilitude to this account, below are some instances of this kind of collusion, taken from Nigeria, Taiwan and Indonesia. We may note at this point that each of these three countries falls in the bottom half of the Transparency International Corruption Perception Index, Taiwan being ranked 29th, Indonesia 45th and Nigeria 54th out of the 54 countries represented. The Index is a composite one based on various measures of corruption, as perceived by private sector business people.

The first example is taken from an anthropological narrative, referring to a village in south-east Nigeria.

> When the tax man came the following day, the (village council) had not met to decide how to welcome him; the food, drinks and money usually offered to mitigate the harsh tax assessment were not ready. When the tax man left, the elders and teenagers who had been exempted from the tax the previous year were now enroled to be taxed [*Iyam, 1995: 170–71*].

Since no gifts were available for him at the meeting, the tax man was able to punish the villagers by exercising his legal discretion on the question of which persons were liable to head tax in the way least favourable to their interests.

Another description of the same problem, this time from Taiwan, is as follows:

> It is this unintentional 'flexibility' of the tax laws that has yielded discretion to individual tax officials in interpreting the law. From the taxpayer's point of view, this arbitrariness means that the tax officials can raise hell with anyone they pick, and that 'anyone' could very well be the one that fails to buy them out. Unless the taxpayers receive extremely unfair treatment, they are usually reluctant to bring their cases to court [*Chu, 1990: 394*].

The situation was similar in Indonesia in the early 1980s.

> We had a dense forest of overlapping regulations that no one really understood. It could take years to figure out which laws were in effect and which ones had been superseded. This put businessmen and individual taxpayers at the mercy of tax officials ... The result was that businessmen needed to develop personal links with individual officials to ensure that all went well ... Of course, you had to pay a lot to this person to be certain he'd take good care of you [*Winters, 1996: 165-6*].

The exercise of discretionary power as a method of extracting bribes from taxpayers seems to be quite widespread in Africa and Asia.

The Strategy of Tax Simplification

It is in order to prevent this sort of outcome that the strategy of simplifying the structure of the tax system has been widely adopted in the current wave of tax reform in developing countries. Needless to say, the tax simplification strategy has more than this one objective. Other objectives include increasing total tax revenue by broadening the tax base, improving horizontal (if not vertical) equity and minimising tax-induced distortions of the economy. But in addition to these aims, tax simplification was expected to pay dividends in terms of the reduction of corruption. According to the head of the HIID tax reform mission to Indonesia in the mid-1980s, 'it was expected that simplification would reduce the scope for corruption, since the complexities and ambiguities in tax law were used by tax collectors and taxpayers alike to cloak their transgressions' [*Gillis, 1989: 93*].

One of the benefits of a less complex tax structure and a less ambiguous tax law is that it should reduce the frequency of face-to-face interactions between tax officials and taxpayers. There is much support in the tax literature for such a reduction, on the grounds that it reduces the temptation and the practical scope for tax officials to solicit bribes or to accept those offered. The introduction of withholding systems (like pay-as-you-earn) and presumptive assessments (where liability is assessed by reference to publicly monitorable factors) are effective ways of reducing the need for face-to-face interactions. Another benefit of tax simplification should be that the number of separate but overlapping tax jurisdictions are reduced, and that this reduces the degree of discretion that individual tax officials are allowed to exercise. This decreases the area of uncertainty about true liability, and thus the taxpayer's incentive to offer a bribe for a wrongly reduced settlement. 'Public officials who are in direct contact with their clients and those who can exercise discretion tend to figure more prominently' in the corrupt practices of revenue-raising agencies, according to one study of seven Asian countries [*Alfiler, 1986: 39*].

Is there a conflict between the two anti-corruption tactics of reducing face-to-face interactions between tax officers and taxpayers and reducing official discretion over liability assessments? Does not the resort to presumptive methods of assessment widen the tax officer's discretion? The answer is that it does not, provided that the presumptive rule is well defined and is based on available and transparent data. Consider the example of a tax which is intended to fall on incomes in the agricultural sector. Given that households' annual crop yields and the costs of producing them vary from year to year, it might be decided that regular on-farm inspections were needed to determine liability, and that tax inspectors should be allowed discretion to estimate the off-farm income of the farmer. Suppose that this method gave rise to corruption. A presumptive assessment method is then substituted for regular site inspections. Henceforth liability is determined by the size of the farm household's land holding, after allowance is made for the fertility of the soil. If there are accurate numbers from a recent cadastre of the size of all farm holdings, plus a transparent official classification of agro-climatic zones, presumptive tax liabilities can be calculated at once with no inspections and no scope for official discretion. What suffers in such a change is horizontal equity. Less discretion may cause more arbitrariness, for example, as between farmers who are able to cultivate their holding fully and those who are not. The reduction of corruption may have to be traded off against the degree of horizontal equity in a tax-simplifying reform, if extensive resort is had to presumptive methods.

Value-Added Tax and the Costs of Tax Simplification

Another trade-off exists between tax simplification and collection costs. The simplification of the tax system does not necessarily make it less costly to administer: it may make it more so. The proposition that tax simplification can raise the cost of revenue collection may be illustrated by reference to a policy of transition from assorted indirect taxes to a value-added tax (VAT). In the first place, it is clear that the introduction of a VAT does typically involve a great simplification of the structure of indirect taxation, in that it normally replaces a number of different existing indirect taxes. These are export taxes, excises (both specific and *ad valorem*), sales taxes (at manufacturing and/or wholesale and/or retail levels), selective taxes on services (usually those defined as luxuries) or, indeed any indirect tax that the government has thought fit to impose. Each of these different existing taxes will typically have its own structure of rates, its own list of exemptions, its own set of compliance requirements and so on. Many rate structures will be excessively differentiated. There will be many examples of overlapping incidence, leading to an irrational and inefficient distribution of the tax burden as well as the wide scope for official discretion that is conducive to corruption. Compared with all this, a VAT of the tax credit type is an immense simplification.

But this does not necessarily imply that adoption of a tax credit type of VAT will lower the costs of collecting the previous amount of revenue. All VATs which use tax credits, and therefore incorporate the potential anti-evasion advantage of the ability to cross-audit, i.e. to check the declarations of one taxpayer by reference to the declarations of others, are likely to require:

(1) a more extensive taxpayer registration than pre-existing taxes, as efficiency benefits depend on comprehensiveness of coverage (as well as simplicity of rate structure). In addition, the work of registration is heavier, for both parties, than registration for other types of taxes.

(2) the establishment of a refund or credit facility, partly for those taxpayers whose purchases and sales volumes are 'lumpy', that is, discontinuous and variable in size, but particularly for those whose sales are wholly or mainly for export, and therefore zero-rated.

(3) a significant upgrading of tax officers' skills to operate this more sophisticated method of indirect taxation. This will involve high training costs, particularly in countries that previously relied more heavily on revenue from excises than from sales taxes.

Thus simplification by means of transition to a VAT is likely to generate additional recurring costs. This has some interesting implications.

In principle, such costs can be traded off against the efficiency gains that tax simplification brings by reducing economic distortions, and this sets a limit to how much simplification is worthwhile. Also, the acceptable level of the costs of simplification will be affected by the size of the government's revenue target. If the government wants to raise more revenue than it did before, the distortion costs of persisting with the previous system of assorted taxes will rise at the margin, and this will make the additional costs of moving to a broad-based tax system like VAT more acceptable [*Gemmell, 1991*]. Tax reform inevitably requires achieving a balance between progress towards a number of different objectives, of which minimising collection costs is only one.

Will a Credit-type VAT Reduce Corruption?

We have already referred to the fact that the tax credit form of VAT makes cross-auditing a possibility. Cross-auditing means the ability to use information from one taxpayer's returns to check on the accuracy of the information supplied in another taxpayer's returns. This possibility arises because every transaction involves both a buyer and a seller, and under a comprehensive VAT both buyer and seller will have to file returns, each recording one side of an identical transaction. Also, the incentive to mis-declare the amount of tax paid works in opposing directions. A buyer may want to over-state the amount of VAT in her purchases of inputs, because that amount may be deducted from her own VAT liability. But a seller will not be willing to collude in this, because she can only do so by raising her own tax liability.

How in principle a cross-audit can be done is illustrated by the following table. In Table 1, the rows represent the stages of production, starting at the top and working down. To make this less abstract, one can visualise a farm growing wheat, a mill milling the wheat into flour, a bakery using the flour to make bread and a sandwich shop using the bread to make sandwiches to retail to the public. The columns represent the build up of gross costs of production, including VAT, at each of these stages of the production of retail sandwiches. In the fifth column, it can be seen that the seller's tax payment at any stage should be equal to the claim for tax credit of her buyer, who is also the seller of another product with additional value-added at the subsequent stage of production. If there are four stages of production from a to d, if VAT a = 1, then VAT credit b = 1; if VAT b = 10, then VAT credit c = 10; and if VAT c = 13, then VAT credit d = 13. Observed inequality of any of these three required equalities indicates error or, more likely, malfeasance. So much is well known and has been much discussed. But how far is this cross-audit feature of VAT likely to reduce corruption in practice, when corruption takes the form of collusion between dishonest tax officials with dishonest taxpayers? There are two major considerations which derive from two characteristic features of a credit-type VAT: the desirability of comprehensive coverage and the need for a refund facility.

CORRUPTION AND DEVELOPMENT

Stage of Production	(a) Raw Material	(b) Manufacturing	(c) Wholesale	(d) Retail
Value of purchases	0	11	110	143
VA added by stage	10	90	30	70
Cumulative VA	10	100	130	200
Tax due at stage (10%)	$1 - 0 = 1$	$10 - 1 = 9$	$13 - 10 = 3$	$20 - 13 = 7$
Cumulative VAT	1	10	13	20
Sale price to next stage	$10 + 1 = 11$	$100 + 10 = 110$	$130 + 13 = 143$	$200 + 20 = 220$

Source: Authors.

As emphasised earlier, the VAT has many advantages that make it a good form of taxation, whether it reduces corruption or not. It is income elastic, very productive of revenue with much reduced distortion of economic incentives, and neutral with respect to vertical equity. But these benefits are realised in full only if coverage is made as comprehensive and uniform as possible. There are good reasons, then, apart from a government's desire to raise the portion of its income that it 'earns', for the desire to register and tax as many small businesses as possible. The question is how far to go in this direction. To exclude entirely the retail stage, as was initially done in some francophone African versions of VAT, is probably to be too pessimistic about what can be done.

The difficulty of their inclusion, however, arises from the illiteracy and poor record-keeping of many retailers and owners of small businesses in developing countries. Their inclusion by use of the *forfait* (or negotiated assessment) procedure, while increasing the efficiency benefits of the tax and augmenting its revenue, can easily lead to bribery and corruption. It introduces into the new system the face-to-face meeting and the wide permitted discretion that opened the door to corruption in the old. It is particularly vital that, if resort is had to the *forfait*, it should be confined to sales, and not applied to purchases. Tax credits should be permitted against actual invoices only [*Due, 1976: 179*]. The collection of the latter is not onerous, even in a world of tropical rainstorms and hungry rats, and it provides an important reality check on the negotiated assessment of sales volumes. But the best solution is probably to steer clear of *forfait* altogether, and instead grant outright exemption to some small firms and farms with less than a stated threshold value of sales.

With the exception of the *forfait*, when used, the VAT operates by taxpayer self-assessment, based on records of sales and purchases. For every transaction, therefore, two independent records should be available to the VAT administration. In an ideal world taxpayer returns could be extensively, but not completely, cross-checked by computer, as a means of identifying discrepancies and possible delinquencies. In most developing countries, that time is still distant. In practice, the much-heralded cross-audit is so onerous as to be, with rare exceptions, useless as a means of policing self-assessment. There are still too many cash transactions without invoices or receipts [*Chu, 1990: 404*]. Moreover, a market in forged invoices can quickly develop. Bear in mind also that the cross-audit does not, in any event, detect every possible form of VAT evasion. Therefore, much of the success in reducing corruption still depends on more low-tech, and thus more fallible forms of audit and inspection.

It is usually impossible to audit every taxpayer every year, so a selection has to be made. Although the choice of who to audit, and who to ignore should be made on rational and impersonal criteria, this does not always happen. It is clear that discretion about who to audit will be a residual source of corruption. There have certainly been cases of policy failure in the auditing of VAT returns. The ratio of inspectors to taxpayers may be acceptable, and numerous audits and inspections may take place. Yet these may be quite ineffective where clear audit priorities are not established, a system for reporting findings does not exist and the regular reviewing of audit work by senior officials is absent, as is all too often the case. This kind of laxity will act as a breeding ground for corruption even when a VAT is in place.

But much more damaging is the fact that, without a workable cross-audit facility, there is nothing in the pure mechanics of a VAT that would stop the tax inspector and the tax payer meeting in advance to agree the level of the assessment, and then hiring corrupt accountants to prepare false paperwork which appeared to validate the wrongly reduced assessment. It is, after all, still in the interest of both the taxpayer and the tax official to agree on a wrongly reduced assessment and a bribe smaller than the amount of the reduction. Where corruption is already endemic, as in Indonesia, some collusion is likely to survive the introduction of VAT. In Taiwan, apparently, the existing system of regular pay-offs to the local tax office can be relied upon to secure at the very least an under-statement of the amount of evaded tax, if evasion is detected and reported from an audit [*Chu, 1990: 397*].

Do Corrupt Tax Officials Rationally Resist the Tax Simplification Strategy?

A final difficulty of implementing a tax simplification strategy is that, alongside the various pressures on government to move forward on tax reform, which have already been noted, other pressures exist that deter them from moving very vigorously and wholeheartedly [*Bird and Casanegra de Jantscher, 1992: 100*]. One of the reasons for this may be the existence of corruption in the tax administration. It is a matter of great interest, therefore, to enquire whether corrupt tax officials try to resist policy-makers' efforts to bring in reforms that restrict their meetings with taxpayers and the scope of their discretion, and if so whether they can succeed.

The focus here is on the Indonesian tax reform of the 1980s. The original aim of the technocratic economics ministers who conceived the tax reform was to modernise a tax system which had become over-complex, income-inelastic and administratively lax through years of high-level neglect. But as the oil price declined from its 1979–80 peak, the motivation for the reform came to include the enhancement of 'earned' government income, as well as squeezing out corruption within the tax administration. Both of these objectives were to be served by a drastic tax structure simplification centred on the introduction of a VAT.

> The second part of the Indonesian tax reform was the replacement of its complex sales tax structure with a more general credit-type VAT. The drastic simplification of the rate structure (to only one basic rate) and the elimination of many exemptions and other forms of special treatment reduced much of the discretionary authority of the tax officers ... Equally important in this regard was the built-in incentive under the credit-type system for taxpayers to engage in self-monitoring of tax collections [*Flatters and Macleod, 1995: 409*].

Flatters and Macleod testify to the active opposition of the tax officials:

> The Indonesian customs service and the sales tax office strongly resisted both of these aspects of the tax reform. Similar stories could be told about resistance of tax collectors, in Indonesia and elsewhere, to simplifications in property tax administration, income tax laws and tariff structures [*Flatters and Macleod, 1995: 409*].

Flatters and Macleod's story of bureaucratic resistance is corroborated by one of the key Indonesian tax reformers, as follows:

> The strongest resistance to tax reform, as it turns out, came from the tax officials themselves. They had the most to lose from the depersonalisation and simplification of the system. It was the same with customs. Before we could go ahead with tax deregulation, we had to replace the director general of taxes. Without this move, we could achieve nothing [*Winters, 1996: 166, n.62*].

Despite this clear documentation of the tax reformers' view that the resistance of the tax officials to tax simplification in Indonesia was strong, it has been argued that the resistance was more apparent than real, and that the tax officials were content with mere shadow-boxing. The tax reformers' view could, after all, be criticised as complacent, on the grounds that, if the tax officials had not resisted, this would show that the design of their reforms were in fact inadequate to prevent corruption, and seen by insiders to be toothless. By the same token, the tax officials would have been obliged to do some shadow-boxing, if they were not in effect to admit publicly that they saw the reforms as toothless against corruption, and thus push the reformers into trying more effective measures. We should be wary of accepting the tax reformers' view without considering some of the subtleties of political signalling that might be involved. How can we check the likelihood that the resistance of the Indonesian tax officials was rationally motivated by fear of the anti-corruption impact of the tax reform?

The weight of the evidence is on the side of the view that Indonesian tax officials did see the reforms as a threat, and that fear was a rational one given that they did indeed have a corruption-reducing effect within the tax system. We would not go so far as to claim that corruption in Indonesia has declined in the last decade: corruption may have decreased in the tax system and increased elsewhere in the economy. But a decline within the tax system does seem probable, for the following reasons. The Indonesian VAT was designed to be as simple a VAT as existed anywhere in the world. It did not extend below the importer and manufacturer levels, not even to wholesalers. There are very few exemptions, and there is only one rate of levy, ten per cent. Perhaps most important of all

> nearly two-thirds of the base of the tax passes through three bottlenecks that are easily accessible to the government, and therefore the tax administration: the customs house, sales of refined petroleum products by Pertamina ... and sales of the 200-odd government-owned enterprises ... Given these bottlenecks, the tax administration is in a position to collect more than half the potential VAT revenues with minimal expenditure of administrative resources, thereby allowing enforcement efforts to be focused on the remaining, less accessible portions of the tax base [*Gillis, 1989: 99*].

In these circumstances, and given also that the task of certificating the value of all Indonesian imports has been contracted out to a European firm, it is hard to argue that the same or a larger percentage of potential indirect tax revenue would be lost through corruption than was previously the case. Second, the VAT revenue figures are too high to be consistent with a constant or increasing level of leakage. This can be shown by a simple calculation. The nominal proceeds of a single-rate VAT with completely comprehensive coverage have to increase at the same rate as the total of value added at current prices, i.e. the nominal rate of economic growth. Between 1985 and 1995, the real rate of growth of GDP in Indonesia was approximately seven per cent per annum, while the GDP deflator was approximately eight per cent per annum. If nominal GDP was growing at 15 per cent per annum, the tax base for a comprehensive single-rate VAT would be growing at 15 per cent also.

According to the IMF *Government Finance Statistics Yearbook 1996* (p.192) the revenue from 'general sales tax, turnover or VAT' amounted to 2,327 billion rupiahs in 1985, and had grown to 18,335 billion rupiahs in 1994. This is a rate of growth of approximately 22 per cent per annum. It follows from this that the degree of exploitation of the VAT tax base was growing rapidly and significantly in the period 1985–94, at a rate of around seven per cent a year. Although in an initial transitional phase, this rate of growth could theoretically occur while the degree of revenue leakage was rising, growth of the exploitation of the tax base *plus* increasing revenue leakage could not persist over the longer term. There must come a point of inflection in both growth functions after which both decelerate as the limits of the VAT tax base are reached. Under the collection conditions described, it seems likely to us that the revenue leakage already has been, and will continue to be, squeezed.

Third, the obvious success of the VAT in revenue enhancement, deriving from the inherent income elasticity of the tax base as well as the increase in the degree of exploitation of that base, created a virtuous circle. Once the government had succeeded in putting in place a 'cash machine' of this degree of productivity, short term revenue pressures were reduced. The temptation to set revenue targets for other types of taxes, and allow discretion as to the means by which they are met, becomes less urgent and easier to resist.

CONCLUSIONS

One very frequent practical obstacle to the successful implementation of a strategy of tax simplification is that the tax authorities are rarely left alone to develop simpler and more productive revenue-gathering systems. They are often the victims of a policy-activism that is dictated by considerations of visibility rather than effectiveness. Governments often make sudden highly visible changes in tax policy, which look dramatic but are undertaken primarily to demonstrate that 'the government is doing something about it', whatever 'it' may happen to be at the time. The real impact in solving the chosen short-run problem may be small, but the side effects on the task of simplifying the tax system may be large. A good example of this is the proliferation of different rates and exemptions within a VAT in response to the agitation of particular socio-economic groups. Another example is the existence of short term pressures for extra revenue which lead to the retention or introduction of taxes that are productive of revenue but quite undesirable from the viewpoint of the other goals of taxation [*Gray, 1989: 2*]. It is worth noting, with reference to the Indonesian reform, that neither of these things happened.

In the 1980s, there has been a particular kind of policy activism, which goes under the name of structural adjustment. The reform of the budget or tax system was a condition in over two-thirds of the World Bank's structural or sectoral adjustment loans in the period 1980–86 [*Mosley, Harrigan and Toye, 1995: 44*]. Inevitably in the circumstances, in some countries schemes of tax simplification themselves came to be regarded as a quick fix for a burgeoning fiscal deficit. Guatemala's 1983 tax reform may be cited as an example of this. Under the guidance of the IMF, the government decided to increase revenue by replacing the existing turnover sales tax and a stamp duty with a tax credit method VAT. The VAT became operational one month after it was announced, leaving no time to organise and train the tax administrators or to educate the taxpayers. Far from being 'self-enforcing', as the authorities seemed naively to believe, the VAT got into immediate difficulties because the administration received a flood of refund requests, most of which were believed to be fraudulent, but which there was no capacity to audit. The refunding was suspended, re-introducing cascade effects, public confidence was lost, the VAT rate was drastically lowered and the stamp duty brought back to fill the consequent revenue gap [*Bird and Casanegra de Jantscher, 1992: 79–83*]. This was *not* the way to simplify the Guatemalan tax system!

Much ground would be gained in the war of attrition against corruption if politicians could be weaned away from their habit of pursuing the politics of visibility in taxation decisions. There is an obvious link between the adoption of tax policies that look good to the median voter and the maintenance of extensive bureaucratic discretion. This is because tax policies that look good to the median voter would be unworkable if their regulations were to be enforced as written. This is true of income taxes with an extremely steep rate of progression, for example. Such taxes would be very difficult to collect without allowing enough bureaucratic discretion to ensure that the effective progression of the tax incidence is much milder than the nominal rate schedule would lead one to expect. Thus the pursuit of visibility politics in taxation is not merely compatible with bureaucratic tax discretion, it is symbiotic with it. The symbiosis is, needless to say, strengthened when the proceeds of bureaucratic tax corruption are partly siphoned off by politicians. However, what looks good to the median voter (assuming here the success of the democratisation agenda) need not remain fixed and unchanging. Electorates may learn eventually that all that glistens is not gold, and that democratic politicians, like conjurors, win the applause of their parties by the extravagant practice of mis-direction. As Abraham Lincoln memorably put it: 'you can fool some of the people all of the time and you can fool all of the people some of the time, but you cannot fool all of the people all of the time'.

The Indonesian case shows that tax reform does not always fail, and that the tax simplification strategy can bring some anti-corruption dividends. However, the Indonesian case, in tax reform as in structural adjustment policy more generally, has unusual features which mean that it is not easy to draw easily applicable policy lessons for other developing countries. For one thing, Indonesia since 1966 has benefited from an economic leadership that is far-sighted and technocratically skilful. The lesson of Indonesia is not that there are technical fixes for cultural dispositions that hinder development, but that what is required is a long-lasting political drive from a very high level to a particular vision of development, and that vision must be technically well informed.

Where such political pre-conditions are lacking, however, second best and n-th best solutions have to be considered. These involve some toleration of corruption, but also an attempt to limit the damage that it can do to a government's efforts to 'earn' more of its income. Under this scenario, corruption will never disappear, and anti-corruption policy will always be a matter of containment, a little more or a little less.

Flatters and Macleod [1995] analyse this problem using a model of collusion between tax collectors and taxpayers to reduce the latter's liability, the difference between this and the true liability being divided between them. They argue the case for limited toleration of this corruption, when four conditions apply. They are that:

(1) the government cannot pay tax collectors more than the normal civil service rate;
(2) the tax collectors have better knowledge of the true tax liability than is available to the Finance Minister;
(3) for the collectors, bribes are a perfect substitute for wages;
(4) collectors exert more effort to establish true liability when they are paid higher wages-plus-bribes.

In these conditions, if the Finance Ministry tolerates limited corruption, it can overcome the handicap imposed by poor knowledge of individual tax liabilities. It can collect more revenue compared with a situation in which the tax collectors are uncorrupted, but also unmotivated to exploit their superior knowledge to increase the Finance Ministry's revenue total. Corruption of tax officials may be one problem, this model is telling us, but personal integrity when it is combined with a minimal incentive to work is another.

This is a good warning against the practical consequences of taking an excessively moralistic approach to policy-making, and in that sense it follows a familiar tradition in political economy. The four assumed conditions are not wholly implausible individually, and there may indeed be countries where all hold good at the same time. The Indonesian case certainly shows that they are not universally true, and that the strategy of tax simplification ought to reduce the need to tolerate corruption because it reduces the asymmetry of information between the Finance Ministry and the tax officials.

Even where the conditions of the Flatters and Macleod model do hold, and limited corruption does augment government revenues, the government remains vulnerable to the evaporation of its revenues, unless it is able to enforce its chosen limits to corruption. It must at all times be able to exercise powers of dismissal and financial penalty over both excessively lazy and excessively greedy tax collectors. If it cannot do these two things, the revenue benefit of its Faustian bargain will disappear. Maybe the disciplining of the excessively greedy tax collectors will prove easier than it seems. In this connection, one is much heartened by the true story of the developing country government that introduced a system of self-assessment for import duties, stood down all its customs officers and found that its customs revenue sharply increased.

NOTES

1. For sources, see Moore [*1998*].
2. The use of the concept of 'earned income' is indeed a logical extension of the term 'rentier': rentier income is 'unearned' in the language of classical political economy.
3. It would be a major undertaking, because many other factors are involved.
4. Horizontal equity refers to the equal tax treatment of equally placed individuals, or companies: it requires the like treatment of like. Vertical equity requires that differently situated individuals (or companies) are treated differently and in a manner appropriate to their differences. What is appropriate is controversial. Some argue for proportionate taxation, that is tax payments proportionate to income, while others argue for progressive taxation, where the tax rate rises as income increases, on the grounds of the declining marginal utility of income. The distorting effects of taxation on the economy arise if the tax element in the prices of goods and services is not strictly proportional to the non-tax element. In this case, the relative prices of goods and services will be changed by the taxation, and people's economic behaviour will be distorted away from the pattern that they would freely choose in the absence of taxation, and which ipso facto they regard as preferable. The neutral impact of VAT, as shown later in Table 1, is therefore a highly desirable feature of any tax, but which very few other taxes have in the same degree as VAT.

REFERENCES

Alfiler, C.P., 1986, 'The Process of Bureaucratic Corruption in Asia: Emerging Patterns', in L.V. Carino, *Bureaucratic Corruption in Asia: Causes, Consequences and Controls*, Quezon City: JMC Press.

Bardhan, P., 1997, 'Corruption and Development: A Review of Issues', *Journal of Economic Literature*, Vol.XXXV, Sept., pp.1320–46.

Besley, T. and J. McLaren, 1993, 'Taxes and Bribery: the Role of Wage Incentives', *Economic Journal*, Vol.103, No.416, pp.119–41.

Bird, R.M. and M. Casanegra de Jantscher (eds.), 1992, *Improving Tax Administration in Developing Countries*, Washington, DC: International Monetary Fund.

Chaudhry, K.A., 1989, 'The Price of Wealth: Business and State in Labor Remittance and Oil Economies', *International Organization*, Vol.43, No.1, pp.101–45.

Chu, C.Y.C., 1990, 'A Model of Income Tax Evasion with Venal Tax Officials: the Case of Taiwan', *Public Finance/Finances Publiques*, Vol.XXXXV, No.3, pp.392–407.

Due, J.F., 1976, 'Value-added Taxation in Developing Countries', in N.T. Wang (ed.), *Taxation and Development*, New York: Praeger.

Flatters, F. and W.B. Macleod, 1995, 'Administrative Corruption and Taxation', *International Tax and Public Finance*, Vol.2, pp.397–417.

Gemmell, N., 1991, 'Tax Collection Costs and the Choice of Tax Base in Less Developed Countries: A Geometric Note', University of Nottingham, Credit Research Paper No.91/3.

Gillis, M., 1989, 'Comprehensive Tax Reform: The Indonesian Experience, 1981–1988', in M. Gillis (ed.), *Tax Reform in Developing Countries*, Durham NC: Duke University Press.

Goldscheid, R., 1958 (1925), 'A Sociological Approach to Problems of Public Finance', in R.A. Musgrave and A.T. Peacock (eds.), *Classics in the Theory of Public Finance*, London and New York: Macmillan.

Gray, C.W., 1989, *Issues in Income Tax Reform in Developing Countries*, World Bank, Working Paper Series No.267.

Iyam, D.U., 1995, *The Broken Hoe: Cultural Reconfiguration in Biase Southeast Nigeria*, Chicago, IL: Chicago University Press.

Moore, M.P., 1998, 'Death without Taxes: Democracy, State Capacity, and Aid Dependence in the Fourth World', in M. Robinson and G. White (eds.), *Towards a Democratic Developmental State*, Oxford: Oxford University Press.

Mosley, P., Harrigan, J. and J. Toye, 1995, *Aid and Power: The World Bank and Policy-based Lending*, second edition, Vol.1, London: Routledge.

Thorp, R., 1996, 'The Reform of Tax Administration in Peru', in A. Silva (ed.), *Implementing Policy Innovations in Latin America: Politics, Economics and Techniques*, Social Agenda Policy Group, Inter-American Development Bank, Washington DC.

Toye, J., 1989, 'Tax Reform in South Asia: Yesterday and Today', *Modern Asian Studies*, Vol.23, Part 4, Oct., pp.797–813.

Wade, R., 1985, 'The Market for Public Office: Why the Indian State is not Better at Development', *World Development*, Vol.13, No.4, pp.467–98.

Winters, J.A., 1996, *Power in Motion: Capital Mobility and the Indonesian State*, Ithaca, NY: Cornell University Press.

Fighting Systemic Corruption: Social Foundations for Institutional Reform

MICHAEL JOHNSTON

While institutional reforms enhancing transparency and accountability in state and economic institutions are indispensable parts of any anti-corruption strategy, they also need a long-term social foundation, particularly where corruption is systemic. Social empowerment – expanding and protecting the range of political and economic resources, and alternatives, open to ordinary citizens – is one way to address this task. Social empowerment entails strengthening civil society in order to enhance its political and economic vitality, providing more orderly paths of access and rules of interaction between state and society, and balancing economic and political opportunities. Development strategies aimed particularly at hitherto-excluded people and regions within a country are of particular importance. Social empowerment does not involve wholly new remedies, but rather the judicious coordination of a variety of familiar development and anti-corruption policies. Where it is successful, social empowerment will not totally eradicate corruption. It can, however, provide necessary support for institutional reforms, weaken the combinations of monopoly, discretion, and lack of accountability that make for systemic corruption, and help institutionalise reform for the long term by linking it to lasting interests contending in active political and social processes.

INTRODUCTION

In many countries where corruption is the exception, not the rule, reformers have several advantages. Anti-corruption laws, agencies and organisations are in place and enjoy broad-based support, as do independent courts, auditors and news media. Citizens and organisations are willing to confront the problem directly [*Alam, 1995*] and elected officials cannot ignore them without the risk of losing office. New episodes of corruption may feature novel tactics of venality but they are generally limited in scope. Government is broadly

Michael Johnston, Department of Political Science, Colgate University, Hamilton, NY 13346, USA. Tel: 1 315 228 7756, Fax: 1 315 228 7883, E-mail: mjohnston@mail.colgate.edu.

legitimate; civil liberties, systems of accountability, property and contract rights, and the rule of law are credible. Ineffective policies and the marked deterioration of governmental functions can be addressed without a crisis, for it is possible to change the government without bringing down the regime [*Przeworski and Limongi, 1993*].

In such settings, we generally respond to corruption through institutional reform. A range of familiar and well-tested options is at hand. Some address operational problems through improved controls over discretion and resources; more transparent procedures; strengthening of internal and external accountability systems; improved recruitment, compensation, training and retraining for officials; and creating channels of appeal for clients, for example. Where problems lie at the level of basic structures, rather than with operations, redesigned institutions may be needed as replacements for, or additions to, existing ones. Winning support for, and implementing, institutional reforms can be far from easy: corrupt interests with a stake in the status quo can strongly oppose changes, while reform advocates may be divided among themselves as to the nature of the problem and the best remedies for it. Public support for reform, while critical to its success, is often transitory and diffuse. Still, institutional reforms have a good track record in those nations where government is generally legitimate and effective, and corruption is a problem with limited scope and many foes.

Unfortunately, institutional reforms by themselves do not fare as well where corruption problems are worst. Corruption in many of those nations is not only more extensive but is also a qualitatively different problem, embedded in political and economic systems in ways that both reflect its impact and help sustain its force. Particularly in developing or transitional societies where the challenge of limiting corruption is most urgent, new institutional forms and procedures – like the ones they replace, in many instances – are often deprived of the administrative and political support and underlying normative consensus that they require for success. Thus, even where corruption is reduced for a time, it has a way of reasserting itself. This is systemic corruption, and it poses reform challenges which are institutional as well as social in nature.

If the limited corruption of more advanced countries represents a formidable challenge, what if anything can be done where it is the rule, and where routine political and economic processes sustain rather than resist it? Where real power is not won through open, honest competition, nor exercised through transparent, accountable processes and institutions, where can reformers begin? And where people find it prudent to respond to corruption by avoiding the problem or through corruption of their own [*Alam, 1995*], where can reformers find significant support? Finally, how can reform and reductions in corruption be made sustainable, rather than just short-term or superficial?

I argue that social empowerment – expanding and protecting the range of political and economic resources, and alternatives, open to ordinary citizens – is an essential part of any attack upon systemic corruption. Where grassroots communities and the people within them deal with corrupt officials because they have few alternatives, and respond to corruption in evasive or illicit rather than direct ways [*Alam, 1995*], we must search for ways of reducing their political and economic vulnerability and of giving them more effective means of recourse. Institutional reforms designed to increase accountability and transparency in the operations of the state and major economic institutions, and measures to counteract specific corrupt practices, will always be worthwhile; in no way does social empowerment supplant these approaches. But major political and economic institutions must engage with viable social processes, including political and economic contention, and become linked to enduring incentives and interests if they are to be sustainable and to yield their full potential benefits.

Social empowerment does not so much involve a whole new set of anti-corruption measures as an integration of development policies, many of them familiar, aimed at enhancing the vitality of political and economic life and of civil society, particularly in those segments of a country which have been excluded from development or exploited. In part because the renewal of interest in corruption as a problem in development is relatively recent, social empowerment as a comprehensive anti-corruption strategy has yet to be implemented anywhere (though such empowerment has long been a general development-policy goal, and the anti-corruption debate has devoted renewed attention to the value of a viable civil society [*Cooter, 1997*]). However, a number of countries have reduced corruption historically through the development of civil society and enhanced political and economic competition; changes which, while often not planned or coordinated as reforms *per se*, incorporate some of the elements of social empowerment. Thus at various points in this analysis I will discuss examples illustrating the potential of the strategy. This discussion will not arrive at 'the answer' to corruption problems in the developing world, or even in any one country; indeed, social empowerment strategies will have to be tailored to the structure, problems, current lines of conflict and development potential of specific societies. For that process, there is no substitute for a detailed knowledge of a country and its people. But I do hope to identify a general strategy for building solid social foundations for institutional reform, and for strengthening forces and processes which can sustain reductions in corruption over the long term.

CORRUPTION, VULNERABILITY AND CHOICE

Sustainable anti-corruption reform is critical to the future of developing and transitional societies. Corruption is not just a 'growing pain' associated with development; even less is it a sort of facilitating process. Evidence is mounting that corruption slows economic growth [*Ades and di Tella, 1994; Mauro, 1997; Murphy, Shleifer and Vishny, 1993; Rose-Ackerman, 1996, 1997; Rose-Ackerman and Stone, 1996; World Bank, 1997*] and serves as a heavy tax upon investment [*Wei, 1997*]. It is often at its worst in relatively closed economic and political systems [*Elliott, 1997*]. Corruption undermines political development, flourishing where national institutions and guarantees of basic economic rights are weak [*Knack and Keefer, 1995*] and ethnic divisions and conflicts are particularly deep [*Easterly and Levine, 1996*]. As economies and markets become more interdependent, corrupt agents can extend their dealings across borders, quickly shifting illicit profits out of poor countries into numbered bank accounts elsewhere. Corruption reduces the effectiveness of aid-funded projects [*IMF, 1995; Isham, Kaufmann and Pritchett, 1995, 1996; Rauch, 1995*] and further weakens political support for aid within donor countries. Countries suffering from corruption cannot make the best use of their human and natural resources; instead, they will likely remain vulnerable to and dependent upon outside interests and markets, and be unable to implement effective development strategies of their own. Because corruption, as a form of influence, requires scarce resources – money, access, expertise – it will tend to favour the interests of the 'haves' in a given setting, usually at the expense of the 'have-nots' [*Johnston, 1982: Ch.2*]. For this reason, even seemingly 'petty' corruption, as judged by the sums of money changing hands or the ordinary nature of the situations and participants involved, can be part of a pervasive syndrome of problems that helps keep poor countries poor.

Corruption does not explain all that is wrong with developing societies, nor does it negate all that is right in them. It is not something that 'happens to' a country, but rather a symptom of deeper difficulties. In many respects, it is not just a 'development problem', but also a profoundly *social* process involving real people in concrete situations. Looked at one way, corruption is a problem of official ethics and public dealings; but viewed another way, it is a function of the opportunities and alternatives people have in life. While institutional reforms focus – rightly – upon the opportunities and alternatives open to officials, it makes equal sense to consider those available to citizens, both as they affect their vulnerability to corruption and as they shape possible opportunities for responding to it.

In advanced societies, where economic and political vitality and a strong civil society can often be taken for granted, the importance of social foundations for institutional reform can easily be overlooked. In developing and transitional societies, by contrast, the indifferent track record of reformed institutions (and particularly those of liberal democracy and market economics) in many places gives citizens little reason to trust them or to use them to defend themselves. The major institutions of the state and the economy must win broad-based legitimacy and support. For these reasons, it will not do simply to propose democracy and market economics as solutions to systemic corruption. Comparative statistical evidence suggests that democratic rights and processes by themselves do not significantly reduce corruption [*Isham, Kaufmann, and Pritchett, 1995; 1996*] and are linked to economic growth in only limited and indirect ways [*Barro, 1995; Przeworski and Limongi, 1993*]. Moreover, democracies and advanced market economies have corruption problems of their own (if typically less pervasive and harmful to development). For serious cases of corruption, reform from the bottom upwards, opening up political and economic alternatives and bringing excluded segments of society into an active mainstream, is an essential counterpart to increased official transparency and institutional change.

Definitions

No issue is more enduring in the corruption debate, and none has so frequently preempted promising discussions, as that of definitions. Despite the fact that most people, most of the time, know corruption when they see it, defining the concept does raise difficult theoretical and empirical questions [*Johnston, 1996*]. We are unlikely ever to arrive at a single definition which accurately identifies all possible cases. Moreover, if a significant proportion of the population regard a person, process or regime as corrupt, or if they believe corruption is inevitable in their daily lives, that is an important social and political fact, whatever an analyst might say about the situation. In cases of systemic corruption, however, we encounter a lasting and pervasive pattern of abuses that few would hesitate to call corrupt. Therefore I will simply define corruption as the abuse of public roles or resources for private benefit. The terms 'abuse', 'public', 'private', and even 'benefit' [*Thompson, 1993; 1995*] may be contested in actual cases, and in fact such disputes can be indicators of the sort of political contention that we might want to encourage; but this definition fits cases of systemic corruption without major difficulties.

Systemic corruption is not a special category of corrupt practice but rather a situation in which the major institutions and processes of the state are routinely dominated and used by corrupt individuals and groups, and in which many people have few practical alternatives to dealing with corrupt officials. Examples might include contemporary Nigeria and Mobutu's Zaire; Haiti's *tonton macoute*; the deeply-rooted corruption Scott [*1972: Ch.4*] analysed in 1960s' Thailand; the political machines found, often during phases of rapid urbanisation, in American cities and elsewhere (for Palermo, see Chubb [*1981*]); and – within certain segments of economies or policy systems – the entrenched systems of patrimonialism that still exist even in relatively developed countries [*Theobald, 1992*]. In such settings, political will to pursue reform is often feeble, and corruption may be monopolistic, organised and

coordinated and thus 'entrenched' [*Johnston, 1997a*]. The near-inevitability of
official abuses may be as much a matter of expectations as a positive fact –
expectations created by a climate of intimidation, perhaps, or cultivated by
'middlemen' with a stake in maintaining the value of their 'services'
[*Oldenburg, 1987; Sacks, 1976*]. Still, corruption that is pervasive is no longer
an exception to the political or administrative norm.

The Broader Setting: Conditions Sustaining Systemic Corruption

Systemic corruption is so persistent and difficult to combat not only because
of its inner workings but also because it is embedded in a wider political and
economic situation that helps sustain it. The relationships between corrupt
practices and the broader situation are reciprocal: corruption contributes to
delayed and distorted political development, weakening competitive processes
and major institutions [*Johnston, 1997b*], while that environment renders
people more vulnerable to corrupt exploitation – or dependent upon its petty
rewards, in the absence of better political and economic opportunities – and
thus less able to resist it. Corruption becomes embedded in the range of
interrelated development problems noted above. Prolonged slow or negative
growth, or even rapid growth if monopolised by a few well-connected factions,
perpetuates the scarcity of economic alternatives for the many while
reinforcing dependency upon corrupt officials. Political monopoly power puts
civil liberties at risk; elections and trials can be rigged. Intimidation and the
perception that corruption is inevitable weaken mass support for would-be
reformers, who may conclude there is nothing to gain, and much to lose, by
remaining in opposition, and throw in their lot with the powerful.

    Martin Shefter's [*1976*] account of the rise of New York's Tammany Hall
machine offers one account of the growth of systemic corruption in a rapidly-
changing society. During the 'Rapacious Individualism' of the first half of the
nineteenth century a number of politicians and their followers – often based in
the many volunteer fire companies of the day – fought for political power,
often physically. Followings were loose-knit and poorly disciplined and
leaders had to bribe followers repeatedly in order to be confident of their
support. Competition was disorderly: those who won power did not hold it for
long and entrepreneurs who paid bribes often got little in return.

    A 'consolidation' phase followed, paralleling the rise of business
oligopolies. Political leaders tightened discipline somewhat by eliminating
competitors at the polls (or in back alleys), while businessmen searching for
reliable political deals became partners in some of the remaining political
combines. Tammany itself had a businessman-boss in this phase. During the
mature-machine phase (1880s and after), Tammany held a virtual monopoly
over New York City politics. It disciplined its followers ruthlessly – for they
had no real political alternatives – and treated business, too, as a prime target

for exploitation. Corruption became more concentrated in very large deals at the top of the machine, as business interests bought major contracts and franchises from political leaders with a tight hold on power. The high prices and arbitrary nature of these deals, and the lack of prospective political alternatives, led many business figures – by now, becoming more managerial in approach, and shifting their emphasis beyond the boundaries of New York – to become prominent in the antimachine movement [*Shefter, 1976*].

INSTITUTIONALISING REFORM THROUGH SOCIAL EMPOWERMENT

Widening citizens' political and economic resources and alternatives and giving basic protection to their political and economic activities can reduce their vulnerability to exploitation, enhancing their ability to participate effectively in politics and to check the self-interested behaviour of official decision-makers and of each other in the process. Where this occurs, corrupt officials will find it more difficult to maintain the political and bureaucratic monopolies and discretion and the weak mechanisms of accountability which Klitgaard [*1988: 75*] identifies as basic causes of corruption. Social empowerment is a complex, long-term anti-corruption strategy, and may well involve increased corruption problems in early stages. It is in no way a substitute for reforms at the organisational, personnel and administrative levels: indeed, social empowerment and 'macro-level' policies must work together. Moreover, social empowerment can entail considerable political contention, particularly where the rules and boundaries defining corruption are changing or unclear. But moderate levels of conflict, and widespread debate (and even scandal) over the rules of public life, can be healthy things: the Collor de Mello scandal in Brazil, for example, mobilised new public opposition to corruption [*Keck, 1992: 4–7*], much as machine corruption in American cities gave rise to a reform movement. Over time, social empowerment can help sustain reform, both within institutions and at the level of day-to-day economic and political activity.

What various examples of social empowerment in differing societies will have in common is the emerging strength of the groups and interests which make up civil society – that is, organisations, enterprises, and informal social networks active in the realm between individuals and government. Even when such groups do not have overt political agendas or allegiances, they play very important roles. Where social empowerment is effective, institutional reforms, and the official rules of decision-making and administration, can converge with social values, and thus grow in legitimacy and effectiveness. Conflicts over the rules of politics and government may grow out of the self-interests of private parties, but the settlements that can emerge among private and public parties will be the more legitimate and durable precisely *because* those interests have been engaged. In this way, social groups and private interests can become, not the instigators or targets of corruption, but 'law merchants' [*Cooter, 1997: 191*] supplementing official laws with strong social norms and aiding in a transition towards the rule of law. Society will not be completely free of corruption – far from it – but over the long run, social and legal values can become interlinked in a 'system of public order' [*Rogow and Lasswell, 1963: 67*].

Pursuing Social Empowerment

A discussion such as this one can only point in general terms towards social trends and groups which may prove helpful in the struggle against corruption. In exploring the connections between social empowerment and reform, there is no substitute for the experience and judgements of officials and scholars deeply familiar with the specific personalities and conflicts, problems and opportunities involved in a nation's politics. None the less, we can point to three major challenges.

(1) State and Civil Society: Both the fundamental strength of civil society and the overall balance between it and the state are critical aspects of any reform strategy. Where the groups, interests and organisations of civil society are vigorous, they can serve as political and communication links (both upward and downward) between government and people. They can monitor the conduct of officials, and of each other, and through conflict and competition can reach settlements regarding acceptable political practice that engage private interests in the reduction of public corruption. This is a critical development: while anti-corruption campaigns are obviously important, institutionalising reform means linking it to enduring incentives. The same interests that had previously contributed to corruption, either as instigators or as paying victims, can come to inhibit it to the extent that they are numerous and well-organised, experience a healthy competitive balance among themselves, and become better able to insist upon less exploitative treatment by officials.

The state–society relationship can become imbalanced in a variety of ways. Where civil society is weak, citizens and private interests are vulnerable to exploitation by political and/or bureaucratic monopolies and, because they lack the political means and organisational strength to insist on their formal rights, often respond to corruption in evasive or illicit ways [*Alam, 1995*], minimizing its costs or fighting it with more corruption. People and firms will have little reason to think that if they were to refrain from corruption others would do the same. On the other hand, where the state is poorly institutionalised, government power and public officials can be exploited by powerful interests in civil society – as arguably occurs in many liberal democracies – and there, the balance tilts in the other direction. Politics and administration may be permeated by sectoral interests and become 'privatised' in the worst sense of that term. Where state and society are in balance, however, it is more difficult for either side to exploit the other..

Civil society is not a unified entity in its own right; strengthening it is a complex, group-by-group process whose details will differ from country to country. This must be done in order to speed the development of countervailing political interests and to institutionalise both boundaries and channels of access between government and people, legitimating the former while drawing it into more extensive but orderly interactions with the latter. This is by no means a simple task: if social interests gather strength faster than do the institutions defining boundaries and paths of access between state and society, we may create an apparent surge in corruption, as once-concealed practices come to light, elite consensus breaks down (as happened to Italy's anti-communist coalition after the end of the cold war, with the *mani puliti* and *tangentopoli* scandals among the results), whistleblowers begin to feel free to speak, and organised corruption gives way to more fragmented and disruptive practices. But these can be indicators of a breakdown in the old systemic corruption. Thus, while institutional reforms without a firm social foundation are unlikely to succeed, the cultivation of civil society is not a substitute for institution-building. The two must work together.

The development of civil society will be disorderly, particularly as compared to the immediate aftermath of anti-corruption coups or official crackdowns. But vibrant civil politics is inherently disorderly, and indeed this helps us understand why anti-corruption coups do not work. Attempts to fight corruption by seizing central control and cracking down from above – even where the anti-corruption intent is genuine, as it often is not – may temporarily put a chill on corrupt activities. But in the long run they inhibit the very processes – political competition, overt and self-interested conflict over rules and standards, and the free mobilisation of social groups around issues of scandal – that are needed to build a new system of public order. Sustained political leadership and support from international aid partners will be more effective at increasing the political and economic competition, and the strengthened civil society, needed to weaken the monopolies underlying systemic corruption. There is no guarantee that the system will never revert to its bad old ways, but political competition will strengthen elites' incentives to confront the problem directly, and the improved economic performance likely to result from reduced corruption can create incentives sustaining the overall process [*Rose-Ackerman, 1996*].

A strong civil society can also be a check upon official conduct, and critical to accountability, because 'transparent' procedures mean little if no one outside the state can demand a meaningful accounting backed up by credible threats of political or legal sanctions. The anti-Collor public protests in Brazil, already noted, hardly eradicated the deeper causes of corruption [*Keck, 1992: 7*]; but without them, many political officials would have found it easier to avoid confronting the president. Similarly, the corruption convictions of two former South Korean presidents in recent years were a harrowing experience for that society, but when these cases are viewed within the context of the country's gradual democratisation they can also be seen as indicating a significant degree of pluralisation and the emergence of significant anti-corruption forces outside the state. But without a strong civil society to energise them, even a full set of formally-democratic institutions will not produce accountability. At a lower level of aggregation, a weak civil society will provide little sustaining force or protection for free social interaction. Cooter [*1997*] shows that where people freely and repeatedly interact, they tend to form strong and legitimate social norms. Survey and interview research on popular conceptions of right and wrong suggest that most citizens judge public dealings, as well as each other, by social norms learned in everyday situations [*Johnston, 1991*]. In advanced economies business and professional groups promulgate codes of good practice and can impose anti-corruption sanctions of modest scale relatively quickly, on a lower burden of proof than those required in court.[1] Where civil society is weak, by contrast, vital social support for limits on corruption is lost.

(2) Orderly Interaction and Access: A second major task is to foster more extensive interaction between private parties and government, in such a way as to encourage each side to respect the autonomy of the other. I use 'autonomy' in Huntington's sense – not to refer to complete independence or isolation of government from society, or *vice versa*, but rather to the ability of each to maintain its boundaries and prerogatives while dealing with the other. Mutual autonomy thus implies not only that citizens know and value the duties and functions (not to be confused with personal power) of officials, but also that officials respect the rights of citizens, and that both come to regard legitimate procedures as serving mutual ends. Private individuals and groups will be better able to insist on their rights; and where official processes become more transparent and access to those agencies is made easier, 'gatekeeping' officials and functionaries will be less able to create contrived shortages, manipulate monopoly positions and bureaucratic bottlenecks, or otherwise exploit their roles.

What of the citizens' commitment to established rules? I have already suggested that where private interests are not only well organised but also numerous and competitive, they may be able to monitor and check each other. But it is also important to give citizens a direct stake in process as well as in outcomes. This can be done through more effective taxation: when the continuing costs of governmental processes are tangible and perceptible, people will acquire a stake in knowing how government does its business, rather than just caring about outcomes. Historically, effective taxation did more than just enhance revenues; indeed, for Weber [*1946 edn: 204-9*], it was a 'presupposition of bureaucracy' allowing regular salaried compensation for officials and weakening the notion of personal service to patrons as the primary obligation of office. Regular salaries based upon revenues collected and distributed by full-time administrators created incentives to effective administration and record keeping, and helped pave the way for a permanent, efficient civil service enforcing its own codes of behaviour with salaries as an important means of control. The growing effectiveness of these functions meant, in turn, that further revenues could be collected, reinforcing the trends already underway. Theobald [*1992: 22-4*] argues that the *absence* of this self-reinforcing cycle in poorer nations today sustains corruption: administratively weak states are less able to extract revenues, and therefore less able to foster economic development, which means that such economic surpluses as *are* created remain in small-scale, difficult-to-tax segments of the economy. Meanwhile, government salaries remain grossly insufficient and therefore officials devote much of their energy to finding illicit income rather than to carrying out their nominal duties.

A related idea would be to institute officially-recognised fees for government services. Not only would this reduce corruption in a definitional sense, by making legitimate many side-payments that are already taking place and are undermining respect for established procedures; it might also mean that citizens would encounter officials more as equals and come to expect value for money – a form of accountability, after all – rather than accepting the terms dictated by corrupt officials. More effective taxation and legitimate fees for service could also raise the salaries of bureaucrats who, in some countries, have little choice but to increase their incomes by any means necessary including corruption. Many of today's low-corruption democracies passed through phases in which fees for service were the norm; such relationships were a significant step in the development of stable mutual expectations between citizens and officials.

To the extent that relationships and encounters between individuals and social interests on one side, and officials on the other, become more orderly and predictable, both sides are more able and likely to think in terms of, and to plan for, the longer term. At that point, people and businesses can begin to perceive the long-term costs and risks of corruption and to calculate them against its apparent short-term benefits. Corruption, after all, is an expensive and risky form of influence; corrupt officials often do not 'stay bought', and a person or group which benefits from corruption today may be its victim tomorrow. If and when those groups in civil society come to believe that they can pursue their goals by other means, the reduction in risk and expense attending a reduction in corruption may become decisive incentives. Corruption can be risky to officials as well, particularly if entrenched corruption networks have begun to weaken; if positive systems of legitimate incentives can be substituted for bribe income, some officials may find pressures to accept the latter less compelling [*Mookherjee, 1997*]. These incentives can be intangible as well as monetary: Gruber [*1987*] reminds us that bureaucrats' motivations are complex and critical to the question of political accountability. Most care about the functions they are supposed to perform; once assured of a living wage they may respond positively to changes that increase their effectiveness, professional status, and sense of personal security.

(3) Balancing opportunities: Social empowerment also requires finding a balance between political and economic opportunities. Huntington [*1968*] argues that where economic opportunities are relatively plentiful and political opportunities scarce, people may try to buy their way into political power; and where political opportunities are plentiful and economic advantage more difficult, people are more likely to use political power to enrich themselves. Thus, economic and social development must take place in a rough balance, or else growing strength in either sector will foster more corruption in the other [*Johnston, 1997c*]. This 'balance' is both important and particularly difficult to identify in practice; it will differ in its details from place to place, and the judgements of experienced observers will be needed to assess the state of play in any nation. Suffice it for now to say that while many nations need economic growth first and foremost to address human needs, it is also needed to revive civil society as a counterbalance to the state, to open up legitimate economic opportunities beyond the control of corrupt monopoly combines, and to end the 'zero-sum' competition over material necessities that so often makes corruption a necessity for survival. Huntington's injunction is a reminder that if economic growth is not accompanied by wider political access and opportunities, we may simply be trading one mechanism of corruption for another. The 'balance' notion also applies *within* the economic and political sectors: a diverse economy is likely to have fewer 'bottlenecks' that can be exploited in monopolistic fashion, while the more competition and non-violent conflict within a political system, the better it will be able to provide political checks upon corruption in the middle to long term, and the more difficult it will be to contrive and exploit political or bureaucratic monopolies over access, influence and distribution.

Such a balance of opportunities raises difficult questions of priorities and sequencing. Scarce and unbalanced political and economic opportunities are ultimately a product of uneven development and insufficient competition within the political and economic realms, and of a lack of clear boundaries and orderly paths of access between them. (This argument is developed in more detail in Johnston [*1997b*].) If corruption is indeed a symptom of deeper and broader development problems and imbalances, broad-based, long term strategies are required for reform. But the fundamental nature of those underlying problems, together with the very real and immediate power of political and economic interests with a stake in continuing corruption, make it difficult to identify the 'entry points' for reform. If every aspect of the problem is connected to every other, many things may need to be done at once; but if political and economic competition are weak, and civil society is exploited and dependent upon entrenched interests, what opportunities have would-be reformers got?

Meaningful civil liberties are a place to begin. An independent press and opposition groups will more likely develop if accorded basic civil liberties, as will sustained social interaction. Civil liberties also allow losers from corruption to take direct countervailing action, rather than responding in illicit or evasive ways which further perpetuate corruption and weaken opposition to it [*Alam, 1995*]. On the economic side, the first step would be credible guarantees of property and contract rights [*Keefer, 1996; Knack and Keefer, 1995*]. Over time we would expect this to increase economic alternatives, weakening dependence upon corrupt officials and helping strengthen civil society. Similarly, aid for emergent sectors of the economy and for the most deprived regions of a country (admittedly complicated tasks) can create new economic opportunities outside of established corrupt networks and empower new political constituencies.

Where civil liberties are reasonably secure, public opinion can be mobilised against corruption. Hong Kong's Independent Commission Against Corruption (ICAC) used extensive innovative social strategies to complement its impressive investigative and prosecutorial powers by producing significant changes in public attitudes. Corruption in pre-ICAC Hong Kong was certainly entrenched. Worse, most citizens saw it as inevitable and resistance as futile. Over the quarter-century between its creation and the return of Hong Kong to China, the ICAC's massive, well-produced public relations and civil society campaigns broke the belief that corruption was inevitable. Television advertisements published a telephone number for complaints and promised protection. In these campaigns and in materials distributed to school children, corruption was portrayed as harmful to families, to the economy, and to traditional Chinese values. ICAC–funded concerts and sporting events fostered social interaction with an anti-corruption theme, particularly among the young. People began to report abuses to the ICAC, and by the 1980s young people in Hong Kong took a stricter view of corruption than did their elders – a contrast found in few other societies. The ICAC's future is unclear, but it changed for the better a social environment that tolerated corruption and helped sustain it [*Clark, 1985; Manion, 1996*].

Broadened political alternatives also weaken corrupt monopolies. One approach is to establish independent arenas of appeal against corruption and other abuses, chiefly in the courts but also in the form of mass media, investigative agencies and ombudsmen open to public complaints and scrutiny. The goal is to encourage, protect, and follow through upon direct countervailing action. The second, much broader, task is to foster significant and institutionalised political competition, creating opportunities for political forces to win and lose significant power through publicly visible processes. Competition will be beneficial even if some parts of society are not initially included. England's seventeenth century parliaments, for example, played major roles in resisting the abuses of royal patronage both before and after the Civil Wars, even though they were strikingly unrepresentative by modern standards [*Peck, 1990*]. Alternatives must be meaningful, but structured: one party presents no choice at all, but 20 or 30 of them are unlikely to have agendas much broader than the personal interests of their leaders, or to be able to win enough power to resist corruption.

The 'Old Corruption' tradition of electoral abuses in Britain was ended in part through enhanced political competition. At the beginning of the nineteenth century British elections featured extensive vote-buying and intimidation. Electorates were small – in many constituencies, no more than a handful of people had the franchise – and landlords and urban patrons built local political monopolies through a mixture of threats and bribes. Farm tenants could lose their livelihoods if they did not vote the right way, while the few urban residents who could vote were often paid for their support. Frequently the patron or a crony stood unopposed; even where there was opposition, patrons held extensive leverage because the ballot was not secret.

But the 'old corruption' was vulnerable to reform. Controls on campaign spending helped but even more important were two changes which significantly increased political competition: the expansion of the electorate and the secret ballot. Reform Acts in 1832, 1867, and later expanded the franchise, at first marginally and then greatly, creating an electorate too big to bribe. Parties had to become more organised, both to mobilise thousands of voters and, once in government, to deliver on the public commitments that took the place of bribes. Parties competing nationally for parliamentary majorities fielded candidates and campaigned in more constituencies, wiping out local monopolies and giving voters meaningful alternatives. The 'old corruption' hung on for a time, but its death knell was the secret ballot instituted in 1872. Now, a patron had no way of knowing whether voters stayed 'bought' or intimidated, and the voter could more freely change from one party to another, intensifying competition even in remote areas. By the century's end the 'old corruption' was largely a thing of the past [*O'Leary, 1962*].

A focus on the excluded offers another point of entry. Important as enhanced political and economic opportunities (and a balance between them) are, the internal political economy of growth and change is also a critical issue. I have suggested above that the widening of political and economic opportunities within societies is an important aspect of the struggle against systemic corruption, and a way to institutionalise reform over the long run. The economic and political strands are intertwined: broad-based growth is likely to strengthen civil society and social interaction, which in turn is a necessary (if not sufficient) step toward greater political competition; such competition, to the extent that it weakens corrupt monopolies, is likely to aid further (and broader-based) economic development, and so on.

This suggests that planners, aid partners and officials in charge of economic development should pursue policies that open up opportunities for hitherto excluded groups and regions – not just for their own sake, but as a way of increasing the strength of civil society and broadening the base of political and economic activity. Admittedly, these are not simple polices to formulate and execute, and even enlightened political leaders will look askance at economic development proposals likely to strengthen opposition interests. But it is worth emphasising here that a number of development ideas of considerable merit in their own right may also have long-term anti-corruption benefits. These would include literacy and other education programmes, particularly those aimed at women and young girls; micro-credit initiatives that not only provide economic resources but also help build local organisations; broader development schemes that as far as possible are aimed at the poorest people and regions, and encourage development that is not dependent upon corporate or bureaucratic 'middlemen' for success; transportation and communication schemes that link peripheral areas more closely to the rest of society, and so on.

There is nothing intrinsically new, and surely nothing simple, about any of these proposals; but what they have in common is the goal of increasing the number, and the autonomy, of interests in society, and reducing their vulnerability to and dependence upon the monopoly practices and petty favours of corrupt officials. It may well be that, in addition to careful reforms and oversight of political and bureaucratic institutions, one of the most effective ways to combat systemic corruption and to institutionalise reform in the long run is to build a society that is less easily exploited by the holders of wealth and power.

CONCLUSION: ANTI-CORRUPTION EFFORTS AND DEVELOPMENT
POLICY

In recent years something approaching a consensus has emerged regarding the harmful effects of corruption upon economic and political development. A parallel view – less than a consensus, but for now the dominant outlook nonetheless – has emerged around the value of economic and political liberalisation as the way forward for international development. At first glance, the reform approach proposed here may appear simply to be just more liberalisation. Certainly enhanced political and economic competition are the cornerstones of the argument, though the goal is not just competition for its own sake, but rather to break down corrupt political and economic monopolies and to open up paths of political and economic participation for people and groups hitherto exploited by, and dependent upon, those monopoly interests.

But social empowerment as I envision it is not just liberalisation. Instead, it is based at the level of everyday life, and focuses upon the range of options and resources open to ordinary citizens. Moreover, it involves a substantial component of institutionalisation: in civil society, as interaction fosters stronger social norms, and in the state–society relationship, as open paths of access between state and society bring about a balance between both while boundaries between public and private resources, processes and interests are made clearer and more legitimate.

Institutionalisation is not a part of this strategy simply for reasons of analytical symmetry, but also because of a fundamental problem raised by the drive toward liberalisation. That gap, essentially, is one of values: if liberalisation is our basic prescription for development, where if anywhere are its limits to be drawn? What is *not* to be put up for sale via liberalised economic or political processes? Do both politics and economics become a free-for-all, with ends justifying the means? Admittedly this is something of a caricatured view: but if it contains an element of truth it suggests that without a healthy measure of institutionalisation we will encounter real problems in placing limits upon the exercise of market and political power, and that any reductions will be accomplished mostly by repealing the rules rather than by improving the workings of society and its political and economic systems. If we do that we will simply have exchanged one set of development problems for others, perhaps far more serious. In that sort of competition poor people and poor countries will be very much the losers. For this reason, then, I have tried to emphasise (and reiterate here) the potential for building new, more legitimate and effective, norms and standards through orderly political and economic contention in civil society – norms and standards that, as suggested at the outset, are prerequisites for effective institutional reform.

We have also, in recent years, seen an increased concern with 'good governance'. This is only to be welcomed to the extent that it implies a recognition that a peaceful, orderly society is required for effective development, and that some ways of attaining that kind of order are vastly preferable to others (see, for example, UNDP [*1997*]). But our conceptions of governance have often been quite narrow. While some aid agencies look at governance in general terms – emphasising participation, the rule of law, and the soundness of policy and institutions – some of the largest lenders for a long time saw governance primarily as a matter of orderly project implementation and reliable repayment of loans. Few would deny that these are important, and that they are arguably among the results of good governance, but it may be time for all concerned with sustainable development to look at the broader connections between government and society, and between political and economic development, that are proving to be so important in the research of recent years. 'Governance' might include the state and openness of political and economic competition, the vitality of civil society, and the security of civil liberties and of rights of property and contract.

Brautigam [*1992*] proposes three dimensions of governance: accountability; openness and transparency; and predictability and the rule of law. An OECD [*1995*] document likewise points to 'the form of political regime; the processes by which authority is exercised in the management of a country's economic and social resources; and the capacity of government to formulate and implement policies and discharge government functions'. A broader definition of governance, emphasising social empowerment, the vitality of political and economic competition and the soundness of the institutions linking and delineating those spheres – perhaps 'the degree of institutionalisation and openness of the political and economic processes through which social-development decisions are made'? – might produce a worthwhile shift in emphasis from the administration of projects towards the broader-based assessment of a country's political and economic capacity for development.

There are few if any new tricks for dealing with corruption, any more than there are compelling 'solutions' to development problems. Social empowerment as a component of anti-corruption efforts has yet to be tried in any conscious, integrated way. But its basic components are well known, for the most part, and while the reform goals spelled out above are far from easy they are also familiar to us. The way forward may lie less in what we do than in how we understand our reasons for doing it, and the ways in which various strategies interrelate in particular kinds of societies. Sustainable reductions in corruption are possible; but direct attacks upon it as an institutional problem require a sound social foundation if they are to succeed, and if they are to be sustained over the long term. This means that anti-corruption forces must understand and attack the long-term development problems of societies in which corruption is often embedded, and of which it is a symptom. Doing this, while difficult, is not only the most promising way to attack corruption; it also focuses our attention and resources upon many of the reasons why corruption is important to begin with.

NOTE

1. I am indebted to Peter Eigen for his comments on this point.

REFERENCES

Ades, Alberto and Rafael di Tella, 1994, 'Competition and Corruption', *Working Paper*, Oxford University, Institute of Economics and Statistics (March).
Alam, M.S., 1995, 'A Theory of Limits on Corruption and Some Applications', *Kyklos*, Vol.48, No.3, pp.419–35.
Barro, Robert J., 1995, 'Economic Freedom and Political Democracy', *Swiss Review of World Affairs*, 3 Jan., pp.20–22.
Brautigam, Deborah, 1992, 'Governance, Economy, and Foreign Aid', *Studies in Comparative International Development*, Vol.27, No.3, pp.3–25.
Chubb, Judith, 1981, 'The Social Bases of an Urban Political Machine: The Christian Democrat Party in Palermo', in S.N. Eisenstadt and R. Lemarchand (eds.), *Political Clientelism, Patronage and Development*, London: Sage, pp.91–124.
Clark, David, 1985, '*Dirigisme* in an Asian City-State: Hong Kong's ICAC', paper presented at the Thirteenth World Congress, International Political Science Association, Paris.
Cooter, Robert D., 1997, 'The Rule of State Law Versus the Rule-of-Law State: Economic Analysis of the Legal Foundations of Development', in Michael Bruno and Boris Pleskovic (eds.), *Annual World Bank Conference on Development Economics 1996*, Washington, DC: The World Bank, pp.191–217.
Easterly, William and Ross Levine, 1996, 'Africa's Growth Tragedy: Policies and Ethnic Divisions', unpublished manuscript, The World Bank, Washington, DC.
Elliott, Kimberly A., 1997, 'Corruption as a Global Policy Problem: Overview and Recommendations', in Elliott (ed.) [*1997: Ch.11*].
Elliott, Kimberley A. (ed.), 1997, *Corruption and the Global Economy*, Washington, DC: Institute for International Economics.
Gruber, Judith E., 1987, *Controlling Bureaucracies: Dilemmas in Democratic Governance*, Berkeley, CA: University of California Press.
Huntington, Samuel P., 1968, *Political Order in Changing Societies*, New Haven, CT: Yale University Press.
IMF (International Monetary Fund), 1995, 'Unproductive Public Expenditures: A Pragmatic Approach to Policy Analysis', *IMF Pamphlet Series 48*, Washington, DC.
Isham, Jonathan, Daniel Kaufmann and Lant Pritchett, 1995, 'Governance and Returns on Investment: An Empirical Investigation', *Policy Research Working Paper 1550*, Washington, DC: The World Bank, Poverty and Human Resources Division.
Isham, Jonathan, Daniel Kaufmann and Lant Pritchett, 1996, 'Civil Liberties, Democracy, and the Performance of Government Projects', unpublished manuscript.
Johnston, Michael, 1982, *Political Corruption and Public Policy in America,* Monterey, CA: Brooks-Cole.
Johnston, Michael, 1991, 'Right and Wrong in British Politics: "Fits of Morality" in Comparative Perspective', *Polity*, Vol.XXIV, No.1, pp.1–25.
Johnston, Michael, 1996, 'The Search for Definitions: The Vitality of Politics and the Issue of

Corruption', *International Social Science Journal*, No.149, pp.321–35 (English language version).

Johnston, Michael, 1997a, 'What Can Be Done about Entrenched Corruption?', paper presented to the Ninth Annual Bank Conference on Development Economics. Washington, DC: World Bank.

Johnston, Michael, 1997b, 'Corruption and Distorted Development: Competition, Institutionalization and Strategies for Reform', paper presented to the USAID Conference on Economic Growth and Democratic Governance.

Johnston, Michael, 1997c, 'Public Officials, Private Interests, and Sustainable Democracy: Connections between Politics and Corruption', in Elliott (ed.) [*1997: ch.3*].

Keck, Margaret E., 1992, 'Brazil: Impeachment!' *Report on the Americas*, Vol.XXVI, No.3, pp.4–7.

Keefer, Philip., 1996, 'Protection Against a Capricious State: French Investment and Spanish Railroads, 1845–1875', *Journal of Economic History*, Vol.56, No.1, pp.170–92.

Klitgaard, Robert, 1988, *Controlling Corruption*, Berkeley, CA: University of California Press.

Knack, Stephen and P. Keefer, 1995, 'Institutions and Economic Performance: Cross-Country Tests Using Alternative Institutional Measures', *Economics and Politics*, Vol.7, No.3, pp.207–27.

Manion, Melanie, 1996, 'Policy Instruments and Political Context: Transforming a Culture of Corruption in Hong Kong', paper presented at the Annual Meeting of the Association for Asian Studies, Honolulu.

Mauro, Paolo, 1997, 'The Effects of Corruption on Growth, Investment, and Government Expenditure: A Cross-Country Analysis', in Elliott (ed.) [*1997: Ch.4*].

Mookherjee, Dilip, 1997, 'Incentive Reforms in Developing Country Bureaucracies: Lessons from Tax Administration', paper presented at the Ninth Annual Bank Conference on Development Economics, The World Bank, Washington, DC.

Murphy, Kevin M., Shleifer, A. and R.W. Vishny, 1993, 'Why is Rent-Seeking So Costly to Growth?', *American Economic Review*, Vol.83, No.2, pp.409–14.

O'Leary, Cornelius, 1962, *The Elimination of Corrupt Practices in British Elections, 1868–1911*, Oxford: Clarendon Press.

OECD (Organisation for Economic Cooperation and Development), 1995, 'Participatory Development and Good Governance', OECD, Paris.

Oldenburg, Philip, 1987, 'Middlemen in Third-World Corruption: Implications of an Indian Case', *World Politics*, Vol.39, No.4, pp.508–35.

Peck, Linda Levy, 1990, *Court Patronage and Corruption in Early Stuart England*, Boston, MA: Unwin Hyman.

Przeworski, Adam and F. Limongi, 1993, 'Political Regimes and Economic Growth', *Journal of Economic Literature*, Vol.7, No.3, pp.51–69.

Rauch, James, 1995, 'Bureaucracy, Infrastructure, and Economic Growth: Evidence from US Cities During the Progressive Era', *American Economic Review*, Vol.85, No.4, pp.968–79.

Rogow, Arnold A. and Harold D. Lasswell, 1963, *Power, Corruption, and Rectitude*, Englewood Cliffs, NJ: Prentice-Hall.

Rose-Ackerman, Susan, 1996, 'When is Corruption Harmful?', unpublished manuscript, The World Bank, Washington, DC.

Rose-Ackerman, Susan, 1997, 'The Political Economy of Corruption', in Elliott (ed.) [*1997: Ch.2*].

Rose-Ackerman, Susan and Andrew Stone, 1996, 'The Costs of Corruption for Private Business: Evidence from World Bank Surveys', Washington, DC: World Bank.

Sacks, Paul Martin, 1976, *The Donegal Mafia: An Irish Political Machine*, New Haven, CT: Yale University Press.

Scott, James C., 1972, *Comparative Political Corruption*, Englewood Cliffs, NJ: Prentice-Hall.

Shefter, Martin, 1976, 'The Emergence of the Political Machine: An Alternative View', in Willis D. Hawley *et. al.*, *Theoretical Perspectives on Urban Politics*, Englewood Cliffs, NJ: Prentice-Hall.

Theobald, Robin, 1992, 'On the Survival of Patronage in Developed Societies', *Archives Européenne de Sociologie*, Vol.XXXIII, No.2, pp.183–91.

Thompson, Dennis F., 1993, 'Mediated Corruption: The Case of the Keating Five', *American Political Science Review*, Vol.87, No.2, pp.369–81.

Thompson, Dennis F., 1995, *Ethics in Congress: From Individual to Institutional Corruption*, Washington, DC: The Brookings Institution.

UNDP (United National Development Program), 1997, *Corruption and Good Governance*, Discussion Paper No.3, UNDP, Management Development and Governance Division, New York.

Weber, Max, 1946 ed., 'The Presuppositions and Causes of Bureaucracy', in H.H. Gerth and C. Wright Mills (eds.), *From Max Weber: Essays in Sociology*, New York: Oxford University Press.

Wei, Shang-Jin, 1997, 'How Taxing is Corruption on International Investors?' mimeo, Kennedy School of Government, Harvard University.

World Bank, 1997, *The State in a Changing World: World Development Report 1997*, Oxford: Oxford University Press.

Criteria for Sustainable Corruption Control

FREDRIK GALTUNG

Curbing corruption is now a major focus of institutional reform. In the context of endemic corruption, reforming institutions might contribute to short-term success, but this needs to be complemented by what one might call sustainable corruption control, making corruption an incidental problem over the long term. The first section aims to justify and define this goal and to suggest a set of useful indicators. The following contribution draws attention to three criteria for achieving and maintaining low levels of corruption, the stakeholders, the feasibility and credibility of the process and the international dimension of control.

INTRODUCTION

If endemic corruption was long held to be a cultural, moral and historical problem [*Wraith and Simpkins, 1978*] by the 1990s it has clearly become an institutional one. There are hardly any newly elected governments in Latin America, Africa and Asia that do not promise sweeping legal and administrative reforms to reduce corruption. International organisations and bilateral agencies support this trend and have recently linked corruption control to the disbursement of aid or loans. Before corruption became depoliticised in the mid-1990s such initiatives would have been impossible.[1] Now endemic corruption is understood to be one of the major institutional impediments to sustainable development.[2]

It is a sobering reflection on the utility of the law that most countries in the world provide criminal sanctions against those involved in corruption, yet when corruption is endemic, the laws are widely flouted and sanctions are infrequently imposed. 'When they are, they tend to be directed against small fish rather than big fish' [*Pope, 1996: 2*]. Reforming corrupt institutions is therefore both a critical and a necessary step. The most comprehensive notion

Fredrik Galtung is a founding staff member of Transparency International and currently a Ph.D. candidate in the Faculty of Social and Political Sciences, University of Cambridge. This work was first presented as a paper at the 'Workshop on Corruption and Development' organised by the Institute for Development Studies at the University of Sussex. The author benefited greatly from the numerous comments of the participants, in particular from Mark Robinson, Gordon White and Michael Johnston. The author also wishes to thank Peter Eigen and Jeremy Pope for their support and comments over the years. He remains entirely responsible for the contents.

to emerge in this recent debate is the national integrity system. It involves strengthening and supporting five main 'pillars' (public programmes, civil service reform, law enforcement, public awareness and the creation of institutions to prevent corruption) to create a 'holistic' anti-corruption strategy [*Pope, 1996; Langseth, Stapenhurst and Pope, 1997*]. These measures, which are broadly aimed at increasing transparency and strengthening accountability in the public sector, are currently being introduced in public sector anti-corruption strategies with support from Transparency International (TI) and the World Bank.

The argument of this study is that the reform of institutions is a crucial but not a sufficient step in tackling this problem. It might contribute to short-term successes, meaning anything from one to ten years of effective, if localised, corruption reform. This strategy is unlikely to outlive the first generation of reformers, however. These approaches need to be complemented by what one could call sustainable corruption control[3] – strategies that reduce endemic corruption to levels that are tolerable and sporadic and keep things that way. In the first section an effort is made to justify and define this goal and to suggest a set of indicators to measure progress or failure. Section II calls attention to criteria that might contribute to achieving and maintaining low levels of corruption.

I. SUSTAINABLE CORRUPTION CONTROL: GOALS AND INDICATORS

Corruption needs to be reduced to levels that are both tolerable and incidental. This may seem like a modest goal when the discourse of political reformers today often addresses the need to 'eradicate' and conduct a 'war' against corruption. Still, 'the wise reformer knows that corruption can never be entirely eliminated' [*Pope, 1996: vii*]. A number of authors have pointed out that the costs of eliminating corruption completely - quite aside from the ahistorical nature of the undertaking[4] – would be prohibitive [*Rose-Ackerman, 1996; Pritzl, 1997*]. It would simply not be worthwhile in economic terms. In addition to the financial costs, the mechanisms needed to eradicate corruption would be incompatible with the liberal traditions that influence democracies. In short, the future will never be quite 'free of corruption' [*Johnston ,1993: 3*].

What, then, are the indicators of this approach? Corruption is a crime in which the direct parties to the transaction benefit and most if not all negative externalities are externalised.[5] As a result, the incentives for secrecy have always been high. This creates obvious difficulties from anyone aiming to create a set of measures and it may never be possible to develop a set of objective indicators: for example, the number of investigations in the press would reveal more about the freedom of the media than it would about the incidence of corruption. The same could be said for the independence of the judiciary in a tally of the successful court cases against malfeasance by public officials or public companies. All else being equal, a survey of the German *Länder* or US states could use indicators of this kind, but one would need to control at the very least for population and the region's share of the country's GNP to provide an accurate basis of comparison. Even then, such surveys 'do not necessarily reflect the reality of corruption ... since the dark or hidden area of bureaucratic corruption (i.e. unreported and unknown incidents) might be in existence behind the reported incidents' [*Kim, 1994: 112*].

The best available measure to date probably remains the Transparency International (TI) Corruption Perception Index (CPI), published annually with Johann Graf Lambsdorff of Göttingen University since 1995.[6] The TI CPI is a 'poll of polls' that captures the perception of thousands of international business leaders, risk analysts and business journalists, on the relative degree of corruption in over 50 countries. Countries are included in the CPI if they are covered by at least four polls. Their score is averaged on a scale of 0 to 10, where 0 would be entirely corrupt and 10 a perfectly 'clean' state. In the 1997 CPI Nigeria (1.76) and Denmark (9.94) ranked as the most and the least corrupt countries respectively.

Lancaster and Mantinola (quoted in Quah [*1997: 16*]) ... recommend this index because it is 'robust' and 'captures more than a single indicator' and 'combines several measures of political corruption for each country'. There is a widespread recognition that this is perhaps the most useful indicator of corruption we currently have.[7] At best, however, this survey can measure two things: trends over time and relative positions *vis-à-vis* other countries. It does not capture the absolute amount of corruption in any one country. Also missing from this Index is the role of the bribe-givers in international trade. The CPI measures perceived levels of corruption in the public sector but it says nothing about the export behaviour of the leading industrialised countries.[8]

Public opinion polls are nothing new. In the latter half of the twentieth century, they have emerged 'as an effective device for promoting accountability and responsibility in government' [*Hickock, 1995: 10*]. For several years now *Poder Ciudadano*, an Argentine NGO, does regular 'corruptometers'. Using a respected international polling company, they survey both people at large and the business community in particular to measure trends in the incidence or perception of corruption [*Ocampo, 1993*]. This barometer of corruption has been useful when *Poder Ciudadano* sought to target specific areas, like the health care sector, which were of particular concern to the public. The independent commissions against corruption in Hong Kong and New South Wales, Australia, have also made use of polls both to investigate trends in the perception of corruption in the public administration and to measure their own impact in the community [*ICAC, 1995*].

Polls of corruption could also include a ranking of the percentages paid in commissions (both legal and illicit) for public contracts. In major international contracts these can range from a few percentage points to a third or even half the value of the project in which case grand corruption with high-ranking officials is assumed to take place [*Moody-Stuart, 1994*]. Interesting as it might be, a poll of this kind could be counterproductive. It could serve as a guide not only to investors seeking markets with lower commissions but also as an international benchmark for politicians demanding bribes. If politicians in country X receive 20 per cent and those in country Y only 15 per cent, the latter might soon demand a 'raise'. Furthermore, the cost of corruption is not measured in the amount of commission paid. Projects that are inherently uneconomical divert scarce resources from areas where they are needed most, meaning that the real cost could be a manifold of the project itself [*Frisch, 1995*].

The cost of corruption can also be measured econometrically. Shang-Jin Wei's [*1997*] study on the impact of corruption on investment flows from 14 source countries to 45 recipient countries in the early 1990s shows the taxing effect of corruption to international investors, largely based on a regression of the TI CPI. Wei shows that a one percentage point increase in the marginal tax rate reduces inward investment by about five per cent and that other things being equal, an 'increase in the corruption level from that of Singapore to that of Mexico is equivalent to raising the tax rate by over twenty percentage points' [*Wei, 1997: 1*]. The study also finds that corruption in high growth East Asian countries turns off foreign investors as much as it does in other parts of the globe.

For the full economic cost of corruption to be measured, the complete benefits and costs associated with economic agents engaged in a corrupt transaction would need to be accounted for – not just the utility function of the actors directly involved. In other words, all the externalities would need to be internalised in the function. The existence of substantial negative externalities in a corrupt transaction is a fundamental reason for the current wave of anti-corruption measures seen in so many countries [*Colombo, 1995*]. For the policy-maker, significant externalities create a '*prima facie* case for departures from non-interventionist industrial or trade policies, since without intervention it seems likely that the externalities will not be taken into account in resource allocation' [*Stewart and Ghani, 1991: 587*]. Corruption is not perceived to be a victimless crime. It is a transaction which carries substantial social, political and economic costs. This is felt intuitively when political elites become tremendously wealthy within a few years; it is obvious when managers and civil servants collude to produce unnecessary or disproportionate infrastructure; it is also clear when the tax base of a country falls systematically over the years because of corrupted tax inspectors or fails to rise in spite of a growing formal sector. Where institutions are at their weakest, 'individual rationality generates negative externalities and comes into conflict with collective rationality' [*Schedler, 1995: 12*]. As Stewart and Ghani [*1991: 585*] have pointed out, 'if policy interventions are to be justified on the basis of externalities, it is necessary to have some idea of the potential orders of magnitude involved, in principle before decisions are made'. What makes it difficult to measure, is that the real cost is not in these monuments to corruption, nor in the percentages paid as commissions, but much rather in the direct misallocation of resources from those areas where they would have been needed most. To this one must add the damage to political legitimacy, especially in new and emerging democracies. It remains to be seen whether economists and policy makers can develop functions that usefully internalise these externalities.

II. CRITERIA FOR SUSTAINABLE CORRUPTION CONTROL

In what follows I will suggest that there are at least three areas or levels to a sustainable anti-corruption approach: it must define and actively engage the key stakeholders in the process; the qualitative dimensions of feasibility and credibility of anti-corruption measures should be considered; and there is a global dimension to corruption control which is evolving but is far from complete.

The Stakeholders

In the classical legal definition of corruption there is a bribe giver and a bribe taker. If we look away from scenarios where there are multiple recipients, the essential point is that it takes two parties for a transaction to qualify as bribery – a corrupter and one who is corrupted. One of Robert Klitgaard's [*1988*] most interesting contributions to the study of corruption was to depart from this notion and point out that there are not just two but always three actors involved in any corrupt transaction: a principal (P), an agent (A) and a client (C).

FIGURE 1
KLITGAARD'S P-A-C MODEL

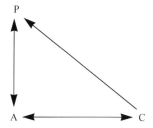

In other words, to take an example from corruption in the tax administration, a tax collector (A) abuses the power given by the state (P), when accepting money from a tax payer (C) to reduce the latter's tax burden.

Most definitions of corruption cover both transactions between A and C (for example, bribery, extortion) and the direct abuse of A's relationship to P (for example, internal fraud, theft of government property). If C abuses his or her relationship with P (for example, through tax fraud, illegal capital transfers) this is not considered to be corruption since it does not include the active (or passive) collusion of an agent of the state.

In Klitgaard's work [*1988*], P plays the determining role in any reform process: P selects A; P sets A's rewards and penalties; and P affects A and C's moral costs of corruption. In any fundamental institutional reform it is important to appreciate from the outset that if the political will is lacking - both for change and for rigorous implementation at all levels of government - no legislative or administrative changes can ever be effective in containing corruption [*Schedler, 1995*]. While the model is useful in a number of ways, its dependency on P reveals one of the greatest obstacles to reform. It lies at the very heart of government, with the politicians and the political interests in power. These will almost invariably see moves towards greater transparency and accountability as an erosion of their own power, as indeed they are [*Pope, 1995*]. Principals – like the former president of Mexico – might on the one hand take initiatives to curb corruption, while on the other hand engaging in wholesale corruption. In other words, they can be both principals and agents, depending on the circumstances. The principal, agent, client model of corruption needs to be extended to include these distinctions and account for the roles of all key stakeholders in the process. The figure below illustrates this.

FIGURE 2
A TWO-LEVEL P-A-C MODEL OF CORRUPTION (AND FRAUD)

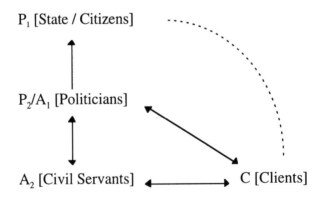

In this model P_1 is the state and its citizens, based on Benjamin Constant's [*1988*] notion that civil society can be sovereign in one respect and subject in another. In practice these two relations are always confused. P_2 is a principal in Klitgaard's sense, with the power to define and influence both its relationship to agents and clients and their relationship to each other. P_2 (for example, a minister) can also become an agent, however, either by assuming this role illicitly (for example, by interfering in public contracts) or because another P_2 (for example, a head of state), redefines the P_2's position. A_2 are civil servants and the clients are referred to here as civil society.

TABLE 1
ILLUSTRATIVE CATEGORIES OF CORRUPTION (AND FRAUD)

	P_1	P_2/A_1	A_2	C
P_1	[No corruption]	–	–	–

P_2/A_1	• embezzlement
	• theft of public
	  funds
	• vote rigging
		• bribery
		• extortion
		• sale of public
		  office
			–	–

A_2	• embezzlement
	• abuse of public
	  goods
		• personnel scams
		• internal pay-offs
		• corruption of
		  internal
		  investigations
			• personnel scams
			• nepotism
				–

C	[Fraud]
	• tax evasion
	• public procure-
	  ment cartels
	• illicit capital
	  transfers
		• 'grand corruption'
		• extortion
		• 'collusion'
		• sale of public
		  office
		• vote buying
		• illicit party
		  funding
		• clientelism
			• bribery
			• extortion
			• 'collusion'
			• facilitation
			  payments
			• clientelism
			• backsheesh
				[Private sector
				corruption]

Based on this two-level P-A-C model we can develop the following categories of corruption (Table 1). This categorisation does not aim to be complete since the terms used to cover corruption vary widely and there is sometimes disagreement as to what constitutes corruption, legally, historically and culturally [*Heidenheimer et al., 1989*]. In the discussion that follows we need to note that what we refer to as endemic corruption are varying levels of corruption within and between all the levels of this diagram, with the exception of those areas where there cannot be any abuse of public power for private gain: P_1 cannot cheat itself; if C abuses its relationship to P_1 it is a matter of fraud or cartels, but not of corruption; and if Cs bribe each other, it is private, not public corruption.

Recent experience indicates that the initiative for reform can come from actors other than principals. A handful of *Mani puliti* ('Clean Hands') judges in Milan, under the leadership of Antonio Di Pietro, stumbled across a minor episode of embezzlement in early 1992, and eventually contributed to the downfall of large segments of the Italian political and business elite [*Sapelli, 1994; della Porta, 1996*]. One of the key prosecutors, Gherardo Colombo [*1995: 196*], characterised this action against grand corruption in Italian public and private life as entirely 'spontaneous'. They are a striking example of agents taking initiative into their own hands.

Social movements and NGOs have also contributed to the downfall of corrupt political establishments in a number of countries in recent years. In Bangladesh they choked the streets to Dhaka to bring down president Ershad. In Brazil thousands of 'painted faces' took to the streets and deposed president Collor. During the supreme court hearings of president Pérez, the housewives of Caracas beat their pots and pans every evening in protest because they feared the trial was rigged.

Hong Kong is used by many as an illustration of a country that turned the tide on corruption. It was a systemic problem and it has become an incidental one. From the outset reformers were aware of the need to change public attitudes both towards the law and the institutions meant to implement and guarantee it. The Independent Commission Against Corruption (ICAC) has three departments: Operations (investigation); Corruption Prevention; and Community Relations (education). The last department alone has 200 officers providing publicity spots, private sector seminars, civic education, etc. [*de Spelville, 1996*]. This illustrates the emphasis the ICAC gives to all the stakeholders in the corruption process (and of the costly nature of this form of corruption control).[9] A remarkable illustration of the Hong Kong ICAC's ability to involve key stakeholders directly to increase both accountability and credibility is its stringent system of checks and balances through four advisory committees. The membership is drawn from all sectors of the community (A's and C's) and was appointed by the Governor (for our purposes, the principal). Initially, these committees were chaired by the ICAC Commissioner. This was changed so that chairs would be drawn from the committees themselves with the objective of improving their independence. As an illustration of the advisory committees' importance, the ICAC cannot desist from pursuing a case once investigations have started without their formal approval.

Transparency International (TI) has introduced an anti-corruption mechanism called the Integrity Pact (TI-IP) which would also have the effect of engaging key stakeholders, while creating a level playing field for those companies caught in a classic prisoner's dilemma: if one company commits itself not to pay bribes it cannot trust its competitors to do likewise [*Galtung, 1995*]. The TI-IP would function as follows: a government, when inviting contractors or suppliers of goods and services to tender for a specific, usually large public contract, informs the potential bidders that their tender offer must contain a commitment signed personally by the bidder's Chief Executive Officer (CEO), not to offer or pay any bribes in connection with this contract. The government on its part will commit itself to prevent extortion and the acceptance of bribes by its officials and to follow transparent procurement rules. The monitoring and compliance process will be accompanied by the principal, the agents and the clients (that is, the competing companies), as well as NGOs active in this field (for example, TI national chapters).

In essence the TI-IP is nothing more than a commitment to respect and invoke the existing laws of the country, but with a difference. The bidders who violate their commitment not to bribe will be subject to significant sanctions, such as loss of contract, liability for damages (to the government and the competing bidders) and forfeiture of the bid security. The government could also blacklist the offender from all government business for an appropriate period of time. In other words, all the sanctions are commercial. This creates the strongest incentive for the bidders to enforce the sanctions themselves, through the courts or by international arbitration. The TI-IP also involves the CEOs personally. This procedure requires them to certify the amounts of payments to third parties so they will not be able to disclaim knowledge of malpractice as is presently often the case. At present the TI-IP is in the first stage of being introduced in eight countries in Central and South America, Asia and Africa at the request of the national governments and with the technical support of TI and the national chapters of TI in the respective countries.[10] In the past year the World Bank [*1997*] has become supportive of this approach and now advocates the inclusion of what it calls 'no bribery pledges' in the bidding and contract implementation processes.

TI is also promoting national integrity working groups which draw together all the stakeholders within the state (executive office, public service, investigations, prosecution, judiciary, education, information and key vulnerable departments, such as customs, procurement, revenue collection, local government) together with coalition partners from outside government (NGOs, religious leaders, private sector, relevant professional bodies, etc.) [*Pope, 1996: xi*]. Based on an analysis of the existing framework and by identifying areas for reform, the working group develops short, medium and long-term goals and assigns responsibilities for follow-up action and reporting back to the working group. In Tanzania and Uganda the establishment of the working group and its overall plan have been publicised, soliciting inputs from the wider public. All this has taken place with the endorsement of the political leadership.

FIGURE 3
THE TI INTEGRITY PACT

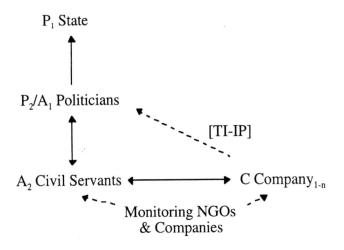

A further example comes from the Bolivian capital, La Paz. When Ronald MacLean Abaroa became the first freely elected mayor over ten years ago the municipality had developed into one of the great centres and sources of corruption in his country. Property taxes were in principle one of its main sources of revenue and the declared value of properties had not kept pace with the hyperinflation of the early 1980s, meaning revenues for the city were negligible. Under the fiscal circumstances, the properties had to be adjusted for their value in US dollars. A small army of over a hundred public servants promptly declared themselves volunteers in what they recognised to be a recipe for corruption since the civil servants had a wide discretion on the evaluation of the property and there was minimal accountability. What would invariably happen is that after negotiation, the owner of a property would agree with the agent that his house was worth, say $10,000, even if its real worth was closer to $100,000. The agent could earn up to a year's wages on a single transaction of this kind [*MacLean, 1994*]. The likelihood that someone would detect this behaviour was low. These were often public officials with long experience in the municipality who knew that they were unlikely to get caught. And even if they were caught, the worst that could happen to them would be dismissal or transfer to another function without criminal charges being pressed.

MacLean consulted with the then president, Paz Estenssoro, to get backing for a new undertaking. Starting with the assumption that the citizens are basically honest and that they are forced to bribe to defend themselves against

FIGURE 4
REVENUE COLLECTION IN LA PAZ

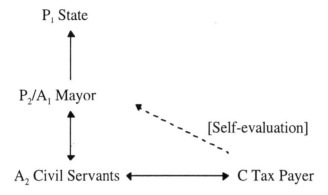

a corrupt system, he introduced a legal provision enabling people to self-evaluate their property. He assumed that the best judge of the value of a property would be its owner. This measure was combined with a threat: if the property was undervalued, the city reserved the right to buy it. This process was monitored by a handful of close associates of the mayor. The legal basis for this threat was weak, however, since no one could in effect be forced to sell their property. Still, people gave values to their property which by far surpassed the city's most ambitious goals. The dollar value of the city's revenues in the third year of the administration – this reform took one year to introduce – were 18 times higher than those of the first year. MacLean left after his first term to become the country's foreign minister. Shortly after a new mayor took office, the system he had introduced was discarded and corruption is as rife as it was before.

Credibility and Feasibility

The argument in this section is that there are two basic qualitative ingredients in any lasting reform effort. These are credibility and feasibility. Credibility presupposes two conditions: sound incentives and a high degree of moral integrity [*Schedler, 1995*]. Feasibility is based on a certain degree of viability within the legal, economic, political and cultural realm. Combining both is less obvious that it might first seem. Often, these are factors which only develop over time. The qualitative value of individual initiatives can also change considerably and time is the essence of any sustainable strategy or theory. The following figure offers a model for these two ingredients which must be considered in any serious reform effort.

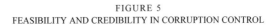

FIGURE 5
FEASIBILITY AND CREDIBILITY IN CORRUPTION CONTROL

Feasibility

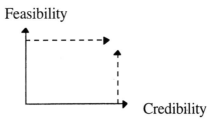

Credibility

In 1977 a new law was introduced in the Ivory Coast modelled on the new French anti-corruption legislation at the time. The law was passed by parliament (under one-party rule) but the basic mechanisms needed to implement it were never introduced. This non-law just celebrated its twentieth anniversary. This measure was feasible but it did not add credibility to the government's faltering anti-corruption efforts.

In the early 1990s legislation drafted by the Russian Duma included a conflict of interest clause which would have limited all public servants – whether top-ranking officials or primary school teachers – to their one public position. Since teachers often earn less than a living wage, forbidding them from giving after-hour private lessons was not only impractical, it would not contribute to curbing corruption. A law which cannot be enforced, however impressive it might first seem, will neither be credible nor for that matter feasible.

Some initiatives might seem credible but for lack of feasibility, they do not make it into the text books. In South Africa there was a proposal to reverse the burden of proof on civil servants 'living beyond their means'. This is a measure that has proved effective in Hong Kong and Singapore where public office holders with unusually high standards of living might have to 'prove their innocence' by documenting how they acquired their wealth. In the new South Africa, this approach was deemed to be unconstitutional. During the administration of Thomas Sankara (1984–87) in Burkina Faso, directors of public companies and ministers were often brought in front of popular tribunals where, without legal assistance, they were required to justify their wealth. Because of the excesses of the reversal of the burden of proof during those years, such a measure cannot be considered by corruption reformers in the country today.

In Benin, during the administration of president Nicéphore Soglo in the early 1990s, the head of state declared his assets and liabilities upon taking office, as is required by the constitution. Following the constitution, he did so directly to the high court, without publishing the results. This was feasible and accorded with the letter of the law but it did not give his act any credibility. After a long period of one-party rule, doing more than the law requires would have added much credibility to an otherwise weak administration. Throughout his term, there were requests from the media and NGOs for him and his ministers to be more transparent and to declare their assets publicly. The president resisted this pressure and lost the subsequent election to his predecessor. This can be contrasted with president Benjamin Mkapa of Tanzania, elected in 1996. He publicly disclosed his assets, his income and coupled this with a similar declaration for his spouse. She does not hold public office but top politicians have been widely suspected of transferring their assets in their wife's name to avoid detection. This is within the realm of the feasible and it is one of the more outstanding demonstrations of personal commitment by any head of state.

The temporal specificity of these criteria is best illustrated by the Hong Kong case. When the ICAC was established in 1974 it was by no means credible nor did it look like the task it had taken upon itself was going to be wholly feasible. Major scandals involving corruption in the police itself were part of the impetus for forming the ICAC. The first to protest publicly against it were the police officers worried they would be investigated. Then followed an innovative amnesty law to clean the slate. It is worth quoting in full:

> Notwithstanding section 12 (*jurisdiction*), the Commissioner shall not act as required by paragraphs (a), (b) and (c) of that section in respect of alleged or suspected offences committed before 1 January 1977 except in relation to:
>
> (a) persons not in Hong Kong or against whom a warrant of arrest was outstanding on 5 November 1977;
>
> (b) any person who before 5 November 1977 had been interviewed by an officer and to whom allegations had been put that he had committed an offence;
>
> (c) an offence which the Governor considers sufficiently heinous to warrant action
>
> (cited in Pope [*1996: 106*]).

The first effect of the amnesty law was to reduce the credibility of the effort considerably, while increasing its feasibility. The trial and extradition from the UK for corruption of the former police commissioner was a significant victory, made possible under a clause in the amnesty law for grand scale corruption. It increased the credibility of the ICAC enormously. Over time, the ICAC had successfully convinced its original detractors, including the police and significant parts of the private sector, that it can act both efficiently and credibly.

The Globalisation of Corruption Control

The Spanish sociologist José María Tortosa's [*1995*] book on corruption opens with the observation that to analyse corruption in any one country one has to understand the world system in which it functions. In recent years there does seem to be an international dimension to most cases of grand corruption: the bribe-giver might be a transnational corporation (TNC); a corrupt politician might seek refuge from prosecution abroad; and, most common of all, the proceeds of corruption can be secreted to numbered accounts in foreign destinations. None the less, most anti-corruption activity and a substantial part of the literature on corruption, focuses almost exclusively on the use of national measures to control a national or local problem. This is as true for the Hong Kong ICAC as it was for the municipality of La Paz or indeed all the other illustrations given in this article so far. And yet just as narcotics prevention and control is now inevitably transnational in nature, efforts are being made to extend the scope of corruption control beyond a country's borders. Corruption control is currently evolving in ways that seek to make full use of the panoply of local, national, regional and international mechanisms. Credible moves in this direction only started in the early 1990s. In a simplified fashion, the table below tries to capture the diversity of areas in which these tools are being applied.

TABLE 2
THE INTERNATIONAL DIMENSION OF CORRUPTION CONTROL

	National Corruption		International Corruption	
	Acting locally/ nationally	Acting internationally	Acting locally/ nationally	Acting international
Using local and national tools	(1) ++	(2) +/–	(3) +	(4) +/–
Using international tools	(5) +/–	(6) +	(7) –	(8) ++

Box (1) above is entirely national (or local) in scope: the corruption it addresses is national as are the mechanisms and the area it seeks to control. This is the classic sphere of corruption control as it is for most social reforms. The (++) symbolises an area of high and lower (+) activity, respectively, as opposed to (+/–), where they are still not systematised; in the case of (–)

mechanisms are still on the drawing boards. The argument of this section is that control mechanisms are being introduced at all levels of international control in recent years but that some areas remain weaker than others and are in obvious need of strengthening.

Through its network of almost eighty national chapters, registered in their respective countries as national NGOs, Transparency International (TI) acts internationally against national corruption using endogenous institutions (2). The recent activities of the World Bank and other development organisations can to an extent also be seen in this light when they support national institutions (both governmental and non-governmental) since 'solutions can only be home-grown' (Wolfensohn quoted in Langseth *et al.* [*1997: iii*]).

The best known national measure against international corruption (3) is the US Foreign Corrupt Practices Act of 1977. It imposes criminal penalties on US-based corporations bribing foreign officials to obtain contracts abroad. If the US FCPA is aimed at the bribery of their corporations abroad, Singapore has a mechanism to protect itself against being bribed. In 1996 Singapore barred five transnational manufacturing and engineering corporations from government contracts for five years in the wake of a corruption scandal [*McDermott, 1997; Taylor, 1996*]. The US FCPA and Singapore's blacklisting are the exceptions, however, since few countries are willing or able to take such unilateral action for fear that they might incur a commercial competitive disadvantage. This has led to allegations by US companies that they lose numerous international contracts to less scrupulous competitors - over $20 billion worth in 1996 alone [*FAZ, 1996*]. To some extent, this contradicts Wei's [*1997*] analysis of the propensity of major exporting countries to bribe abroad since he shows that the FCPA has a minimal impact on US export behaviour. TI's Integrity Pact is one of the few attempts to introduce a mechanism against international grand corruption using national mechanisms (4). The World Bank [*1997*] is now also supportive of this approach, but it remains to be seen how effective this mechanism will be.

Only the use of a multilateral system (8) has meant that other countries are now following the example of the FCPA to prohibit bribery by their companies abroad. The most mature mechanism is perhaps the process started in 1989 at the OECD, which led to the signing of a convention in December 1997 to criminalise bribery abroad. Another multilateral action is the Organisation of American States' 1996 convention against corruption signed by 23 member states. It should assist both in controlling international (8) and national corruption (6) since it includes extradition arrangements and mutual legal assistance procedures. The European Commission has issued directives against intra-community, transborder corruption (8) [*TI Brussels, 1996*], covering areas previously outside the bounds of legal prosecution. The Council of Europe - with its membership in both Western and Central and Eastern Europe

- is also engaged in drawing up a convention for its members which could be extended to non-member countries. Since it will take several years for these mechanisms to be ratified and implemented it is too early to tell whether they will be effective. What is striking is that they are all based on regional membership (that is, the Americas, the European Union, OECD). The UN General Assembly approved a declaration calling on member states to 'take effective and concrete action to combat all forms of corruption, bribery and related illicit practices in international commercial transactions'; it is not attempting to draft a universal convention against corruption. This regionalisation of international corruption control is a pragmatic compromise between unilateral action and a global convention. State actions in this area are complemented by efforts of non-governmental organisations, like the International Chamber of Commerce's principles for corporate codes of conduct. All activities in (7) depend on the implementation of the multilateral projects in (8), meaning that it will be the weakest link in this template for the foreseeable future.

On a bilateral basis there is already a promising example of international corruption using international mechanisms (8), however. Mali's recent breakthrough in bilateral judicial assistance covers three variations on the theme of international corruption control mentioned in the beginning of this section. The director of the Mali state tobacco monopoly, Boubacar Dembélé, was paid over $2 million by a leading TNC for 'consultations' rendered over several years [*Fall, 1997*]. A protracted trial led to a death sentence for grand corruption in March 1995. Key evidence was provided with the investigatory help of a Swiss magistrate and a decision by the Swiss government to lift banking secrecy laws for his two accounts. A year later he succeeded in escaping from prison and found refuge in neighbouring Senegal. From Dakar he applied for refugee status, alerting the UN High Commissioner for Refugees and Amnesty International that he faced the death penalty if he was extradited. Senegal is bound by the Geneva Convention which would in principle make an extradition impossible on humanitarian grounds. A year after his escape the Senegalese government nonetheless found a contested legal procedure to send him back. Two weeks later the Swiss government transferred the money in the two accounts back to Mali, a first for any developing country [*ibid.*].

There are several international actions against national corruption using international tools (6). The International Anti-Corruption Conference, held bi-annually since it was started by the Hong Kong ICAC in the 1980s is a good example. At the last meeting in Lima, Peru, there were 1,200 participants from over 90 countries, representing government agencies, the private sector, professional associations, NGOs and multilateral institutions. While the focus was on national corruption issues, international mechanisms were also raised.

Using entirely different means, TI's Corruption Perception Index also contributes to this international debate.

International anti-corruption tools used to tackle national corruption on a national level (5) are only just evolving. In 1997 the IMF invoked its 'good governance clause' in Argentina, Cambodia and Kenya with demands for demonstrable anti-corruption measures. As an 'operational directive' the clause is not a formal conditionality since the IMF's Articles of Agreement stipulate that it should not deal in matters that are political in nature. Negotiating officers can none the less insist on its compliance. In Kenya the IMF suspended $220 million in loans over concerns about the allocation of power contracts and on the grounds that the government had failed to combat corruption. 'The suspension led to a fall in the value of the [Kenyan] shilling, reduced investor confidence, reduced aid flows from other donors, and caused higher inflation as the price of imports, particularly fuel, increased in the shops' [BWU, 1997: 9]. The IMF agreed with the Kenyan government that it would have to fulfil the following sweeping preconditions for the release of further finance: strengthen management of the energy sector; safeguard the independence of the Kenya Revenue Authority; ensure that the Kenya Anti-Corruption Authority will be fully independent and have a wide mandate to investigate corruption and to bring both civil and criminal investigations; and establish full accountability with regard to past financial infractions. To date, there is no publicly available report to confirm that these reforms have been implemented.

Mechanisms in (5) could also work at two other levels: One, there could be international codes, say for professional bodies, which could be used in a national reform scenario. The world federation of engineers (FIDEC) has, for example, passed a code of conduct designed to prohibit engineers from passing substandard works. The International Bar Association may follow suit, having recognised the link between corruption and the abuse of human rights. Second, there could be international databases, perhaps organised by consumers protection organisations on the internet, providing information on corrupt practices by TNCs.

If we look at these international control mechanisms in the light of the three classic problem areas cited in the beginning of this section - corruption by international agents (for example, TNCs), extradition and mutual legal assistance and repatriation of the proceeds of corruption - then it is clear that we are likely to make progress in some areas more rapidly than in others. Most of the mechanisms in Table 2 are aimed at controlling international corruption by TNCs, both through the abolition of the tax-deductibility of foreign bribes, as in the recent convention signed by the OECD, and its eventual criminalisation in the image of the FCPA. In the first stage this will exclude high-growth companies from countries such as Brazil, South Africa or

Malaysia, but once the mechanisms are in place there would be considerable pressure for them to abide by the same rules.

Extradition and mutual legal assistance will be considerably more difficult to implement. The only realistic approach is a gradual one based on regional conventions, such as the OAS or the Council of Europe project. For a global convention the sanctions and judicial methods are too varied, however. For example, numerous countries, like Mali, Vietnam, Cambodia and China, impose the death penalty for grand corruption (in some cases seen as anything above $10,000). In spite of the success (*sic*) in Mali, punishment of this kind would make it impossible for most countries to implement extradition procedures.[11] A variation on this theme is a method that has been used with limited success, namely restricting the freedom of movement of authoritarian and corrupt leaders and their entourage. Zaire's Mobutu Sese Seko was refused entry visas to most European countries (France and Belgium included) over a number of years and the same currently applies to the ruling junta in Nigeria.

Finally, the most pressing concern in many capital cities - Kinshasa, Islamabad, Manila, Cotonou and Bamako included - remains the repatriation of the proceeds of corruption. This is the weakest link by far as the unique success in Mali demonstrates.[12] Since the sums alleged to be hidden in numbered accounts in Switzerland alone would go a long way towards alleviating the debt of some of the least developed countries [*Ziegler, 1990*] both a prospective and retrospective approach have to be explored. Prospectively, the obvious basis for an international approach would be to gain from the experience of the international Financial Action Task Force (FATF) which regulates money laundered from the proceeds of drug trafficking. This method has serious limitations, however. First, there are the banking havens whose sole comparative advantage is eluding most international conventions. Secondly, even with the best of intentions, it would be impossible for a bank or a national supervisory body to vet all deposits by politicians, civil servants or their proxies to ascertain that the source is not a corrupt one. In short, this approach has limitations. Retrospectively and prospectively, a gradual country-by-country approach, might be the most promising. In the Dembélé case in Mali, Swiss Development Cooperation made SFr 300,000 available to cover the legal proceedings and investigation on the Swiss side. The sum they were able to release to Mali was a tenfold of this. This precedent and the recent Nazi Gold scandal might stimulate the necessary political will in the government and the Federal Banking Commission to improve the prospects of mutual legal assistance for other countries as well. National lobbies might then be the most effective means of introducing similar procedures in other banking secrecy havens.

CONCLUSIONS

Until the early 1990s, much of the literature on corruption was relativist, if not functionalist: 'what counts as corruption in country A is perfectly legal and morally permissible in country B' [*O'Donnell, 1997: 23*]. A couple of years ago, Lord Young, then Chairman of Cable & Wireless, argued that European-based multinationals should not impose the moral standards of their home countries on the business they do elsewhere. In the end, he argued, 'the moral problem is simply jobs'.[13] Olusegun Obasanjo has argued strongly against the 'myth' in the North 'that a traditional culture of appreciation and hospitality [in Africa] fosters corrupt practices'.[14] While there are still some grey areas - even established democracies debate these in their media regularly - a certain dysfunctional core has almost become universally recognised. This applies to the direct embezzlement of public funds, grand corruption, personal enrichment from party funds, and so forth. The broad consensus across regions on these core issues is one of the bases for the anti-corruption 'eruption' the world has seen since the early 1990s [*Naim, 1995*].

A focus on institutional mechanisms, though crucial, will not be sufficient to turn the tide on endemic corruption. There are two radical approaches to controlling corruption at the 'interface of the public and the private sectors' [*Rose-Ackerman, 1996: 1*]. Gary Becker [*1994; 1997: 10*] claims that 'the only way to reduce corruption permanently is to drastically cut back government's role in the economy'. The evidence to support this hypothesis is not as forthright as it may seem. With a couple of exceptions, the ten countries with the highest perceived degree of integrity on the 1997 TI CPI (Denmark, Sweden, Finland, New Zealand, Canada, Netherlands, Norway, Australia, Singapore and Switzerland) do not read like a who's who of capitalist laissez-faire. And those who have liberalised and deregulated their economies in the past few years already had low levels of corruption before.[15]

The reverse experiment was attempted in numerous countries by doing away with the private sector. Some even succeeded in maintaining remarkably low levels of corruption (for example, China after 1949) but the success did not last more than ten years [*White, 1996*], nor was the political context of these revolutionary reforms what one might call polyarchal. Evidence of corruption in the Soviet Union became increasingly apparent in the last few decades but it is ironically in the transition to capitalism that corruption is reaching unparalleled proportions. A recent survey by Control Risks, a consulting firm, said European and US executives now viewed Russia as the most corrupt country in the world. The worst six offenders includes the former Soviet republics of Ukraine, Azerbaijan, Uzbekistan and Kazakhstan [*Reuters, 1997*]. The choice of doing away with either the state or the private sector does not seem to be one that is practicable or even desirable for most states today.

Furthermore, the systemic corruption problems industrialised countries such as Italy, France, Spain and Japan have faced in the 1990s should silence critics who claim that corruption is a historical (some say necessary) rite of passage states pass through on their way to modernisation.

The above analysis has sought to suggest some new ways of thinking about controlling corruption over the long term. This is based on three basic criteria. First, the actors or stakeholders in the process must be clearly identified and have a sense of common purpose and shared responsibility. Klitgaard's [1988] main case study of successful corruption control is the Philippines Bureau of Internal Revenue under Marcos. It was a success at the time, but did not outlive its creative and principled administrator. As the examples above show, initiatives for corruption reform can be taken by principals, agents and clients, but lasting reform can only succeed if all three are actively engaged. The La Paz scenario failed in the long run because it was based on the notion that to reduce corruption, the agents would have to be circumvented. It created a direct link between the clients and the principal which only worked as long as it enjoyed the full backing of the mayor. In the Hong Kong ICAC and the Transparency International Integrity Pact (TI-IP) there is a sense that corruption reform can be extended to include all key stakeholders in the process – the principal, its agents and the clients but also civil society or NGOs. This is the case in the interplay of the Hong Kong ICAC's various organs and the advisory committees which 'guard the guardians'. It is too early to tell whether the TI-IP will be effective but it makes an effort to be inclusive and to extend the monitoring capacity both to companies which are invited to monitor each other and to NGOs that can test the transparency of the procurement process. Since the TI-IP will initially be used in a few select public contracts it is a first-step scenario and not one that aims to be sustainable in itself.

Second, for reforms to be successful over time they must navigate a difficult gradient between what is feasible and credible. One-off measures like declarations of assets, new legislation, reversal of the burden of proof, and so on, can all be categorised fairly neatly for their relative levels of credibility and feasibility. The examples from Benin, Burkina Faso and South Africa make it clear that what might be credible or feasible in one context might not be in another. The Hong Kong ICAC's experience in successfully controlling endemic corruption over a longer period of time, illustrates the give-and-take reformers might have to go through, balancing measures which gradually increase the institution's operational capacity and its credibility.

Third, the Achilles' heel of efforts to stem grand corruption is currently the tremendous loopholes provided by the international system. Significant new initiatives are currently being developed and implemented to control one aspect of international corruption - bribery by TNCs to gain contracts abroad.

Still, the extradition of corrupt public officials and the repatriation of the proceeds of corruption remain difficult, to say the least.

The overall point is that these three criteria need to be located in specific institutional arrangements for them to be effective. There is no basis for complacency on this front since there is considerable scope for improvement. At the same time, there has probably never been a more propitious climate for reforms aimed at this resilient dysfunction of the state system.

NOTES

1. As late as 1990 it was still felt that work on corruption would be a clear 'violation of the political abstinence prescribed by the [World] Bank's charter' [*Eigen 1996: 159*].
2. Some of the authors who have argued this point are Eigen [*1995a; 1995b*], Frisch [*1995*], Galtung [*1995*], Gould and Amaro-Keyes [*1983*], Klitgaard [*1993; 1996*], Moody-Stuart [*1994*], Parfitt [*1991*], Rose-Ackerman [*1978*], Trzyna [*1994*], World Bank [*1989; 1991; 1992*]. The best econometric work in this area is Elliott [*1997*], Mauro [*1995*], Wei [*1997*] and Lambsdorff (this volume).
3. This will also be the subject of the next book in the TI Sourcebook series by Jeremy Pope, forthcoming in 1998. Alan Doig [*1994*] also mentions the need for 'sustainable anti-corruption strategies'.
4. LeVine [*1990*] offers a brief but excellent summary of some of the historical attempts to eliminate corruption by political and religious zealots. With the possible exception of modern-day Singapore, none of the examples he gives seems to have remained 'clean' for more than 25 years, that is, one generation. Historically speaking, the only other exceptions seem to be the top-ten countries on the TI Corruption Perception Index (1997). They have been 'clean' for more than a generation and give few indications of deteriorating.
5. The only negative externality the parties internalise is the moral one, but this is an area that will be covered in this study.
6. The Transparency International (TI) Corruption Perception Index (CPI) can be consulted at www.transparency.de.
7. The leading econometric work on corruption in recent years is all based at least in part on the TI Index, see Elliott [*1997*], Mauro [*1995*], Wei [*1997*]. See Lambsdorff (this volume).
8. A 'bribery index' of this kind is planned by TI for 1998.
9. Many things will undoubtedly have changed for the Hong Kong ICAC since July 1997. The examples based on the success of the ICAC are no less relevant as illustrations, however.
10. The first reports on the TI-IP's effectiveness as well as the World Bank 'no bribery pledge' should be available by late 1998.
11. Swiss law, for example, would only allow the extradition of a foreign official for corruption committed abroad if the maximum prison sentence is no more than one year (Art. 35, 1st al., EIMP, quoted in Lampert [*1995: 160*]).
12. On the 10th anniversary of the 1986 'people power revolution' in the Philippines, Imelda Marcos gave the following prayer at a public gathering: 'May the Lord enlighten … the Swiss banks that they might preserve the laws of confidentiality, trust and basic decency between the banks and their clients' (*The Guardian*, Dar es Salaam, 27 Feb. 1996).
13. Lord Young, quoted on a BBC World Report, broadcast in May 1994 (TI Newsletter [*June 1994*]).
14. Olusegun Obasanjo, 'Positive Tradition Perverted by Corruption', *Financial Times*, 14 Oct. 1994.
15. An article on the 'rampant corruption' in Latin America concludes that 'free markets and democracy have done little to stem the growing tide of scandal', Matt Moffett and Jonathan Friedland, 'A New Latin America Faces a Devil of Old: Rampant Corruption,' *Wall Street Journal*, 1 July 1996.

REFERENCES

Becker, Gary S., 1994, 'To Root out Corruption, Boot out Big Government', *Business Week*, 31 Jan.
Becker, Gary S., 1997, 'Want to Squelch Corruption? Try Passing out Raises', *Business Week*, 3 Nov.
Borghi, Marco and Meyer-Bisch, Patrice (eds.), 1995, *La corruption, l'envers des droits de l'homme*, Fribourg, Switzerland: Editions universitaires.
BWU, 1997, 'Corruption Rises up Bank/Fund Agendas', *Bretton Woods Update*, Oct.–Dec.
Colombo, Gherardo, 1995, 'Les enquétes de la magistrature italienne dans les crimes contre l'administration publique. Les méfaits de la corruption', Borghi and Meyer-Bisch [*1995: 195–208*].
Constant, Benjamin, 1988, *Political Writings*, Cambridge: Cambridge University Press.
de Spelville, Bertrand E.D., 1996, 'The Experience of Hong Kong in Combating Corruption', paper presented at Uganda International Conference on Empowerment of Civil Society in the Fight Against Corruption, Mweya Lodge, Uganda, 21–25 April.
della Porta, Donatella, 1996, 'Partidos políticos y corrupción: reflexiones sobre el caso italiano', *Nueva Sociedad (Venezuela), No.145*.
Doig, Alan, 1994, 'Sustainable Anti-Corruption Strategies: The Role of Independent Agencies', unpublished paper, University of Liverpool.
Eigen, Peter, 1995a, 'Das Nord-Süd Gefälle der Korruption', *Kursbuch*, Vol.120, pp.155–70.
Eigen, Peter, 1995b, 'La corrupción en los países desarrollados y en desarrollo – Un desafío de los '90', *Contribuciones, CIEDLA*, Vol.4.
Eigen, Peter, 1996, 'Combating Corruption Around the World', *Journal of Democracy*, Vol.7, No.1, pp.158–68.
Elliott, Kimberly Ann (ed.). 1997, *Corruption and the Global Economy*, Washington, DC: Institute for International Economics (IIE).
Fall, Elimane, and Cherif Ouazani, 1997, 'Le magot de Démbélé', *Jeune Afrique*, 8–14 Oct.
FAZ, 1996, 'Mickey Kantor zieht gegen die internationale Korruption zu Felde', *Frankfurter Allgemeine Zeitung*, 31 July .
Frisch, Dieter, 1995, 'Les effets de la corruption sur le développement', *TI Working Paper*, No.7.
Galtung, Fredrik, 1995, 'An der Korruptionsfront, *Kursbuch*, Vol.120, pp.171–82.
Gould, David J. and Jose A. Amaro-Reyes, 1983, 'The Effects of Corruption on Administrative Performance: Illustrations from Developing Countries', *World Bank Staff Working Paper No.580*.
Heidenheimer, Arnold J., Johnston, Michael and Victor T. LeVine (eds.), 1989, *Political Corruption: A Handbook*, New Brunswick, NJ: Transaction.
Hickock, Eugene W., 1995, 'Accountability of Public Officials', in Seymour Martin Lipset (ed.), *The Encyclopedia of Democracy*, London: Routledge.
ICAC (New South Wales), 1995, *Community Attitudes to Corruption and the ICAC 1995*, Sydney, NSW: Independent Commission Against Corruption (ICAC).
Johnston, Michael, 1993, 'Social Development as an Anti-Corruption Strategy', *VIth International Anti-Corruption Conference*, Cancún, Mexico, Nov.
Kim, Young Jong, 1994, *Bureaucratic Corruption: The Case of Korea*, Seoul: Chomyung Press.
Klitgaard, Robert, 1988, *Controlling Corruption*, Berkeley, CA: University of California Press.
Klitgaard, Robert, 1993, 'A Framework for a Country Programme Against Corruption', in Fredrik Galtung (ed.), *Accountability and Transparency in International Development*, Berlin: Transparency International and DSE.
Klitgaard, Robert, 1996, 'Preventing Corruption: A Practical Handbook for Dealing with Municipal Malfeasance', monograph, Feb.
Lampert, Jean, 1995, 'Fisc et corruption', Borghi and Meyer-Bisch [*1995*].
Lancaster, Thomas D. and Gabriella R. Mantinola, 1997, 'Toward a Methodology for the Comparative Study of Political Corruption', unpublished paper.
Langseth, Petter, Rick Stapenhurst and Jeremy Pope, 1997, 'The Role of a National Integrity System in Fighting Corruption', *EDI (Economic Development Institute of The World Bank) Working Papers* , No. 400/142.
LeVine, Victor T., 1990, 'Controlling Corruption: A Review Essay', *Corruption and Reform*, No.5, pp.153–57.

MacLean Abaroa, Ronald, 1994, 'El estado y la prevención de la corrupción', *Conference Organised by the Presidential Commission on Ethics in the Public Service*, Santiago, Chile, June.

McDermott, Darren, 1997, 'Singapore Imposes Ban on 5 Overseas Contractors', *Wall Street Journal*, 15 Feb.

Mauro, Paolo, 1995, 'Corruption and Growth', *Quarterly Journal of Economics,* No.110, pp.681–712.

Moody-Stuart, George, 1994, *Grand Corruption in Third World Development*, Berlin: Transparency International (TI).

Naim, Moises, 1995, 'The Corruption Eruption', *Brown Journal of World Affairs,* Vol.2, No.2, pp.245–61.

Ocampo, Luis Moreno, 1993, *En defensa propia: Como salir de la corrupción*, Buenos Aires: Editorial Sudamericana.

O'Donnell, Guillermo, 1997, 'Horizontal Accountabilty in New Polyarchies', Third Vienna Dialogue on Democracy, 'Institutionalizing Horizontal Accountability: How Democracies Can Fight Corruption and the Abuse of Power' , Vienna, 26–29 June 1997.

Parfitt, Trevor W., 1991, 'Corruption, Adjustment, and the African Debt', *Corruption and Reform,* Vol.6, pp.25–44.

Pope, Jeremy, 1995, 'Containing Corruption in International Transactions: The Challenge of the 1990s', in Commission on Global Governance (eds.), *Issues in Global Governance*, London: Kluwer Law International.

Pope, Jeremy (ed.), 1996, *National Integrity Systems: The TI Source Book,* Washington, DC: TI and EDI.

Pritzl, Rupert F. J., 1997, *Korruption und Rent-Seeking in Lateinamerika*, Baden-Baden: Nomos.

Quah, Jon S. T., 1997, 'Combating Corruption in Asia: Comparing Anti-Corruption Agencies in South Korea, Taiwan and Thailand', Third Vienna Dialogue on Democracy, Institutionalizing Horizontal Accountability: How Democracies Can Fight Corruption and the Abuse of Power, Vienna, 26–29 June.

Reuters, 1997, 'Russia Tops Roster of Nations with Highest Corruption', 5 Nov.

Rose-Ackerman, Susan, 1978, *Corruption: A Study in Political Economy*, New York: Academic Press.

Rose-Ackerman, Susan, 1996, 'The Political Economy of Corruption: Causes and Consequences', *Viewpoint,* No.74.

Sapelli, Giulio, 1994, *Cleptocrazia: Il 'meccanismo unico' della corruzione tra economia e politica*, Milano: Feltrinelli.

Schedler, Andreas, 1995, 'Credibility: Exploring the Bases of Institutional Reform in New Democracies', paper at XIXth International Congress of the Latin American Studies Association (LASA), Washington, DC, 28–30 Sept.

Stewart, Frances and Ejaz Ghani, 1991, 'How Significant Are Externalities for Development?', *World Development*, Vol.19, No.6, pp.569–94.

Taylor, Andrew, 1996, 'Singapore Exposes Tip of Corruption Iceberg', *Financial Times*, 15 Feb. 1996.

TI Brussels, 1996, 'Corruption Control in the European Union', *TI Working Paper,* No.9.

Tortosa, José María, 1995, *Corrupción*, Barcelona: Icaria.

Trzyna, Ted, 1994, 'Attacking 'Grand Corruption,' a Hidden but Growing Barrier to Conservation', *IUCN Environmental Strategy,* No.9, Dec., p.3.

Wei, Shang-Jin, 1997, 'How Taxing is Corruption on International Investors?' Working Paper, Kennedy School of Government, Harvard University.

White, Gordon, 1996, 'Corruption and Market Reform in China', *IDS Bulletin*, Liberalization and the New Corruption, Vol.27, No.2, pp.40–4.

Wiehen, Michael H., 1996, 'The OECD Recommendations on Bribery in International Business Transactions', *TI Working Paper,* No.10.

World Bank, 1989, *Sub-Saharan Africa: From Crisis to Sustainable Growth*, Washington, DC: World Bank.

World Bank, 1991, *World Development Report 1991*, Oxford: Oxford University Press.

World Bank, 1992, *Governance and Development*, Washington, DC: World Bank.

World Bank, 1997, *Helping Countries Combat Corruption: The Role of the World Bank*, Washington, DC: World Bank.

Wraith, Ronald and Edgar Simpkins, 1978, 'Nepotism and Bribery in West Africa', in Arnold J.
    Heidenheimer (ed.), *Political Corruption: Readings in Comparative Analysis*, New Brunswick,
    NJ: Transaction Books, pp.331–40.
Ziegler, Jean, 1990, *La Suisse lave plus blanc*, Paris: Editions du Seuil.

The Political Economy of Anti-Corruption Strategies in Africa

STEPHEN P. RILEY

In the mid-1990s an international consensus in development discourse has emerged: democratisation, public sector down-sizing, and economic deregulation are desirable goals in themselves, but they also reduce the extensive corruption in monopolistic state agencies. This study examines these issues with reference to the politics and practicalities of anti-corruption strategies in several African societies. It is argued that although down-sizing the state and political liberalisation are desirable goals in many African countries, they are necessary rather than sufficient conditions for the reduction of corruption. Extensive public sector corruption can coexist with democratic or quasi-democratic politics (as in Nigeria in the 1980s). Economic liberalisation can also create opportunities for corruption, through the sales of parastatals in dubious circumstances, and the creation of new, corrupt markets, as can the political liberalisation of previously authoritarian regimes such as Kenya in the 1990s. For short-term anti-corruption strategies to be effective in African societies, more attention needs to be devoted to questions of sequencing, the detail of reform and its sustainability in very poor societies, and the exceptional political and managerial commitment necessary to promote and maintain reform.

INTRODUCTION

Two political upheavals in May 1997 are symptomatic of the condition of contemporary African states. The collapse of Mobutu's kleptocratic regime in Zaïre was closely followed by the overthrow of the democratically elected government in Sierra Leone [*Collins, 1997; Gourevitch, 1997; Riley, 1997*].

Stephen P. Riley, Reader in Politics, School of Humanities and Social Sciences, Staffordshire University, Stoke on Trent ST4 2DE, United Kingdom. He has also taught at the University of Sierra Leone in West Africa and two South African universities: Rhodes University in Grahamstown and the University of Durban-Westville. He is the founding co-editor of *Corruption and Reform: An International Journal/Crime, Law and Social Change* and is currently (1998–99) the research co-ordinator of a British government-funded Department For International Development (DFID) research project on the control of corruption in developing and transitional countries.

Mobutu's replacement by the Democratic Republic of the Congo under Laurent Kabila is evidence of much broader and generally progressive contemporary developments in Africa. Ruled in a malign and authoritarian way for 32 years by Mobutu Sese Seko, Zaïre's state was a mechanism for the self-enrichment of a clique which surrounded the president. Contrary to Western notions of the state, which stress impartiality and the public interest, Zaïre was moulded to serve the interests of the few. For some, the emergence of Kabila's government, along with similar developments elsewhere in central Africa, was a sign that an old, essentially corrupt, pro-western political order was coming to an end. It remains to be seen whether Kabila's new government will have the political will and the external funding to reconstruct a modern economy and polity out of Mobutu's devastation.

An equally significant set of events occurred in the much smaller and economically and politically insignificant west African state of Sierra Leone. It initially appeared that a conventional *coup d'état* had taken place in late May 1997, ousting the short-lived, democratically-elected government of Ahmad Tejan Kabbah. But the rebel soldiers were joined by elements of a brutal insurrectionary force, the Revolutionary United Front (RUF), which had been fighting against all Sierra Leonean governments since 1991 [*Keen, 1997; Riley, 1996*]. The RUF's campaign focused upon the corrupt and inegalitarian politics of the central state since independence in 1961. The significance of this insurrection was that it represented the coming to power of a 'lumpen' or under-class, profoundly alienated by the corrupt politics of all post-independence governments. Extensive systemic corruption and mal-administration has been evident in Sierra Leone for many years [*Kpundeh, 1995; Reno, 1995; Riley, 1983a; Zack-Williams, 1983*]. Widespread, debilitating and diverse forms of public corruption have contributed to the regime's precipitous economic decline since the 1970s [*Luke and Riley, 1989; 1991*]. The result of the emergence of the hybrid military/rebel junta in late May 1997 is an internationally isolated, very unstable, brutal, populist regime, challenged by foreign troops outside the capital of Freetown. Consequently, professional alarmists, such as the writer Robert Kaplan, argue that the apocalyptic scenario of 'The Coming Anarchy', with collapsing states, increasing crime and social crises, is confirmed by these events [*Kaplan, 1994; 1996; 1997*].

Whatever the future for Africa as a whole – which could move towards a more progressive, second 'post-neo-colonial' generation of political leaders, or a gloomier scenario of increased crime, social disorder and weaker states – there is no doubt that minimising corruption needs to be a high priority. Gross, high-level and systemic corruption formed the backdrop to the dramatic events in both Zaïre and Sierra Leone. Reducing the debilitating effects of public sector corruption, and countering the damaging effects of other, diverse forms of corruption, ought to be the focus of attention in the late 1990s. Both internal political factors and the external pressures of aid donors are responsible for highlighting the issue in the late 1990s: in addition to the domestic political turmoil that extensive corruption can help create, international institutions with financial commitments in Africa are now increasingly publicly concerned with its damaging consequences for growth on the continent. The international institutions are also responding to reactions by western governments and publics against the conspicuous consumption associated with systemic corruption in Africa, as in the case of the wealth and lifestyle of Mobutu and his clique.

For these reasons, attempts to reduce and control corruption are politically salient objectives for social reformers and civil society groups, concerned African governments and for a number of aid donors, who have recently developed policies on these issues [*OECD, 1997; UNDP/OECD, 1997*]. Surveying these developments, this paper first examines the current academic and policy debate on anti-corruption strategies, particularly with reference to the policy initiatives of the major international institutions, such as the World Bank. Secondly, it considers the experience of a number of African countries with both developed and cosmetic 'anti-corruption' strategies. States such as Botswana, Mozambique and Tanzania have had relatively low levels of 'grand' corruption until recently; their anti-corruption strategies have taken differing forms. Nigeria, Sierra Leone, Uganda and Zaïre are examples of societies where anti-corruption strategies have existed, but their results have been meagre. A third section of the paper evaluates the new anti-corruption consensus against this African experience and examines the implications for policy. Tables 1 and 2 (below) summarise both the anti-corruption strategies that have emerged since the 1960s and the types of corruption typically found in African political economies.

ANTI-CORRUPTION STRATEGIES: ANCIENT AND MODERN

The growing concern to develop effective and preferably short-term anti-corruption strategies is partly because corruption has profoundly inegalitarian effects; it damages the interests of the poor most, whether the corruption is 'petty' or 'grand' in character [*Moody-Stuart, 1997*]. In Africa, as elsewhere, corruption often has a 'Robin Hood in reverse' character: the losers are likely to be the exceptionally poor, female, and marginalised, whilst the winners are already wealthy and part of an inefficient, swollen state. Most African corruption rewards the already wealthy: usually, it is a form of redistribution from those in poverty to the office-holding and consequently relatively or extremely rich. This corrupt misallocation of resources happens where poverty is a product of unequal wealth distribution and where it is also a consequence of the social exclusion of the poor [*UNDP, 1997; Ward, 1989; World Bank, 1997a*]. Since independence, many African states have not acted in an efficient and enabling way to promote equitable development; instead, through corruption and maladministration, some African states and their agents have reinforced the current unequal distribution of opportunities, undermined basic human rights, and created new inequalities. The overall thrust of recent academic studies has tended to challenge the revisionist standpoint of J. S. Nye and N. Leff that the economic benefits of corruption (in helping capital formation, speeding up development, as well as humanising politics) outweigh the costs (Nye and Leff in Heidenheimer, LeVine and Johnston [*1989*]).

As a result of the obvious damage that corruption has done in many African societies, politicians and public management specialists have made numerous attempts to reduce or minimise the effects of corruption with a series of anti-corruption strategies. Serious attempts to control corruption are often as old as corruption itself. A recent study by Sen [*1997*] points to some early examples, but see also Noonan [*1984*]. In ancient China, many public officials were paid a corruption-preventing allowance to try to ensure their continued honesty. This illustration relates to recent debates about the relationship between the low salary levels of junior civil servants and levels of corruption in Africa. Kautilya, a fourth century BC Indian political analyst, sought to identify forty different ways in which public officials could be corrupt. He also developed a system of spot-checks to reduce corruption, which were accompanied by a rewards and penalties system. Such ancient examples of attempted corruption-control are similar to those developed by public officials and academic analysts in recent years, in the period since the 1960s. Broadly, there are four levels or types of anti-corruption strategy which can be identified in operation in post-independence Africa: international; national; local; and populist [*Theobald, 1990*].

Since the mid-1990s a series of international (Type 1) anti-corruption initiatives has emerged [*OECD, 1997; Kaufmann, 1997; Rose-Ackerman, 1997*], but earlier decades saw African countries themselves develop strategies based upon national and local action (Types 2 and 3), including anti-corruption agencies, public inquiries, inspector-general systems, legal and quasi-legal trials, complaints procedures, and public awareness campaigns [*Clarke, 1983; Doig, 1995; Heidenheimer, LeVine and Johnston, 1989; IRIS, 1996*]. Often a key issue in assessing the effectiveness and sustainability of such strategies is the commitment of the powerful to act effectively to curb corruption [*Klitgaard, 1997; Kpundeh, 1997*]. Populist initiatives (Type 4) such as purges of civil servants and former politicians have not had much success, although the issue of corruption has acquired great political salience in recent years due to the actions of NGOs and activism by lawyers and other public interest groups [*Doig and Riley, 1998; Harsch, 1993; Theobald, 1990; Transparency*

TABLE 1
TYPES OF ANTI-CORRUPTION STRATEGY

---

1 INTERNATIONAL
- New World Bank and IMF policies
- OECD efforts to criminalise transnational bribery
- Transparency International's interventions

2 NATIONAL
- Procedures and training within state or public sector institutions
- 'Service Culture' approaches
- 'Islands of Integrity'
- Capacity-building to 'design out' corruption
- Legal approaches, including state funding of parties, controls on 'revolving doors' and patronage appointments
- Anti-Corruption agencies
- Auditor-Generals and Parliamentary oversight
- The Police and 'Inter-Agency Co-operation'

3 LOCAL OR 'CITIZEN' LEVEL
- Minimising small-scale corruption by protection against the extractive and arbitrary nature of the state
- 'Structural reform' (e.g. decentralisation and deregulation)
- 'Legislative sunlight' provisions
- New administrative procedures (e.g. overlapping jurisdictions; multiple providers; customerisation of public services and service delivery surveys)
- Complaints and redress
- Community oversight
- The Media

4 POPULIST
- Purges (e.g. of civil servants)
- 'Making Examples' (public humiliations and executions; quasi-official tribunals)
- 'Moral Rearmament' campaigns and the New Citizen

Source: Compiled by the author but drawing upon Theobald [*1990*], Doig [*1995*], Doig and Riley [*1998*].

International, 1996]. The harsh punishment meted out to former public officials in Ghana and Liberia in 1979 and 1980 – which involved populist revolutions (in effect, *coups d'état*), dubious trials and speedy public executions for several former heads of state, such as President William Tolbert of Liberia – illustrates a general paradox: extensive high-level corruption can contribute to profound political upheavals, but the problem of corruption does not disappear with the removal of those key officials identified as corrupt [*Jeffries, 1982*].

More recently, several African countries have adopted public integrity reforms which are associated with the 'New Public Management' approach to governance in western societies (Type 3). These initiatives are often linked to the influence of aid donors or the activities of pressure groups such as Transparency International (TI). Examples include new administrative procedures such as overlapping jurisdictions (where two or more officials are responsible for an administrative action), service delivery surveys (for example in Tanzania and Uganda, in cooperation with the World Bank), and structural reform, where an administrative machine is decentralised or deregulation takes place. However, there are several potential problems with such strategies. For example, decentralisation, a widely touted remedy for many of the African state's contemporary ills, can also create lower-level corruption unless it is accompanied by some of the range of possible anti-corruption strategies. Nevertheless, aid donors and others hope that these reforms will improve public integrity either directly or indirectly.

Many of the less coercive anti-corruption efforts are based upon the manipulation of incentives for, and the potential punishments to be meted out to, public officials. These modern strategies are often accompanied by attempts to improve both recruitment of public officials who are more likely to be honest and better information upon their preferably honest public conduct, although they are based upon earlier academic and policy studies [*Gould, 1980; McKinney and Johnston, 1986; Klitgaard, 1988*]. The anti-corruption strategy proposed is usually based upon a distinctive view of the causes and character of corruption. There are three distinct approaches to contemporary corruption and anti-corruption strategies: economic analyses; mass public opinion perspectives; and institutional viewpoints. Developed since the 1960s, these are outlined and evaluated in a wide variety of publications [*Heidenheimer, LeVine and Johnston, 1989*]. Economic analyses prioritise the principal-agent market relationship to identify corruption and anti-corruption strategies, whereas mass public opinion perspectives examine the social or cultural context of corruption and suggest as a result mass attitudinal change or civic awareness anti-corruption strategies. These two approaches are well established and well regarded, with an extensive academic literature and some policy applications. A third and newer, institutional approach focuses upon the public sector and institutional reform [*Doig, 1995; Stapenhurst and Langseth, 1997*]. This is important because it enables the analyst of corruption to suggest short-term and specific policy recommendations which focus upon low-level corruption. This newer approach has yet to have a major impact upon policy formation.

Instead, much of the debate on anti-corruption strategy has at its roots neo-classical economic theory and its application and concerns. Thus, for example, Klitgaard's approach, which has been widely promoted and applied in Africa in the 1990s, is based upon principal-agent economic analysis, derived from neo-classical or neo-liberal economic theory, and is evaluated by him in a number of widely differing developing country contexts, particularly in Africa and Latin America [*Klitgaard, 1988; 1991; 1997*]. Klitgaard argues that officials are most corrupt where they have wide discretion in their actions, little accountability, and considerable monopoly power. This enables them to charge what economists call rents. The less diplomatic call it corrupt enrichment. According to Klitgaard, rents can be reduced by decreasing state power, limiting the discretion of officials, and by strengthening the controls exercised over public officials, including accountancy units in ministries. Transparency is also an important notion: opening up previously secret public officialdom and helping generate freer public discussion through a free, questioning press, and an active civil society, can also reduce corruption. Klitgaard's work has been very influential and appears to be at the core of the World Bank's recent analyses, along with that of Susan Rose-Ackerman. Only recently have international institutions such as the World Bank concerned themselves publicly with these issues, although the World Bank did publish one interesting earlier study [*Gould and Amaro-Reyes, 1983; Rose-Ackerman, 1997; World Bank, 1997a*].

THE NEW AGENDA

The academic and policy-orientated debate on the effectiveness of anti-corruption strategies has been changed markedly by events in developing countries and in the former Soviet Bloc in the 1980s. Arguments about curbing corruption take place now in a new context: we are in an era of economic reform, structural adjustment and what Samuel Huntington [*1991*] has called the Third Wave of democratisation in developing and transitional countries. A shaky new international consensus on development emerged as the old Soviet Bloc model of one party states and command economies collapsed: in a unipolar world, there is an expectation that the developing countries reform both economically and politically as aid budgets shrink, external debts grow, and the terms of trade in their primary commodity exports deteriorate [*Hoogvelt, 1997; Randel and German, 1997*].

The relevant parts of this new international consensus can be briefly stated. The new development agenda of the late 1990s involves an expectation of sustained efforts in developing and transitional countries towards the goals of market economies and liberal democratic political systems. More recently, this has also involved the prioritising of the interests of the poor and marginalised in the context of an enabling state and higher ethical standards in donors [*OECD, 1997; UNDP, 1997; UNDP/OECD, 1997; World Bank, 1997a*]. Progress towards these goals therefore means serious attempts to secure better governance and substantially less corruption in developing and transitional countries.

Corruption is most obviously defined as public office, public sector, or institutional corruption, rather than corruption in the private sector, or as the product of the activities of multinational corporations, or even corruption in foreign aid allocations. The assumptions are twofold: first, public sector corruption will be reduced if the size of the state is reduced. Secondly, moves towards liberal, pluralist politics, involving a freer press, competitive party politics, and the revival or creation of other independent institutions, such as the judiciary and professional associations, will also reduce corruption by making it vulnerable to exposure. In this way, corruption will be potentially politically damaging.

The new international policy agenda of the late 1990s also involves the following assumptions. A limited, legitimate, honest and transparent state ought to be at the centre of the development process in both developing and transitional countries. All too often it is not, and the public interest is thereby undermined and human rights infringed. In many cases, the state sector is swollen, inefficient, and corrupt; individual and group private interests have priority over the collective good; and public officials have considerable discretion to accumulate private wealth through exploiting their monopolistic, low and irregularly paid positions, often in collusion with indigenous or foreign businessmen. Corruption frequently takes place in societies where there is considerable discretion for public officials, limited accountability, and little transparency in governmental operations; in such societies, civil society institutions are often weak or undeveloped. This new set of assumptions – the new agenda for controlling corruption – has already been questioned and an alternative research agenda has been articulated [*Harriss-White and White, 1996*].

THE WORLD BANK APPROACH

Many of these new assumptions would be shared by the World Bank. Although the Bank has been concerned with corruption in its projects for some time, it has recently developed an approach to public sector and other forms of corruption while acknowledging the Bank's mandate which formally restricts its activities to economic development issues [*Robinson, 1997; Stevens, 1997*]. In 1997 the Bank changed its own working procedures to include special procurement audits. It is also increasing the number of external auditors. But the Bank argues that corruption inside Bank projects is linked to corruption in the societies in which it works. As a result, it has rejected an 'enclave approach', which would improve only the efficiency of its own operations, and instead has sought to tackle corruption as a more systematic issue. A 20-member Bank working group, headed by Mike Stevens, was established in the aftermath of Bank President James Wolfensohn's speech to the World Bank/International Monetary Fund Annual Meetings in October 1996. Wolfensohn's speech, in which he spoke of the 'cancer of corruption', attracted great attention and led to the re-thinking. The Bank working group developed an initiative which argued that, 'for the Bank, tackling corruption is less a matter of new instruments and more a matter of carrying out existing activities, but with a greater focus upon their potential to reduce corruption'. The working group argued that the problem was that 'corruption is a function of policies created by economic rents and of weak institutions'. It was also argued by the working group during its frequent meetings in late 1996 and early 1997 that 'markets discipline participants more effectively than public sector accountability mechanisms generally can' [*Stevens, 1997: 1–2*].

The World Bank's new initiative was published in mid-1997. It highlights the damaging economic costs of corruption in its lenders, and emphasises the debilitating growth of corruption in Sub-Saharan Africa and the transitional economies of Eastern Europe and the former Soviet Union [*World Bank, 1997b; 1997c*]. It builds upon earlier policy reforms such as governance. The Bank argues that the principal way to reduce corruption is to encourage deeper and more thorough economic liberalisation and deregulation in borrowers, although reforming and strengthening public institutions are also regarded as important.

The aim of the Bank is to tie lending more closely to efforts to reduce corruption. The Bank will create a new lending instrument to support improvements in public sector operations. It will also raise this issue in a more open way with borrowers in policy dialogues, and launch pilot anti-corruption schemes in institutions such as tax and customs departments provided that borrowers agree. A recent Bank internal report accepts that 'the evidence of systemic corruption in itself is not a reason to withdraw the Bank's support' [*World Bank, 1997b: 17*]. Nevertheless, the Bank has been examining in detail the ways of using lending to reduce corruption. If corruption is systemic, is affecting the Bank's projects, and a government is unwilling to act to reduce corruption, the Bank now proposes to reduce sharply or stop lending to the government concerned, although it will continue its support for NGOs and civil society organisations. If the Bank regards corruption as systemic in a society, in future it will always raise the issue with the government and discuss the government's active anti-corruption programme. If a government is unwilling to act to reduce corruption, the Bank will be justified in reducing lending.

The World Bank is clearly using Klitgaard's analysis in its perspective upon corruption. According to the Bank, corruption principally occurs where officials are in a monopoly position (and can extract economic rents or unofficial additional income), have large discretion in their actions, and little accountability. The Bank therefore argues that an effective anti-corruption strategy should encourage the reduction of rents (by means of greater economic liberalisation and deregulation), channel and reduce discretion (through public sector reform and institutional strengthening), and increase accountability (by building up institutions such as accountancy units in government, and by encouraging the growth of a more vibrant, questioning civil society).

The internal report, *Report of the Corruption Action Plan Working Group (CAPWG) – Country and International Strategies, OPC Review Draft, May 1997* – hereafter *World Bank, 1997b* and subsequent public documents [*World Bank, 1997a; 1997c*] synthesise evidence from its own internal project reports and from a survey of the Bank's staff in early 1997. Bank staff appear to be divided about the effects of corruption across the world although they are agreed that it is pervasive, growing in most states, transnational in character, and increasingly linked to organised crime. The major problem areas are in sub-Saharan Africa (especially Kenya, Mozambique, Nigeria, and the former Zaïre) and Eastern Europe. The Bank's staff disagree as to whether or not corruption is damaging in East Asia, where extensive corruption (as in South Korea) does not seem to be a barrier to rapid economic growth. The reports argue that the Bank should adopt a more vigorous anti-corruption effort, despite the political sensitivity of the issue [*World Bank, 1997b; 1997c*].

Cynics would argue that the corruption issue is just another means for the Bank to secure its real goal: greater structural adjustment in those states whose adjustment programmes have been stymied by political pressures. The Bank's new policy plays down other means of reducing corruption. It is less enthusiastic about strengthening public institutions and increasing public education and awareness of the issue. In addition, the Bank's recent policies pay little attention to the various types or levels of persistent and entrenched corruption that exist in African political economies.

CORRUPTION AND ANTI-CORRUPTION STRATEGIES IN AFRICA

The Bank's arguments need to be examined against the African experience. Corruption has been a difficult and systemic problem in many African political economies for decades and has had damaging effects in terms of the public reputation of regimes, economic growth and general development objectives. The economic effects of African corruption are difficult to distinguish from maladministration and incompetence, large-scale fraud, organised, disorganised or business crime, and international theft, especially in those African economies in decline in the 1980s and 1990s [*Ellis (ed.), 1996; Ellis, 1996; Levi and Nelken, 1996*]. Although the seriousness of corruption varies over time and across Africa, a consensual view is that gross corruption has had very damaging effects [*IRIS, 1996; Goudie and Stasavage, 1997*]. Corrupt income in Africa is linked to the growth in external debt and global capital flows, and trade in exchange commodities such as diamonds, gold, weapons and illicit drugs. In the early 1990s, Nigeria became a major transhipment centre in the international illicit trade in cocaine and heroin in addition to its continuing problems with high-level public sector corruption. The proceeds of these trades across Africa as well as corrupt income in general is siphoned off into off-shore tax havens and conspicuous consumption [*Naylor, 1987; 1996; Hampton, 1996; Robinson, 1994*]. In such circumstances, aid donors, responsible public officials, and civic organisations have a difficult task in seeking honest conduct and good governance, even when programmes of economic liberalisation, deregulation and public sector reform have been initiated.

In some African states, like the former Zaïre, corruption 'goes beyond shame and almost beyond imagination' [*Delamaide, 1984: 60*]. In other African states, such as Botswana or Tanzania until the 1990s, corruption has been relatively low level, or petty, in form. As a result an important distinction can be made between incidental, systematic and systemic corruption in Africa and its effects (see Table 2). Incidental corruption (Type 1) is a feature of life in almost all African societies, but it can be systematic in many public institutions (such as customs departments, parastatals and other revenue-generating bodies) in African countries, if not systemic in society as a whole [*DeLeon, 1993; Riley, 1983*]. The more damaging forms of corruption can be both endemic and planned [*Waterbury, 1973*]. Incidental corruption is small-scale corruption and usually involves isolated individuals or small numbers of individuals: very junior public officials, such as policemen and soldiers manning road-blocks on provincial roads in Sierra Leone, customs officials at airports and ports in Nigeria, and tax officials in Zaïre [*Gould, 1980; Riley, 1983a; Williams, 1987*]. This petty corruption does not have a huge macro-economic impact but can be profoundly alienating to the public: as citizens and as consumers of public resources. Incidental corruption is also often hard to curb.

In comparison, systematic corruption in Africa (Type 2) involves larger numbers of public officials and an element of organisation and conspiracy. It is typically found in government departments or parastatals such as procurement agencies and marketing boards. Examples would include the produce marketing boards in Nigeria, Uganda and Sierra Leone in the 1960s. In this form, corruption has a larger developmental impact by the extensive diversion of government revenues and the distortion of priorities. As a result, anti-corruption strategies have often focused upon the reform of such institutions, often by sacking those individual officials thought responsible, or by instituting public inquiries such as the 1962 Collier Commission of Inquiry 'into the affairs of certain Statutory Corporations in Western Nigeria', where there was extensive corruption and maladministration in the produce marketing board [*Forrest, 1993; Riley, 1983a*]. Numerous other anti-corruption strategies have been developed to deal with systematic corruption

TABLE 2
TYPES OF CORRUPTION

---

1 INCIDENTAL
 – Small-scale;
 – Involving individual and very junior public officials such as policemen, customs and tax officials;
 – Little macro-economic cost, but profound public alienation;
 – Often hard to curb.

2 SYSTEMATIC
 – Larger developmental impact;
 – Can affect most or all of a government department, or a parastatal such as procurement agency or marketing board;
 – Can have substantial impact upon government revenues and trade diversion;
 – Sustained reform effort necessary rather than 'individualised' response.

3 SYSTEMIC
 – Wholly corrupt system: Andreski's 'Kleptocracy' or government by theft;
 – Huge developmental impact (Jean-Bedel Bokassa's Central African Republic, Macias Nguema's Equatorial Guinea, Moi's Kenya, Mobutu's Zaïre);
 – In such circumstances, honesty is 'irrational';
 – Reform by fundamental change?

Note: This is an up-dated version of that found in Riley [*1983a: 190–206*]. It also draws upon DeLeon [*1993*].

but they have been ultimately limited in effect. Some forms of systematic corruption concern specific government contracts, such as the famous example of the corruption surrounding the contract which led to a massive over-ordering of external supplies of cement by Nigeria's government in the 1970s. In 1975, the Ministry of Defence ordered 16 million metric tons of cement for supply that year, although the total import capacity of all Nigeria's ports was about 4.5 million metric tons per year. Some observers thought that enough cement had been ordered to cover the entire surface area of Nigeria. Middle-men with connections to the regime made a fortune, and in late 1975 up to 200 cement-laden ships were waiting to off-load in Lagos [*Forrest, 1993; Williams, 1987*]. In this case and other examples of systematic corruption, individuals are often identified by inquiries and press reports as blame-worthy, but a sustained institutional reform effort is necessary rather than simply legal action against individuals.

Systemic corruption (Type 3) is similar to Andreski's [*1968*] notion of 'Kleptocracy: or, Corruption as a System of Government'. Government by theft involves the idea of a wholly corrupt system which is led by a corrupt leadership. Such patterns of corruption have a hugely damaging impact upon development. In such societies, it is irrational to be honest as the diverse forms of corruption are so pervasive. Both Sierra Leone and Zaïre are examples of

African countries where patterns of systemic corruption developed. In Sierra Leone's case, systemic corruption was associated with the personalist rule of President Siaka Stevens (1968–85) during the initially-dominant and later one-party All People's Congress (APC) regime of 1968–92; it rested upon the theft of government revenues and the unusual characteristics of the political economy of Sierra Leone, an economy principally based upon the official and smuggled export trade in alluvial gem diamonds, gold, other minerals and agricultural produce [*Riley, 1983a; Luke and Riley, 1989; 1991*]. From the late 1970s onwards, a huge 'parallel' economy developed, which exceeded the official economy in size, and involved political middle-men and Lebanese and Indian traders. This style of systemic corruption was later conceptualised as a 'shadow state' where corrupt rule existed behind the formal façade of political power [*Reno, 1995*].

The pattern of systemic corruption in Mobutu's Zaïre is probably more well-known, being notorious and based upon a repressive, patrimonial system, an African variant of the European absolutist state [*Callaghy, 1984*]. Similar extensive theft of state resources took place and there is well-documented evidence of how the proceeds of this theft were enjoyed, including expensive properties in western Europe, gifts, luxury travel, and other forms of conspicuous consumption [*Askin and Collins, 1993*]. In Sierra Leone and Zaïre, there have been a variety of reform efforts since the 1960s. Siaka Stevens and Mobutu Sese Seko issued strictures against corruption or promised or initiated reforms, often in response to external criticism of their regimes by aid donors, but such stratagems were of limited effect. In both regimes the problems of systemic corruption and the difficulties of reform were well-known to the donors. In 1979, 18 years before Mobutu's regime finally collapsed, the head of a team of western bankers sent to Zaïre to (unsuccessfully) run the central bank pointed out that it was certain that all reform efforts would fail. Nevertheless, Western support for Mobutu's regime, particularly from the United States, continued until the 1990s [*Collins, 1997; Callaghy, 1984*].

Such donors are now advocating public integrity reforms in African societies which are linked to economic and political liberalisation, as in the case of the World Bank. Harriss-White and White [*1996*] argue that the mid-1990s has seen the emergence of new forms of corruption and new means to combat both its 'old' and 'new' forms. Much contemporary debate rests upon the argument that there is a symmetry between economic and political liberalisation: the free market in economics should be assisted by the free market in politics (in the form of an idealised liberal polity). But there are problems over the compatibility of these goals in the abstract and in the real world of African political economies [*Riley and Parfitt, 1994*].

The relationship between political and economic liberalisation is nowhere near as clear as its advocates suggest and there are major problems concerning the sequencing of such reforms in Africa as elsewhere [*Leftwich, 1996*]. In most African societies, economic reform has preceded political reform. Only African regimes with authoritarian governments, as in Ghana in the 1980s, have been able to sustain economic liberalisation over time. Those regimes which have democratised first have had major problems implementing the economic liberalisation expected of them, as in Zambia from 1991 onwards [*Wiseman, 1995*]. In addition, although a reduced and more efficient state sector is desirable, as is liberal, pluralist politics, the relationship between these goals and the goal of corruption reduction is difficult to disentangle.

Although down-sizing the state and political liberalisation are desirable goals in many African countries, they are necessary rather than sufficient conditions for the reduction of public sector corruption. Extensive public sector corruption can coexist with democratic or quasi-democratic politics in Africa. This was the case in several west African states, including the small enclave state of The Gambia, which had a multi-party system, a relatively free press, and a good human rights record from 1965 until a *coup d'état* in 1994. The ruling Progressive People's Party [PPP] government gradually became enmeshed in a series of high-level corruption scandals as post-coup Public Inquiries demonstrated. West Africa's major oil-producer and most populous state, Nigeria, also suffered from extensive corruption in the early 1980s, when there was a brief period of democratic rule. Under President Shehu Shagari there was substantial commercial and public sector fraud; huge numbers of 'ghost workers' (living workers who claim and receive the salary of imaginary or deceased employees); outright stealing of government property and other assets; and huge illegal transfers overseas. As one contemporary study pointed out, those involved in this massive corruption also covered their tracks: 'the telecommunications building, Africa's tallest building, the ministry of External Affairs and the Accounts Section of the Federal Capital Authority, Abuja, were all burnt following widespread allegations of fraud in these places' [*Falola and Ihonvbere, 1985: 108*].

A series of mysterious – or not so mysterious – fires destroyed the evidence. The civilian government first denied the extent of the corruption and then set up a whole ministry to combat it. No one was prosecuted for the huge frauds and related corruption that was thereby disguised. Although the civilian government did not last long and was replaced by a military regime after a *coup d'état*, its successors have often been as corrupt. A series of anti-corruption strategies were tried by various Nigerian governments but they have been largely ineffectual, even when they have included widespread purges of civil servants in the mid-1970s and an anti-corruption 'War Against Indiscipline' orchestrated by Mohammadu Buhari's military regime in the mid-1980s. At least 10,000 and perhaps up to 12,000 civil servants were dismissed in the aftermath of a *coup d'état* in July 1975, many for vaguely defined offenses including the abuse of office and a decline in productivity. This was during 'Operation Purge the Nation'. The later military government of Buhari also dismissed or retired a larger number of public officials during 1984 and the purge broadened out from the civil service to the police, military and universities [*Williams, 1987; Theobald, 1990*]. Nevertheless, despite these purges and public relations exercises, the public looting and mismanagement of the economy has continued to undermine Nigeria's state sovereignty and contributed to its huge external debt. Even under military regimes publicly committed to probity, and equipped with a range of anti-corruption strategies, private enrichment overtook the public realm.

By comparison, public sector corruption in Tanzania was not a problem in the early years of Tanzania's independence, but in the 1990s growing problems of both petty and grand corruption undermined the economically liberalised, multi-party state. Surprisingly, the regime itself then appointed a Presidential inquiry into corruption [*Mndeme-Musonda, Mjema and Danielson, 1997; Muganda, 1997; Warioba, 1997*]. The Presidential Commission was chaired by J.S. Warioba, a former Prime Minister and first Vice President and had a career civil servant, Alexander Muganda, as both Secretary to the Commission and Director of the existing Prevention of Corruption Bureau. Unlike many such inquiries, the Warioba inquiry took extensive public evidence and reported quickly. It was appointed in January 1996 and reported in December 1996, although its conclusions have not been as rapidly acted upon.

The Warioba report identified 'rampant corruption in the public service' which had escalated at an alarming rate over the past two decades [*Warioba, 1997: 199*]. There was both 'petty' corruption and 'grand' corruption at the highest public levels. Petty corruption was widespread. Muganda argued that it was 'a serious nuisance' and had 'subverted effective service delivery' in Tanzania in the 1990s. It was found in the police and judicial services as in all the social sectors. From the evidence taken in the extensive public hearings of the Commission during 1996, petty corruption affected most members of the public and was the main source of public discontent. Grand corruption was identified in the procurement of goods and services, in the allocation of permits for hunting and mining, and in large public contracts, in particular in road-building and public construction. An assessment of 24 public construction contracts had found substantial cost over-runs: costs had escalated from US$97.4 million to US$154.7 million. In these cases, there was an 'inference of corruption' [*Muganda, 1997: 5*].

The Warioba Commission also addressed the much disputed issue of the causes of corruption. A number of causes for the growth in corruption were identified, including economic deterioration, a decline in public ethics, and the lack of political leadership on the issue. The Warioba Commission accordingly made a number of recommendations to improve public integrity, including proposed amendments to the Leadership Code of Ethics Act, short-term vetting of public officials, disciplinary action against the police and judiciary, and the reinvigoration of the ineffectual Prevention of Corruption Bureau.

This remarkable set of events – very few African governments investigate themselves, though they are very willing to investigate their political opponents – generated an intense debate about the character of corruption in Tanzania. Public discussion of the Commission has focused upon a number of key issues, including the impact of economic liberalisation, the ranking of the causes of corruption examined by the Warioba Commission, the value of the government's Prevention of Corruption Bureau, and questions relating to the outcome of the Commission. It can be concluded that economic liberalisation has significantly contributed to the increase in corruption in Tanzania, although there are many other causes. The Warioba Commission does not rank the causes of corruption in order of severity: all causes are deemed equally important. But unless the causes are clearly identified and ranked, then it is difficult to prioritise effective anti-corruption strategies. Perhaps not surprisingly, there has been slow progress on implementing the Commission's proposals, although some civil servants and politicians have been disciplined or dismissed [*Mndeme-Musonda, Mjema and Danielson, 1997*].

The circumstances surrounding the establishment of the Warioba Commission are worthy of note. 1994 saw many corruption scandals in Tanzania and as a result the government had to react, partly as a consequence of the 1995 elections. These elections also produced many anti-corruption commitments by the politicians involved. The Commission argued that the Prevention of Corruption Bureau was ineffective, but a further problem was the lack of political commitment to give the Bureau the strength and resources to act. Although the Bureau needed complete re-organisation and more power, it was continuously undermined by the clientelistic links between businessmen and decision-makers, particularly prominent ruling-party politicians. The Warioba Commission argued that these links had greatly increased corruption in recent years. In respect of longer-term issues, the Commission argued that law reform was required. Some laws created opportunities for corruption; they had to be amended. A final area of debate generated by the Commission was that of social engineering. Public education, anti-corruption and positive public integrity advertising, as well as general measures to raise public awareness were all required. It was argued that it was important to remind or educate citizens to complain about corrupt acts and to try and prevent politicians from engaging in the bad habits of corruption.

Much of the corruption identified in Tanzania was in the public sector or concerned the character and actions of public officials. However, another important element of corruption is related to the character of African political economies and the attempts of African governments to regulate trade across their boundaries. Customs fraud, which is linked to public sector corruption, is common in many west African states, including Mali and Senegal, which share many similarities such as colonial heritage, state structure and political style, membership of the Franc Zone, and protectionist policies [*Kulibaba, 1997; Meagher, 1997; Stasavage and Daubree, 1997*]. Customs fraud is a complex and difficult instance of corruption to deal with. It can be of various types, including under-declaration of the value of goods, misclassification, and underpayment of taxes due. But in whatever form it occurs, it can have significant economic consequences for such developing states as the revenue base of the state is highly dependent upon the efficient taxation of trade [*Kulibaba, 1997; Luke and Riley, 1989; Meagher, 1997*].

Stasavage and Daubree used standard principal-agent models as a basis for their research, although it was accepted that such models focus upon national level factors and cannot predict for specific customs administrations. Instead, they compare fraud on a product-by-product basis within customs administrations. Their general conclusions are that trade liberalisation had reduced levels of fraud and that pre-shipment inspection 'can be a powerful tool for reducing fraud'. In addition, to reduce customs fraud, donors should support institutional reforms that reduce the discretion of officials and improve monitoring. Customs fraud in many African societies was itself a symptom of specific national political and institutional failures [*Stasavage and Daubree, 1997*].

Customs fraud raises a number of general issues concerning the question of an appropriate anti-corruption strategy, including the irrelevance of the national framework for fighting corruption and the efficacy of pre-shipment inspection companies (such as the Swiss-based Société Generale de Surveillance – SGS) which play a central role in the customs services of several African countries. There is a tension between the costs of such expensive foreign pre-shipment inspection services and the revenue gains for the African state concerned. Considerable controversy concerns the revenue improvements claimed by pre-shipment inspection services, as the revenue gains were in part based upon accompanying reforms in the customs services themselves, particularly improvements in information gathering and assessment and the computerisation of the services [*Stasavage and Daubree, 1997*]. Effective action to reduce customs fraud in states such as Mozambique, as well as Mali and Senegal, is also dependent upon the development of attitudes which support honesty in public conduct, and the reduction of the corrupting influences of foreign businesses [*Hall and Young, 1997; Hanlon, 1996; Stasavage, 1996*].

The issue of customs fraud, like that of corruption in general, is related to the question of low public sector salaries in African states. Other factors aside, the temptation to engage in corruption or ignore business fraud is greater if salaries are exceptionally low or unpaid. However, according to Stasavage and Daubree, the size of public service salaries was less of an issue in Mali and Senegal, when compared with other African countries. Instead, a key problem with the customs services in Mali and Senegal was the lack of funds for non-wage current expenditures, such as basic necessities (including fuel, vehicles, and other administrative costs) for the officials to do their jobs. Low public sector salaries were more of a factor in customs fraud and petty corruption in general in other African countries, including Angola, Côte d'Ivoire, The Gambia, Mozambique, and Sierra Leone [*Reno, 1997a; 1997b; Riley, 1983a; Luke and Riley, 1991; Stasavage and Daubree, 1997*]. But customs fraud and corruption is also related to developments in the wider political economy, including the rise and decline of distinct business groups, and the development of underground economies trading in illicit goods, such as drugs, and the weapons of war. In west Africa, some groups of industrialists and merchants are also losing the political clout to demand protection as economic liberalisation is creating new business groups, which are influencing policy.

Stasavage and Daubree argue that there is a tension between the costs of expensive pre-shipment inspection services and the revenue thereby gained. The improvements secured by pre-shipment inspection services were in part based upon accompanying reforms in the customs services themselves, particularly improvements in information gathering and assessment and the computerisation of the services. This case study, like other research on corruption in government regulation of the economy, points to the need for an integrated, comprehensive approach to reducing corruption which is not dependent upon any particular academic fashion or approach [*Kulibaba, 1997; Meagher, 1997*].

These examples of corruption and attempted corruption control have virtually all taken place in African societies which have liberalised politically in the 1990s. Only Nigeria has resisted the domestic, as well as external, pressures to liberalise and demilitarise its politics. There is thus considerable evidence from these cases that relatively high levels of both petty and grand corruption can coexist with democratic or quasi-democratic politics. A broadly similar coexistence of democratic politics and some high-level public corruption obtains in Zambia where democratisation in 1991 has been followed by economic liberalisation. But Zambia has also been beset by public office corruption. Since 1991, several ministers in Frederick Chiluba's multi-party Cabinet have been implicated in illicit drug smuggling. In Zambia, as elsewhere, economic liberalisation has created opportunities for corruption. The sale of several government parastatals has not been transparent and has left over 80,000 people jobless. Widespread rumours about how Chiluba's ministers and their business cronies have gained from the parastatal sales formed the backdrop to political instability in the aftermath of a contentious election in 1996.[1]

In addition to the impact of economic liberalisation in Zambia, the admittedly imperfect democratisation of previously authoritarian regimes, including Kenya from 1991 onwards, has not led to a substantial reduction in corruption [*Riley, 1992; Wiseman, 1995*]. Many observers would argue that Kenya has in fact seen a growth in corruption in the 1990s, after the moves towards multi-party politics, primarily as a product of the corrupt enrichment of ruling-party politicians and their close associates. For example, much controversy surrounds the fall-out from the so-called 'Goldenberg scandal' of 1992 which involved a gold-exporting scheme backed by senior ruling party members and businessmen. The scheme is alleged to have lost the Kenyan government over US$400 million.

High-level instances of corruption such as these in many African societies have badly damaged or diverted development objectives, undermined long-term economic growth, increased poverty, and contributed to Africa's declining position in world trade. Unlike many Asian states, such as South Korea or Taiwan, where public office corruption has often coincided with high, sustained growth rates, the African cases demonstrate that corruption linked to a top-heavy or swollen state and a predatory ruling group can have extremely debilitating consequences, as seen in polities such as the APC regime in Sierra Leone during the 1970s and 1980s, Moi's Kenya, and Mobutu's Zaïre [*Harriss-White and White, 1996*].

The political realm's centrality in African development, as a rentier state, employer and locus of economic and political power, is part of the explanation for the damaging effects of public sector corruption in Africa. The crimes of the powerful have broad effects: high level corruption has legitimated low level corruption. It can be argued that in these instances of African corruption – whether incidental, systematic or systemic, and whether endemic or planned – the economic and other effects have been profoundly damaging. The brief survey of reform efforts in Africa demonstrates that many strategies have been tried but few have led to consistent and thorough improvements in public integrity. Some of the anti-corruption strategies have been capricious in their effects and some inquiries or campaigns have been politically-motivated or public relations exercises. Recent reforms encouraged by the international institutions have yet to take effect but, given the histories of integrity reform in states such as Nigeria, Sierra Leone and Zaïre, as well as the more promising cases of Botswana and Uganda, the prognosis is not altogether optimistic.

CORRUPTION, ECONOMIC LIBERALISATION AND DEMOCRATISATION IN AFRICA

In many ways, the contemporary debate on corruption, economic liberalisation and democratisation in Africa as elsewhere has been conducted at too high or abstract a level. As Harris-White and White [1996] argue, general arguments about the inverse relationship between economic liberalisation and corruption need to be tempered by recent case-study evidence from China and South Korea which suggests that economic liberalisation displaces, refines and may lead to more corruption. In addition, 'far from improving things in the short and medium term, democratization may actually increase the sources and scale of corruption without strengthening countervailing political or institutional capacity'[ibid.: 3]. Corruption has been decentralised by democratisation in Thailand and the Philippines. Greater opportunities for corruption are also created.

The debate on corruption, economic liberalisation and democratisation thus needs a more precise focus. There are, in fact, a number of more specific questions that need to be considered which derive from this brief survey of African corruption and recent African attempts to control corruption. First, what type or types of corruption are the most damaging? Secondly, what are the relationships between corruption and poverty and how can an effective, enabling state act to reduce corruption and through this assist in poverty alleviation? Thirdly, what forms of anti-corruption strategy are likely to be most effective in the short and long term?

The implication of the first question is that not all types of African corruption are equally damaging or objectionable. Additionally, some types of corruption may be easier to reduce or minimise in their impact. A small number of minor instances of petty corruption by public officials does not have a major macroeconomic effect, although it can be profoundly alienating for citizens and damages their immediate material circumstances. Other forms of corruption, such as the grand corruption of state elites – in both the mild and the malevolent forms of corruption associated with the Houphouët-Boigny and Mobutu families, in Côte d'Ivoire and Zaïre – have had grossly damaging effects in terms of reputation as well as economic growth.

In Africa, some forms of petty corruption may be tolerable, culturally accepted, or tolerated when compared to the costs of corruption control or eradication. Traditional society figures, such as Paramount Chiefs, are often cited as examples of public officials where gift-giving is culturally tolerated. The widespread incidental corruption involving rural police or military forces who supplement their income by an unofficial tax upon travellers and trade is another, more problematic, case [Riley, 1983a; 1983b]. Cultural sensitivity as well as economic analysis is required when developing an anti-corruption approach. Therefore, strategies to deal with different types or levels of corruption have to be developed, and subtlety as well as an appreciation of cultural attitudes is required. Economic liberalisation might remove some petty corruption, by reducing opportunities for junior officials, whereas democratisation has the potential to create a transparency effect and in the longer term reduce larger, more damaging forms of corruption [*Harriss-White and White, 1996*].

The second general question about corruption control illustrates the fact that debates about strategies to control or reduce corruption in African societies have to be considered in the context of the new international development debates of the late 1990s. The relationship between corruption and poverty in African societies is complex and difficult to determine. In the African cases considered, it is evident that corruption is not simply or solely a redistributional system from the poor to the rich. African corruption can also be a result of poverty. This is the case when poorly paid or unpaid public officials ask for and receive corrupt payments because they have to, or when such public officials 'sell' ostensibly free public services such as health care and drug supplies, because of their own poverty.

Many aid donors to Africa would argue that their poverty alleviation objectives in the late 1990s, including literacy programmes and broader educational opportunities, will lead to less corruption. This argument can be developed as follows. African corruption is part of a set of governance problems. One basic issue is the efficient and impartial delivery of public goods to society as a whole; another is the need for the state to secure a stable and equitable resource base to generate growth and development. As part of that society, Africa's poor need sophisticated, sequenced institutional reform and public sector strengthening in the context of a more effective, and empowering, state [*UNDP, 1997; World Bank, 1997a*]. This hypothetical or future state, unlike many current, empirical African states, creates the framework for the delivery of public goods, principally for the poorest citizens. Effective and cost efficient anti-corruption strategies should be considered as part of this broader governance and development goal.

However, corruption and anti-corruption strategies in Africa should also be evaluated in a broader context of social and economic development and societal underdevelopment. The emergence of corruption as an issue is related to the creation of a developed public sphere of life, with a monetised economy, a vigorous civil society and a relatively high degree of socio-cultural homogeneity. Anti-corruption measures are likely to meet with the greatest difficulties in the conditions prevailing in many African societies: a large, peasant-based mainly subsistence sector; a disarticulated and poorly integrated economy; serious primordial divisions; a weak civil society and accordingly high levels of public mistrust [*Ellis (ed.), 1996; Theobald, 1990*]. It is the case that effective corruption control is primarily a product of development which creates wealth, interests and institutions conducive to public integrity [*Khan, 1996*]. Thus these broader social, cultural and historical dimensions of corruption and anti-corruption approaches need to be taken into account in considering this second question. Because there are immense difficulties in securing the effective reduction of corruption in African societies, it is all the more surprising when some successes in corruption control are achieved.

One of the key problems with the attempts by African regimes to control corruption is that diverse strategies have been ineffectively pursued by politically weak governments in exceptionally poor societies. Many approaches, including those at citizen or popular, institutional or procedural, and major contract and senior office-holder levels, have been attempted. But they have often been poorly implemented, partly due to political pressure from individuals and groups with significant interests at stake. In some African societies, procedural or structural reforms, such as those which reduce the arbitrary power of public officials, like customerisation of public services, ought to be considered to limit the opportunities and incentives for corruption whilst raising the risk of detection as well as providing for citizen involvement, complaints and redress. The key issues in assessing anti-corruption strategies are clearly cost, impact, effectiveness and sustainability, whilst also taking into account the relative political and financial strengths of those involved in corruption. What is really needed in the African societies committed to reducing corruption in the late 1990s is a structured and sequenced approach to combatting corruption cost-effectively and in the interests of the citizenry, particularly the poor.

In terms of the relationship between economic and political liberalisation and corruption control, the principal problem with economic liberalisation is that it is essentially a long-term strategy predicated on market forces. It provides no ready means to deliver immediate targeted improvements in public integrity. The problem with political liberalisation is that it will not always appear simultaneously with good governance and may undermine economic liberalisation. In some cases, democratisation has in fact undermined good governance, as was the case in Ghana in the early 1990s when a reforming government was diverted from its original objectives by the desire to win an election. There are also a number of cases where economically liberalising governments have run into difficulties because of the growth of corruption, as in Mozambique and Tanzania, among others [*Hall and Young, 1997; Hanlon, 1996; Mndeme-Musonda, Mjema and Danielson, 1997; Muganda, 1997; Stasavage, 1996*]. Thus it may be the case that the objective of seeking an effective anti-corruption strategy will conflict with the other broader objectives being pursued. Economic liberalisation will not always reduce corruption; nor will the arrival of democratic politics. But combined with institutional reform and political commitment they do provide the foundations upon which a successful anti-corruption campaign can be conducted.

DECIDING A STRATEGY

African reformers – and those in international institutions hoping to minimise corruption in Africa – need to think more about the politics and practicalities of reform efforts rather than relying upon the unpredictable, longer-term effects of economic and political change. Political cunning and real determination is required to deal with the difficult challenge that entrenched corruption presents [*Johnston, 1997*]. Political choices have to be made both by leaderships and by civil society organisations interested in public integrity. The details of the strategy need identifying. Those involved (usually civil servants and politicians, but also journalists and other activists) should identify the types of corruption that exist and their pervasiveness. In Africa in the 1990s, there have been a number of examples of 'workshop' sessions where ideas and suggestions for strategies have been developed, including those run by civil society groups, local and international NGOs, and pressure groups such as Transparency International [*IRIS, 1996*]. A continuing problem is the identification of the structural conditions that have produced the corruption (for example, the type of bureaucracy, its formal rules, and civil service salary levels) rather than a simple identification, condemnation and punishment of the corrupt actors involved. Implementing an effective strategy to highlight the issue of corruption and to try to reduce it involves a number of general issues, relating to timing and sequencing, the consistency of approach, the technical details of the proposed public integrity initiatives and their sustainability, and the ever-present issue of the political or managerial determination and courage to carry through such reforms.

From the point of view of governments, the start of an anti-corruption campaign should be well thoughtout. Few African governments have started by making an example of high-ranking senior officials or politicians. Instead most have issued a general appeal for honesty from civil servants and others or started a public relations campaign. The West African novelist A.K. Armah once compared corruption purges and inquiries in Ghana to unusual fishing nets: the fishing nets caught all the smaller fish but let the bigger fish go free, as was also the case with many corruption inquiries in Sierra Leone in the 1960s and early 1990s [*Armah, 1966; Kpundeh, 1995; Riley, 1983a*]. Making an example of senior figures is a better strategy and will set a good precedent, although the political difficulties involved in this cannot be overestimated. In addition, some African governments have resorted to scapegoats or have been overtly partisan in their official inquiries.

The timing of a strategy also needs to be thought out in connection with economic liberalisation. Losers from structural adjustment are more likely to engage in corruption. Adjustment will alter comparative prices dramatically and will lead to new opportunities and incentives. Thus it is probably better to refine the strategy after an adjustment programme has taken hold, as there are instances where both petty and grand corruption have increased after economic liberalisation. Democratisation can also affect questions of timing and sequencing. A public integrity strategy can be little more than campaign rhetoric, as was the case with campaigners in Nigerian elections. It is of course difficult to distinguish between a merely symbolic and a truly effective plan. But a reforming government with a democratic mandate at least has the popular will behind it. Attempts to improve public integrity must be consistent over time: the stratagem should be well-coordinated and focus upon a particular issue or theme. Some African inquiries have engaged in extensive public consultations or have advocated public education campaigns, as in the case of Tanzania's Warioba Commission which is similar to campaigns in Hong Kong and in the Australian federal states. In order to be consistent, public interest groups should be realistic about what can be achieved. Many African governments, such as Nigeria's in the 1980s, and Sierra Leone's in the early 1990s (which declared a 'war on economic crime'), announced unconvincing, over-ambitious goals that were unrealistic, and doomed to fail. Attempts to control corruption should also operate across the entire political, administrative and business spectrum of activities. An anti-corruption campaign is unlikely to work if it is inconsistent and omits certain public sectors or public officials. Obviously, some areas of government activity (such as customs and taxation divisions) are most prone to corruption but all those who are potentially corrupt or corruptible should feel at risk.

Few African governments or civil society groups have demonstrated the ability to reduce corruption significantly and permanently, although countries such as Botswana have had relatively low levels of grand corruption since independence. However, Botswana has distinctive characteristics, including political stability, sustained economic growth whose benefits are reasonably widely spread, and a relatively unified elite committed to encouraging foreign investment and maintaining public integrity [*Charlton, 1990; Frimpong, 1997; Good, 1994*]. These features are not often found in contemporary Africa. Benin, Burkina Faso, Mali, Uganda and the former Zaïre have taken a series of anti-corruption initiatives recently, including the return of the assets of former heads of state from overseas, and establishing ethics codes and asset declarations procedures [*Harsch, 1997*]. But very few African countries since independence have successfully tackled the problem of corruption.

For reforming governments that seek to deal with corruption, a number of innovations have developed in recent years. These include confidential surveys of private sector businesses with the intention of establishing where corruption exists in the public sector – in customs, public order, procurement, or the wider political system. Such a survey was used in the 1997 World Development Report [*World Bank, 1997a*]. In addition, few African governments or civil society groups utilise the skills of accountants, public finance specialists, or lawyers and their professional organisations. Only recently have African citizen groups started using the services of bodies such as Transparency International (TI). Whilst there are problems with TI, such as the links it has with international institutions and its initially pro-business bias, the advantage of the growth of this organisation is that it can help political leaders and civic organisations who wish to do something about corruption. Public integrity reforms must also be sustainable as well as politically feasible. Politicians have to recognise that they can take action without seriously damaging their own political prospects. In many African societies, they must be able to take the credit and avoid the blame if they are not themselves involved.

Political determination is a crucial aspect of any public integrity strategy. Without a strong commitment to reform and personal examples and commitments from the political leadership, governmental statements of intent, attempted reforms and strategies remain cosmetic devices. There have been many African political leaders who have decried the cost of significant or systemic corruption yet have failed to do anything about it. Obviously, individual politicians, even at the top of political systems, cannot make much of a difference in some cases of systemic corruption. But they can act to demonstrate their own commitment in other cases. They can use their democratic credibility to make some significant changes. Recent studies have suggested examples of how a leader can demonstrate this [*Klitgaard, 1997; Kpundeh, 1997*]. African politicians could demonstrate their commitment to public integrity by dismissing corrupt ministers and announcing the reason for their dismissal, by restructuring law enforcement agencies to fight corruption, and by holding chief enforcement officers accountable for public integrity. It is possible to challenge vested interests. And scandal, as well as clearly illegal cases of corruption, can be used to initiate action, as recent examples in western Europe show [*Levi and Nelken, 1996*].

Democratic politicians, especially in Africa's precarious and fragile newly-liberalised systems of the 1990s, are nervous about taking action where they see no obvious political benefits and fear the political costs. In order for them to act, their political responsibility and determination need to be strengthened. This can include improving the democratic balance in any society [*Johnston, 1997*], creating a public constituency for reform, and enhancing civil society institutions that help the strategy (such as a free press, and the independence of the professions and public agencies). In many African societies, it is also important for civil society groups to humanise corruption: to make clear to all concerned the individual, human costs of misallocations of resources. In

Africa's weak states, with powerful domestic interests opposed to reform, it is obviously hard but necessary to reinforce the political will of democratic politicians to take action on corruption [*Englebert, 1997*].

CONCLUSION

Exceptional political and managerial determination and courage is necessary to enable African states to promote and maintain reform and reduce public sector corruption. This is rarely found, even in the most populist or post-neo-colonial African states. The political and personal risks of a commitment to public integrity are obvious.[2] For many African leaderships, it is much easier to maintain a formal commitment to reform whilst not endangering the interests and corrupt incomes of powerful groups. However, given the new development agenda of the later 1990s, it is also obviously politic for aid-dependent states to take account of these new donor priorities which expect reductions in corruption and better governance. Where African governments do show a determination to improve public integrity, far more attention needs to be given to questions of timing and sequencing, consistency in approach, the details of reform and its sustainability, and the encouragement of the exceptional political and managerial persistence necessary to promote and sustain reform in this area.

In some west African states, including Mali and Senegal, economic liberalisation seems to have helped reduce customs fraud, and the related corruption, when combined with institutional reform and relatively high salaries. In Tanzania, economic liberalisation is part of the explanation for the growth of petty and grand corruption. Some African states have embarked upon comprehensive public integrity initiatives: in Tanzania, the anti-corruption strategy includes expectations of the beneficial effects of long-term growth and literacy efforts, combined with legal reforms and institutional strengthening.

But such ambitious objectives raise important questions about short-term priorities and the inter-relationships between such reform efforts. Almost all the African country experiences examined here raise in one form or another the politics of reform. Does the political leadership have the sustained commitment to improve public integrity or is it engaged in a mere public relations exercise – for citizens and aid donors? In other polities, such as Hong Kong, exceptionally high political commitment, popular support, good administrative organisation and a coherent strategy have yielded results. But there are questions regarding the sustainability and transferability of such an approach to African societies [*Spelville, 1997; UNDP/OECD, 1997*]. Tanzania's recent anti-corruption effort, with its inquiry process, needs to be turned into a sustained political and institutional commitment. In the cases of

Nigeria, Sierra Leone and the former Zaïre we see the political turmoil that gross corruption can cause. There are many anti-corruption institutions in African societies but they are not all like the ICAC in Hong Kong or its institutional near-equivalent in Botswana, or the inspector-general system in Uganda [*Frimpong, 1997; Ruzindana, 1997; Spelville, 1997*].

One obvious if easy generalisation from the experiences of African states is that an ethically motivated and strong leadership is necessary to promote and maintain anti-corruption reform. But African puritans, or African Oliver Cromwells, are hard to find. International institutions, such as the World Bank, have been promoting universal strategies to control corruption, but different African cases demonstrate the difficulties with such universalist solutions [*World Bank, 1997c*]. If elements of a universal strategy are needed, then a number of basic suggestions can be made. In addition to institutional improvements, in almost all African societies the professions should be strengthened – by enhancing their professionalism, independence and technical skills – as part of a strategy to control corruption. Lawyers, accountants, and investigative journalists all need support, from civil society groups and interested individuals, and technical help, including perhaps from external donors. But enhanced professional skills, as well as a commitment to try to control corruption, are more likely to be seen in democratic societies where the pressures of political competition often force politicians to act. Democratisation is thus a necessary but not a sufficient condition for the reduction of corruption. Economic liberalisation is also not a simple panacea for public sector corruption. But reducing the size of the state also reduces the size of the potential corrupt 'take' and enables the public sector to move towards the ideal of an efficient, enabling state. The African experience suggests that sophisticated, well-timed and properly sequenced short-term anti-corruption strategies will contribute to the governance agenda that economic and political liberalisation seek to achieve.

NOTES

1. In early 1997, a popular song on the streets of Lusaka, the capital of Zambia, expressed this mood about Zambia's President and his ruling party: 'Chiluba anaba mupando' (Chiluba stole the seat and should be caged) people sang. The role of folk-song as well as popular sayings and rumours about corruption – what Gunnar Myrdal called the folklore of corruption – has not been frequently studied but is of great importance. In contemporary Mozambique corruption is called '*cabritismo*' (literally 'goatism', from the phrase 'a goat eats where it is tethered'). Similar sayings about voracious goats were expressed about Siaka Stevens and corruption in Sierra Leone.

2. In 1991 Mozambique's Attorney-General raised the issue of corruption in his annual report to parliament. He subsequently received several death threats. In Zaïre in 1979 the head of a team of western bankers sent to run Zaïre's central bank, being critical of Mobutu's kleptocratic ways, was reduced to sleeping with a shotgun under his bed after receiving similar threats from groups of soldiers.

REFERENCES

Andreski, S., 1968, 'Kleptocracy: Or Corruption as a System of Government', in S. Andreski (ed), *The African Predicament*, London: Michael Joseph, pp.92–109.

Armah, A.K., 1966, *The Beautyful Ones Are Not Yet Born*, London: Heinemann.

Askin, S. and C. Collins, 1993, 'External Collusion with Kleptocracy: Can Zaïre Recapture its Stolen Wealth?' *Review of African Political Economy*, No.57, pp.72–85.

Callaghy, T.M., 1984, *The State–Society Struggle: Zaïre in Comparative Perspective*, New York: Columbia University Press.

Charlton, R., 1990, 'Exploring the Byways of African Political Corruption: Botswana and Deviant Case Analysis', *Corruption and Reform*, Vol.5, No.1, pp.1–28.

Clarke, M. (ed.), 1983, *Corruption: Causes, Consequences and Controls*, London: Frances Pinter.

Collins, C., 1997, 'The Congo is Back!', *Review of African Political Economy*, No.72, pp.277–92.

Delamaide, D., 1984, *Debt Shock*, London: Weidenfeld & Nicolson.

DeLeon, P., 1993, *Thinking About Political Corruption*, New York: M.E. Sharpe.

Doig, R.A., 1995, 'Good Government and Sustainable Anti-corruption Strategies: A Role for Independent Anti-corruption Agencies?' *Public Administration and Development*, Vol.15, No.2, pp.151–65.

Doig, R.A. and S.P. Riley, 1998, 'Corruption and Anti-Corruption Strategies: Issues and Case Studies From Developing Countries', in G.S. Cheema and J. Bonvin (eds.), *Corruption and Integrity Improvement Initiatives in Developing Countries*, Paris: OECD.

Ellis, S., 1996, 'Africa and International Corruption: The Strange Case of South Africa and the Seychelles', *African Affairs*, Vol.95, No.380, pp.165–96.

Ellis, S. (ed.), 1996, *Africa Now: People, Policies and Institutions*, London: James Currey.

Englebert, P., 1997, 'The Contemporary African State: Neither African, Nor State', *Third World Quarterly*, Vol.18, No.4, pp.767–76.

Falola, T. and J. Ihonvbere, 1985, *The Rise and Fall of Nigeria's Second Republic, 1979–1984*, London: Zed Press.

Forrest, T., 1993, *Politics and Economic Development in Nigeria*, Boulder, CO: Westview Press.

Frimpong, K., 1997, 'An Analysis of Corruption in Botswana', paper for the UNDP/OECD Development Centre conference on 'Corruption and Integrity Improvement Initiatives in the Context of Developing Economies', Paris, 24–25 Oct.

Good, K., 1994, 'Corruption and Mismanagement in Botswana: A Best-Case Example', *Journal of Modern African Studies*, Vol.32, No.3, pp.499–521.

Gould, D.J., 1980, *Bureaucratic Corruption and Underdevelopment in the Third World: The Case of Zaïre*, New York: Pergamon Press.

Gould, D.J. and J. Amaro-Reyes, 1983, 'The Effects of Corruption on Administrative Performance: Illustrations From Developing Countries', *World Bank Working Paper No.580*.

Goudie, A. and D. Stasavage, 1997, 'Corruption: The Issues', *OECD Technical Paper No.122*.

Gourevitch, P., 1997, 'Continental Shift', *The New Yorker*, 4 Aug., pp.42–55.

Hall, M. and T. Young, 1997, *Confronting Leviathan: Mozambique since Independence*, London: C. Hurst.

Hampton, M., 1996, *The Offshore Interface: Tax Havens in the Global Economy*, Basingstoke: Macmillan.

Hanlon, J., 1996, *Peace without Profit: How the IMF Blocks Rebuilding in Mozambique*, London: James Currey.

Harriss-White, B. and G. White (eds.), 1996, 'Liberalization and the New Corruption', *IDS Bulletin*, Vol.27, No.2.

Harsch, E., 1993, 'Accumulators and Democrats: Challenging State Corruption in Africa', *Journal of Modern African Studies*, Vol.31, No.1, pp.31–48.

Harsch, E., 1997, 'Africans Take On Corruption', *Africa Recovery*, July, pp.26–7.

Heidenheimer, A.J., LeVine, V.T. and M.J. Johnston (eds.), 1989, *Political Corruption: A Handbook*, New Brunswick, NJ: Transaction.

Hoogvelt, A., 1997, *Globalisation and the Postcolonial World*, London: Macmillan.

Huntington, S. P., 1991, *The Third Wave: Democratization in the Late Twentieth Century*, Norman, OK and London: University of Oklahoma Press.

IRIS, 1996, 'Governance and the Economy in Africa: Tools for Analysis and Reform of Corruption', Center for Institutional Reform and the Informal Sector (IRIS), University of Maryland.

Jeffries, R., 1982, 'Rawlings and the Political Economy of Underdevelopment in Ghana', *African Affairs*, Vol.81, No.384, pp.307–17.

Johnston, M. J., 1997, 'What Can be Done About Entrenched Corruption?', paper presented at the Annual World Bank Conference on Development Economics, Washington, DC, April–May.

Kaplan, R.D., 1994, 'The Coming Anarchy', *The Atlantic Monthly*, Feb., pp.44–72.

Kaplan, R.D., 1996, *The Ends of the Earth*, New York: Random House.

Kaplan, R.D., 1997, 'Was Democracy Just a Moment?', *The Atlantic Monthly*, Dec., pp.55–80.

Kaufmann, D., 1997, 'Corruption: The Facts', *Foreign Policy*, No.107, pp.114–31.

Keen, D., 1997, 'Rebellion and Its Functions in Sierra Leone', paper for the conference on 'Identity and Conflict in Africa', University of Leeds, Leeds, 15–17 Sept.

Khan, M.H., 1996, 'A Typology of Corrupt Transactions in Developing Countries', *IDS Bulletin*, Vol.26, No.2, pp.48–55.

Klitgaard, R., 1988, *Controlling Corruption*, Berkeley, CA: University of California Press.

Klitgaard, R., 1991, *Tropical Gangsters*, London: I.B. Tauris.

Klitgaard, R., 1997, 'Cleaning Up and Invigorating the Civil Service', a report for the Operations Evaluation Department, Washington, DC: The World Bank.

Kpundeh, S.J., 1995, *Politics and Corruption in Africa: A Case Study of Sierra Leone*, Langham, MD: University Press of America.

Kpundeh, S.J., 1997, 'Political Will for Anti-Corruption Activities: An Analysis', unpublished paper, May.

Kulibaba, N., 1997, 'Good Governance in Sheep's Clothing: Implementing the Action Plan for Regional Facilitation of the Livestock Trade in West Africa's Central Corridor', Case Study No.3, Implementing Policy Change Project, Washington, DC: United States Agency for International Development.

Leftwich, A. (ed.), 1996, *Democracy and Development: Theory and Practice*, Oxford: Polity Press.

Levi, M. and D. Nelken (eds.), 1996, *The Corruption of Politics and the Politics of Corruption*, Oxford: Blackwell.

Luke, D.F. and S.P. Riley, 1989, 'The Politics of Economic Decline in Sierra Leone', *Journal of Modern African Studies*, Vol.27, No.1, pp.133–42.

Luke, D.F. and S.P. Riley, 1991, 'Economic Decline and the New Reform Agenda in Africa', IDPM Discussion Papers No.28, University of Manchester.

McKinney, J.B. and M.J. Johnston (eds.), 1986, *Fraud, Waste and Abuse in Government: Causes, Consequences and Cures*, Philadelphia, PA: Institute for the Study of Human Issues.

Meagher, K., 1997, 'Informal Integration or Economic Subversion? Parallel Trade in West Africa', in R. Laverne (ed.), *Regional Integration and Cooperation in West Africa*, Trenton, NJ: Africa World Press, pp.165–88.

Mndeme-Musonda, F., Mjema, G. and A. Danielson, 1997, 'Tanzania 1997, The Urge to Merge: The Revival of East African Cooperation', Macroeconomic Report No.7, Stockholm: Swedish International Development Cooperation Agency.

Moodie-Stuart, G., 1997, *Grand Corruption*, Oxford: WorldView.

Muganda, A., 1997, 'The War Against Corruption in Tanzania: An Overview of the Warioba Report', paper for the UNDP/OECD Development Centre conference on 'Corruption and Integrity Improvement Initiatives in the Context of Developing Economies', Paris, 24–25 Oct.

Naylor, R.T., 1987, *Hot Money and the Politics of Debt*, London: Unwin Hyman.

Naylor, R.T., 1996, 'The Underworld of Gold', *Crime, Law and Social Change*, Vol.25, No.3, pp.191–241.

Noonan, J.T. Jr., 1984, *Bribes*, New York: Macmillan.

Organisation for Economic Co-operation and Development (OECD), 1997, 'OECD Actions to Fight Corruption', Paris.

Randel, J. and T. German, 1997, *The Reality of Aid, 1997*, London: Earthscan.

Reno, W., 1995, *Corruption and State Politics in Sierra Leone*, Cambridge: Cambridge University Press.

Reno, W., 1997a, 'African Weak States and Commercial Alliances', *African Affairs*, Vol.96, No.383, pp.165–85.

Reno, W., 1997b, 'Privatising War in Sierra Leone', *Current History*, May, pp.227–30.

Riley, S.P., 1983a, '"The Land of Waving Palms": Corruption Inquiries, Political Economy and Politics in Sierra Leone', in M. Clarke (ed.), *Corruption: Causes, Consequences and Controls*, London: Frances Pinter, pp.190–206.

Riley, S.P., 1983b, 'The Current Political Situation in Sierra Leone', in P.K. Mitchell and A. Jones (eds.), *Sierra Leone Studies at Birmingham: Proceedings of a Symposium*, University of Birmingham, Birmingham, pp.42–63.

Riley, S.P., 1992, 'Political Adjustment or Domestic Pressure? Democratic Politics and Political Choice in Africa', *Third World Quarterly*, Vol.13, No.3, pp.539–51.

Riley, S.P., 1993, 'Post Independence Anti-Corruption Strategies and the Contemporary Effects of Democratisation', *Corruption and Reform*, Vol.7, No.3, pp.249–61.

Riley, S.P., 1996, 'The 1996 Presidential and Parliamentary Elections in Sierra Leone', *Electoral Studies*, Vol.15, No.4, pp.537–44.

Riley, S.P., 1997, 'Sierra Leone: The Militariat Strikes Again', *Review of African Political Economy*, No.72, pp.287–92.

Riley, S.P. and T.W. Parfitt, 1994, 'Economic Adjustment and Democratisation in Africa', in J. Walton and D. Seddon (eds.), *Free Markets and Food Riots: The Politics of Global Adjustment*, Oxford: Blackwell, pp.135–70.

Robinson, J., 1994, *The Laundrymen*, London: Simon & Schuster.

Robinson, M., 1997, Summary Report of the Workshop on Corruption and Development, IDS, University of Sussex, Brighton, 6–7 May.

Rose-Ackerman, S., 1997, 'Corruption and Development', paper presented at the Annual World Bank Conference on Development Economics, Washington, DC, April–May.

Ruzindana, A., 1997, 'The Importance of Leadership in Fighting Corruption in Uganda', in K.A. Elliot (ed.), *Corruption and the Global Economy*, Washington, DC: Institute for International Economics, pp.133–46.

Sen, A. K., 1997, 'On Corruption and Organised Crime', in United Nations Drug Control Programme (UNDCP), *World Drug Report*, Oxford: Oxford University Press, pp.150–3.

Spelville, B. de, 1997, 'A Study of the Policy Initiatives Against Corruption in Hong Kong', Paris: OECD Development Centre.

Stapenhurst, R. and P. Langseth, 1997, 'The Role of the Public Administration in Fighting Corruption', *International Journal of Public Sector Management*, Vol.10, No.5, pp.311–30.

Stasavage, D., 1996, 'Corruption and the Mozambican Economy', Paris: OECD Development Centre.

Stasavage, D. and C. Daubree, 1997, 'Determinants of Customs Fraud in Mali and Senegal', paper for the UNDP/OECD Development Centre conference on 'Corruption and Integrity Improvement Initiatives in the Context of Developing Economies', Paris, 24–25 Oct.

Stevens, M., 1997, 'The World Bank's Approach to Corruption', paper for the Workshop on Corruption and Development, Institute of Development Studies, University of Sussex, Brighton, 6–7 May.

Transparency International (TI), 1996, *National Integrity Systems: The TI Source Book*, Berlin.

Theobald, R., 1990, *Corruption, Development and Underdevelopment*, Basingstoke: Macmillan.

United Nations Development Programme (UNDP), 1997, *Human Development Report*, Oxford: Oxford University Press.

United Nations Development Programme/Organisation for Economic Co-operation and Development – Development Centre (UNDP/OECD), 1997, Report of the conference on 'Corruption and Integrity Improvement Initiatives in the Context of Developing Economies', Paris, 24–25 Oct.

Waterbury, J., 1973, 'Endemic and Planned Corruption in a Monarchical Regime', *World Politics*, Vol.25, No.4, pp.534 –55.

Ward, P. (ed.), 1989, *Corruption, Development and Inequality*, London: Routledge.

Warioba, J.S., 1997, 'Corruption and the State II: Extracts from Joseph Warioba's Report', *Soundings*, No.7, Autumn, pp.198–208.

Williams, R., 1987, *Political Corruption in Africa*, Aldershot: Gower.

Wiseman, J. (ed.), 1995, *Democracy and Political Change in Sub-Saharan Africa*, London: Routledge.

World Bank, 1997a, *World Development Report: The State in a Changing World*, Oxford: Oxford University Press.

World Bank, 1997b, *Report of the Corruption Action Plan Working Group (CAPWG) – Country and International Strategies*, OPC Review Draft, May.

World Bank, 1997c, *Helping Countries Combat Corruption: The Role of the World Bank*, Washington, DC: World Bank.

Zack-Williams, A., 1983, 'A Reflection on the Class Basis of Corruption in Sierra Leone and its Implications for Development', in P.K. Mitchell and A. Jones (eds.), *Sierra Leone Studies at Birmingham: Proceedings of a Symposium*, University of Birmingham, Birmingham, pp.359–62.

Index

accountability, 2, 4, 6, 7, 10, 68–70 *passim*, 86, 87, 91–6 *passim*, 101, 106, 107, 110, 112, 114, 135–8 *passim*
accountancy units, 135, 138
accumulation, 6, 7, 18, 20, 33, 36, 37
Ades, Alberto, 2, 7, 41, 88
adjustment, structural, 7, 81, 82, 134, 135, 138, 152
Africa, 2, 6–7, 9, 10, 20, 66, 72, 76, 105, 113, 129–59 *see also individual countries*
agreements, 13, 42, 43
  extradition, 11, 119
agriculture, 30, 73
aid, 2, 5, 7, 13, 66, 69, 88, 93, 97, 101, 105, 121, 135, 136
Alam, M.S., 85–7 *passim*, 92, 97
Alfiler, C.P., 73
Amaro-Reyes, J., 135
Amsden, A., 31
amnesty, 117
Andreski, S., 140
Angola, 146
anti-colonialism, 18–19, 28, 35
anti-corruption agency, 10, 132
  measures, 1, 5, 6, 9–12, 17–18, 38, 66, 82, 85, 87, 91–4 *passim*, 101, 106, 108–28, 131–5, 137–45, 148–55
antimachine movement, 91
appeal, channels of, 86, 98
appointments, 4, 67, 68
Argentina, 48, 121
Armah, A.K., 152
Asia, 6, 7, 15–39, 72, 73, 105, 113 *see also individual countries*
  East, 7, 12, 17, 21, 31–2, 53, 108, 138
  South, 2, 15, 16, 21–2, 27–31, 34, 38
    Southeast, 12, 15, 17, 21, 32–7
Askin, S., 141
asset declaration, 10, 152
auditing, 77, 85, 136
  cross-, 74–7 *passim*
Australia, 47–51 *passim*, 107, 123, 152
  ICAC, 107
Austria, 49,50
Ayub Khan, 30
Azerbaijan, 123

ballot, secret, 98
Bangladesh, 21, 28, 31, 112
banking sector, 7, 122

Bardhan, P., 28, 41, 70
bargaining power, 25, 26, 28, 32
Barro, Robert J., 89
Becker, Gary, 123
Belgium, 49–51 *passim*, 53, 55n28
Benin, 116–17, 124, 152
Besley, T., 71
Bhutto, Benazir, 9
Bird, R.M., 78, 81
Bolivia, 114–15
bonuses, 70
Botswana, 131, 139, 147, 152, 155
Brautigam, Deborah, 101
Brazil, 9, 91, 94, 112, 121
bribes, 5–6, 11, 18, 20, 22–7 *passim*, 32, 40–44, 51–4 *passim*, 71, 82, 98, 108, 109, 113, 119, 121, 124
  OECD Council on, 42, 119
Britain, 6, 98
Brown, Ron, 42
Buhari, Mohammadu, 142–3
bureaucracy/bureaucrats, 4, 7, 10, 16, 17, 20, 29, 30, 32, 43, 64, 67–9 *passim*, 151 *see also* civil service
Burkina Faso, 116, 124, 152
Business International, 21
business sector, 7, 41–3, 53, 146
BWU, 121

Callaghy, T.M., 141
Cambodia, 121, 122
Canada, 47, 49–51 *passim*, 123
capacity, administrative, 10
capitalism, 15–18 *passim*, 20, 25, 28–38 *passim*
Casanegra de Jantscher, M., 78, 81
caste, 28
Charlton, R., 152
Chaudhry, K.A., 67
chiefs, 148
Chiluba, Frederick, 146
China/Chinese, 2, 10, 17, 33–6 *passim*, 47, 49–51 *passim*, 55n19, 56n35, 97, 122, 123, 132, 148
Chu, C.Y.C., 72, 77
Chubb, Judith, 89
civil liberties, 97, 101
civil service, 6, 10, 95, 106, 114, 116, 132, 142–3, 151 *see also* bureaucracy; officials
civil society, 4, 9, 11, 87, 88, 91–100 *passim*,

Books of Related Interest

Foreign Aid Towards the Year 2000

Experiences and Challenges
Olav Stokke, *Norwegian Institute of International Affairs (Ed)*

> *'Stokke's paper "Foreign aid:what now?" occupies a third of his book, and is an impressive and substantial review of aid in its own right.'*
>
> **International Affairs**

The post-cold war international system is still in the making. This volume aims at taking stock of the effects on North-South relations in general and aid in particular emerging from the revolutionary system transformation taking place in the late 1980s. The changes in the international framework conditions emerging from this source have not affected the aid policy of all donor governments equally strongly or in the same way; nor have they been the only factors that influenced North-South relations or aid policies.

368 pages   1996   0 7146 4713 6   cloth   0 7146 4259 2   paper
EADI Book Series 18

Aid and Political Conditionality

Olav Stokke, *Norwegian Institute of International Affairs (Ed)*

Foreign aid has increasingly become subject to political conditionality. In the 1980s some institutions made aid dependent upon the recipient countries' economic policy reforms. Market liberalisation was the primary instrument and objective. In the 1990s such conditionality was brought one step further; aid was now linked to political reforms, affecting recipient countries' governing systems, requiring democracy, human rights and 'good governance'. This volume looks at these developments and considers the conditionality policies of several European aid donors. Such policies are also considered from recipient perspectives, both from the Third World and Russia, and the issue is also considered from a historical perspective.

416 pages   1995   0 7146 4640 7   cloth   0 7146 4162 6   paper
EADI Book Series 16

FRANK CASS PUBLISHERS
Newbury House, 900 Eastern Avenue, Newbury Park, Ilford, Essex IG2 7HH
Tel: +44 (0)181 599 8866 Fax: +44 (0)181 599 0984 E-mail: info@frankcass.com
NORTH AMERICA
c/o ISBS, 5804 NE Hassalo Street, Portland, OR 97213 3644, USA
Tel: 1 800 944 6190 Fax: 503 280 8832 E-mail cass@isbs.com
Website: http://www.frankcass.com

Arguing Development Policy

Frames and Discourses

Raymond Apthorpe, *Independent Consultant*
and **Des Gasper**, *ISS, The Hague*

This collection shows how policy discourses in the fields of national and international developments are constructed and operate and how they can be analysed. Dominant discourses screen out certain aspects: they 'frame' issues to include some matters and typically exclude important others. More generally, different policy discourses construct the world in distinctive ways, through language that requires deconstruction and careful review.

176 pages 1996 0 7146 4294 0 paper
A special issue of The European Journal of Development Research

The Role of the State in Development Processes

Claude Auroi, *(Ed)*

In recent years the debate on the role of the state in development processes has been characterised by the emergence of the concept of civil society. This book, published with the support of UNESCO, gives an overview of various state interventions in Africa, the Arab world, Europe and Latin America.
264 pages 1992 0 7146 3493 X cloth
EADI Book Series 15

FRANK CASS PUBLISHERS
Newbury House, 900 Eastern Avenue, Newbury Park, Ilford, Essex IG2 7HH
Tel: +44 (0)181 599 8866 Fax: +44 (0)181 599 0984 E-mail: info@frankcass.com
NORTH AMERICA
c/o ISBS, 5804 NE Hassalo Street, Portland, OR 97213 3644, USA
Tel: 1 800 944 6190 Fax: 503 280 8832 E-mail cass@isbs.com
Website: http://www.frankcass.com

Political Conditionality

Georg Sørensen, *University of Aarhus, Denmark (Ed)*

Political conditionality involves the linking of development aid to certain standards of observance of human rights and (liberal) democracy in recipient countries. Although this may seem to be an innocent policy, it has the potential to bring about a dramatic change in the basic principles of the international system: putting human rights first means putting respect for individuals and rights before respect for the sovereignty of states.

134 pages   1993   0 7146 4101 4   paper
A special issue of The European Journal of Development Research

Policy Coherence in Development Co-operation

Olav Stokke, *NUPI* and **Jacques Forster,** *IUED*

In the 1990's, a widely shared conviction emerged among aid donors that their policies should be more coherent than in the past. The drive towards increased policy coherence came as a response to a state of policy coherence.

The shifting grounds of policy coherence in development co-operation are outlined. The policies of some selected donor countries - Canada, France, Germany, the Netherlands, Norway, Sweden and Switzerland - are scrutinised and analysed, with particular reference to the 1990s. Spotlights are also directed towards the European Union, with particular reference to the internal coherence of its development co-operation policy and the common foreign and security policy, and the coherence of EU policies and the bilateral policies of its member states.

256 pages 1998   0 7146 4914 7   cloth   0 7146 4464 1   paper
EADI Book Series 22

FRANK CASS PUBLISHERS
Newbury House, 900 Eastern Avenue, Newbury Park, Ilford, Essex IG2 7HH
Tel: +44 (0)181 599 8866 Fax: +44 (0)181 599 0984 E-mail: info@frankcass.com
NORTH AMERICA
c/o ISBS, 5804 NE Hassalo Street, Portland, OR 97213 3644, USA
Tel: 1 800 944 6190 Fax: 503 280 8832 E-mail cass@isbs.com
Website: http://www.frankcass.com

Cultural Perspectives on Development

Vincent Tucker *(Ed)*

What does cultural analysis have to offer development studies? Is culture a new paradigm for the study of development or a minefield of theoretical confusion? Can we move beyond notions of 'global culture' and 'local culture' to a more refined notion of cultural processes?

This collection of articles addresses these issues providing a diversity of approaches. Two themes in particular run through the contributions: the relationship between culture and political economy and the relationship between local and global processes.

136 pages 1997 0 7146 4337 8 paper

FRANK CASS PUBLISHERS
Newbury House, 900 Eastern Avenue, Newbury Park, Ilford, Essex IG2 7HH
Tel: +44 (0)181 599 8866 Fax: +44 (0)181 599 0984 E-mail: info@frankcass.com
NORTH AMERICA
c/o ISBS, 5804 NE Hassalo Street, Portland, OR 97213 3644, USA
Tel: 1 800 944 6190 Fax: 503 280 8832 E-mail cass@isbs.com
Website: http://www.frankcass.com

For Product Safety Concerns and Information please contact our EU
representative GPSR@taylorandfrancis.com Taylor & Francis Verlag GmbH,
Kaufingerstraße 24, 80331 München, Germany

Printed and bound by CPI Group (UK) Ltd, Croydon, CR0 4YY
11/04/2025
01844012-0013